John Arlott's
100
GREATEST
BATSMEN

John Arlott's 100 GREATEST BATSMEN

Macdonald
Queen Anne Press

A Queen Anne Press Book

©John Arlott 1986, 1989

First published in Great Britain in hardback in 1986 by Queen Anne Press
a division of Macdonald & Co (Publishers) Ltd

This edition published in 1989 by Queen Anne Press

Macdonald & Co (Publishers) Ltd
66-73 Shoe Lane
London EC4P 4AB

British Library Cataloguing in Publication Data

Arlott, John, 1914-
    John Arlott's 100 greatest batsmen. New ed.
    1. Cricket—Batting—History 2. Cricket
    players—Biography
    I. Title
    796.35'826'0922

    ISBN 0-356-17664-9

Photoset in North Wales by
Derek Doyle & Associates, Mold, Clwyd
Printed in Singapore by
Kyodo Printing Co. Pte Ltd

Picture Credits
All-Sport: 12, 13, 31, 40, 52, 53, 54, 55, 83, 89, 93, 100, 122B, 125, 127,
           128, 132, 139, 152, 153, 163, 164, 176, 182, 209, 210, 211, 214,
           216, 238, 263, 264, 280
BBC Hulton Picture Library: Front cover (left), 15, 43, 75, 77, 80
           81, 87, 105, 114, 119, 135, 146, 162, 173,
           178, 186, 191, 198, 246, 258, 278
George Beldam: 118, 151, 169, 226
Colorsport: 18, 30, 44, 61, 63, 70, 130, 142, 166, 205, 218, 220, 236, 253
Patrick Eagar: Front cover (right), 25, 28, 38, 42, 47, 56, 65, 82, 91,
           99, 121, 122T, 123, 124, 126, 149, 156, 172, 200, 212,
           213, 215, 221, 231, 233, 240, 261, 273
David Frith: 16, 86, 147
Hampshire County Cricket Club: 181
Mansell Collection: 10, 50, 51, 150, 170
National Portrait Gallery, London: 49
Photosource: 19, 32, 45, 68, 107, 111, 129, 137, 155, 161, 184, 194, 196,
           203, 204, 219, 251, 267, 275
Press Association: 17, 102, 133, 167, 277
S & G Press Agency: 35, 59, 113, 159, 189, 229
Sussex County Cricket Club: 73
Topham Picture Library: back flap, 21, 22, 34, 58, 71, 90, 94, 96, 97
           108, 110, 116, 141, 143, 144, 207, 224, 243, 244,
           248-249, 252, 255, 268, 271

Tabulated statistics by Bill Frindall
Career records are to the close of the English season 1988
* Not out   † Left-handed batsman   ‡ Left-handed bowler

CONTENTS

INTRODUCTION

If Arthur Chipperfield's 99 in his first Test – Trent Bridge, 1934 – is better remembered than many centuries, nevertheless, all batsmen know – many of them, often ruefully – that a hundred is a hundred is a hundred. That is especially so when a publisher asks for a book on the 100 best batsmen. He does not see 'The Best One-Hundred-and-Twenty-Seven Batsmen' as a title. It must be admitted, too, that while it would have been pleasant to include another twenty-seven, the figure hardly pulls.

Yet, in the back of the mind, there lurk names that sentiment would have put in; the cricketer's urge is to include rather than exclude. Real-life selectors, of course, are realists; even ruthless. The ordinary enthusiast is more weakly human. Especially he has qualms about including so-and-so – whom he knows to be a such-and-such – at the expense of leaving out a nice man. This list was not easy to compile; the original sheet is covered with crossings out. Three batsmen – no prizes for identification – went in and out as many as three times. Indeed, only as this preface was being written was the final alteration made. One man *had* to go in; and it was a heart-searching business to decide who to leave out of what had been the 'final' list. Essentially, though, whatever any critic may 'prove', this is a *personal* list; even if it leaves out some personal favourites.

It may ease some readers' minds to add a list of regretted omissions. There is, for instance, no place for Cyril Walters, the master stylist; the oddly under-estimated Douglas Jardine; quietly firm and polished Ernest Tyldesley; the gamely determined Ian Redpath; the poised and polished Alan Kippax; or four capable England openers – the under-valued and neglected Jack Russell, steady Dennis Amiss, jaunty Cyril Washbrook and, doomed to be remembered as 'Herbert Sutcliffe's partner', that fine competitor, Percy Holmes. Lancastrians will regret the omission of Charlie Hallows and the immortal 'Shake' Makepeace. Five West Indians all but forced their way in – Lawrence Rowe, Roy Fredericks, Seymour Nurse, Larry Gomes and the older Clifford Roach. The senior Nawab of Pataudi, a clear-minded, pragmatic batsman, had his career interrupted by Indian affairs and war. It would be premature to include the spectacularly emergent Indian, Azharuddin – but he must surely soon demand a place – and the omission of the elegant record-breaker Dilip Vengsarkar was a sad decision. For old time's sake I would have been happy to have included the magnificently gritty Bill Edrich; and, above all, the reliable, personable and friendly Colin McDonald.

Perhaps three of the inclusions call for something near explanation for the younger generation of cricket followers, though none for any who watched them. Archie Jackson, the splendid young Australian who died at twenty-three, had already despite the handicap of his terminal illness, shown himself, in glorious fashion and on figures, to be a truly great batsman; it is amazing to contemplate what he might have achieved had he lived. Martin Donnelly after a brief first-class apprenticeship and 'a good war', as the saying is, came to England as, beyond reasonable doubt, the best left-hand bat in the world; unquestionably a master hand. He, like the South African 'Tuppy' Owen-Smith, took himself off to another career. Both, though, had done enough to set themselves in the highest class. The only doubt about either, like Archie Jackson, is as to the height each might have achieved had they played an alloted span in the game.

A cricketing friend suggested that the immensely promising and likeable Graeme Hick of Worcestershire and from Zimbabwe, should have been included. That recalls an earlier response by a very wise old cricketer to a suggestion that a certain young player was 'a great batsman'. 'He is', the elder said, 'extremely promising, but I will tell you if he is a great player when I have seen him play a full series of Tests against the West Indian fast bowlers.' We all look forward to Hick's achievements, which are, surely, a cricketing certainty. To all those whose qualities tempted this selector – as well as those who convinced him – thanks for the pleasure as batsman watched, or as legend relished. 'Great', as Daniel George once said, is a great word.

Figures for current players are correct to the end of the 1988 English season.

BOBBY ABEL

BOBBY ABEL, POPULARLY 'The Guv'nor' despite his lack of height – he was about 5 feet 4½ inches tall – was, after W.G. Grace (for nearly half a century that distinction was necessary), the most outstanding run scorer. He became something of a folk hero of London-South-of-the-River; and in 1902 he was accorded the distinction of inclusion as subject of a cartoon in *Vanity Fair* – the first professional to be so recognized – while Albert Craig, 'the Surrey poet', wrote many broadsheets in praise of him.

Technically, Abel was watchful, quick in reaction, capable of secure defence or of lively attack. Surprisingly for one who suffered much from defective eyesight, he was a cross-batted player; but he was strong on the off-side, hit surprisingly hard considering his lack of height, and had infinite patience and concentration.

Bobby Abel was a natural cricketer who came up uncoached through playing on rough wickets in London parks. He took some time to learn his craft, and he was twenty-three before he played for Surrey, and then largely because of his value in the field. The best description of him has been left by H.S. Altham: 'That curious little figure, surmounted by a somewhat faded and shrunken chocolate cap, the slow half-waddling gait that marked its progress to the wicket, and then the mastery of technique that could reduce all but the very greatest bowlers to frustration.'

To many of his contemporaries only the performances of W.G. Grace made Abel's run-getting credible. His figures would be impressive today, but must have seemed utterly striking then – for instance his 357 not out v Somerset in 1899, which remains the highest individual score ever made for Surrey: he scored 74 centuries: nine of them over 200 (eight for Surrey, one for Players v Gentlemen). He shared in nine partnerships of more than 200 for the first wicket (one with W.G. Grace for South v North in 1889); while in 1899 for Surrey against Yorkshire he and Tom Hayward put on 448 for the fourth wicket. He eight times carried his bat through an innings – once, historically, for England v Australia (Sydney, 1891-92). He played for Surrey for twenty-four years altogether (1881-1904); and in every season from 1895 until 1902 he made more than 2,000 runs with an average always above 40; in 1901, 3309 at an average of 56.

He was shrewd and mentally alert, putting out an autobiography, as well as editing an edition of John Wisden's *Cricket and How to Play It*.

Because of the rare incidence of Test cricket in those days, he appeared in only 13 Test Matches between 1888 and 1902, but he

Robert Abel (1857-1936) Surrey and England
Right-hand bat; slow right-arm round-arm off-break bowler; alert fieldsman anywhere, especially at slip.

must have been an early and automatic choice for an England XI throughout that entire period.

Eventually, to his bitter disappointment, his eyesight failed and, at forty-six, he retired, full of runs and respect. His two sons, T.E. and W.J., both played for Surrey – and the former for Glamorgan also. Neither, however, ever towered over any cricket as their tiny father did over the professional batting of two decades.

FIRST-CLASS CAREER RECORDS

Career	M	I	NO	HS	Runs	Avge	100
1881-1904	627	1007	73	357*	33124	35.46	74

Ct/St	Runs	Wkts	Avge	BB	5wI	10wM
586	6314	263	24.00	6-15	3	—

TEST CAREER RECORDS

Tests	I	NO	HS	Runs	Avge	100	50
13	22	2	132*	744	37.20	2	2

Ct/St	Balls	Runs	Wkts	Avge	BB	5wI	10wM
13	—	—	—	—	—	—	—

The prolific scoring Bobby Abel, who made the first century in England v South Africa Test matches

LES AMES

LES AMES WAS, beyond all doubt, the finest wicketkeeper-batsman the game has ever known; 37,248 runs at 43.51, with 102 centuries; 1,121 dismissals (703 catches, 418 stumpings) prove the point. As a wicketkeeper, he took over from George Duckworth in 1932, and maintained the position until 1938. He took the pace of Harold Larwood and the leg spin of 'Tich' Freeman with equal certainty; indeed, it was said of him that, throughout the 1932-33 – 'Body-line' – tour of Australia, he never missed a chance. Again, his all-round capacity was never better indicated than by his figures of 1928: 121 wickets and 1,919 runs; for 1929, 127 wickets (the highest yet achieved) and 1,795 runs; in 1932, 100 wickets and 2,482 runs. No one has ever seriously approached those all-round figures.

Leslie Ethelbert George Ames CBE (1905-   ) Kent and England Right-hand bat; wicketkeeper; occasional leg-break bowler; cover field.

An easy moving athlete – who played professional football on the wing for Gillingham – he first applied to Kent for engagement as a batsman. He was recommended to add wicketkeeping to his qualifications, and after doing so entered into his amazing partnership with 'Tich' Freeman; the newspaper compositors of cricket scores had 'stumped Ames, bowled Freeman' poised for every Kent match.

Swarthy, with friendly, honest, brown eyes, he was the most amiable of cricketers. He appealed only quietly for a catch or a stumping, and then sped the departing batsman on his way with an almost apologetic smile.

As a batsman he had all the efficiency demanded of a man who scored a hundred centuries. He was sound enough against pace but most spectacular against spin. He would go far and fast down the pitch to drive slow bowling with a long, full, free swing of the bat. His batting always looked the more attractive for the fact that his favourite strokes were the most attractive in the game – the straight, off, and cover drives, and the forward-cut.

In 1935, during The Oval Test against South Africa, he scored the most runs ever made before lunch in a Test: 123; going from 25 to 148. In 1931, he and G.O. Allen put on 246 for the eighth wicket at Lord's against New Zealand. He is, too, the only player twice to win the Lawrence Trophy for the fastest century of the season. He played for Kent in 430 matches between 1926 and 1951 and scored centuries against every first-class county except his own.

He was an England selector from 1950 to 1958; Secretary-Manager of Kent 1957 to 1973 and, in 1976, President of Kent. MCC made him an Honorary Member and took him on to their committee; and he was awarded the CBE in 1973. He liked nothing better, as the years went on, than a break from wicketkeeping, when he enjoyed himself vastly at extra cover and, occasionally, in bowling leg-breaks. He played 47 times for England and scored eight Test centuries.

All through his playing days and afterwards he was helpful and kind to young players: a man who had much from cricket and put much back into it.

FIRST-CLASS CAREER RECORDS

Career	M	I	NO	HS	Runs	Avge	100
1926-1951	592	951	95	295	37248	43.51	102

Ct/St	Runs	Wkts	Avge	BB	5wI	10wM
703/418	721	22	32.77	3-23	—	—

TEST CAREER RECORDS

Tests	I	NO	HS	Runs	Avge	100	50
47	72	12	149	2434	40.56	8	7

Ct/St	Balls	Runs	Wkts	Avge	BB	5wI	10wM
74/23	—	—	—	—	—	—	—

Les Ames, outstanding as both batsman and wicketkeeper, on the 1932 'bodyline' tour to Australia

ASIF IQBAL

ASIF HAS BEEN one of the most charismatic cricketers of modern times. A nephew of Ghulam Ahmed, the former Indian off-spinner, he was brought up in Hyderabad (India) and played for them in the Ranji Trophy from 1959 to 1968, when he emigrated to Pakistan; but he has played much of his best cricket in England for Kent. Bow-legged and wiry, amazingly quick of eye and reaction and fast over the ground, he has always been a lively figure at the crease or in the field. Always prepared to take on bowlers with attacking strokes, to bowl rather better than normal form dictated to turn a match, or to make the unexpected catch, his reputation was created by the number of occasions when – largely on his own – he saved or even won, apparently lost matches; and he went like lightning between the wickets.

In his first Test – for Pakistan against Australia at Karachi in 1964-65 – he went in at number ten and scored 41 and 36 (at number three); and then, even more improbably, opened the bowling with Majid Khan (five good wickets between them).

Asif Iqbal Razvi (1943-   ) Hyderabad, Karachi, P.I.A., National Bank, Kent and Pakistan Right-hand bat; medium pace right-arm bowler; alert fieldsman anywhere and inspirational captain.

The Asif cover drive – a stroke that has spread joy from Canterbury to Karachi

He made his first major mark in a Test when at Lord's in 1967, coming in at number nine, he scored 76, and with Hanif set the Pakistan Test record for the eighth wicket. At The Oval in the same series when Pakistan were 65 for eight, still 159 behind and facing an innings defeat, he made a quite brilliant 146 and, with Intikhab, put on 190 in 175 minutes.

His great year was 1976-77 when he scored four centuries in three different series. In the three-Test home rubber with New Zealand he (166) and Javed Miandad set a fifth wicket Pakistan record of 281. In Australia he scored 313 runs at 78.25, including 152 not out at Adelaide; and 120 at Sydney when Pakistan beat Australia for the first time; and then 135 against West Indies in Kingston, Jamaica.

Again, almost predictably, it was he who alertly and positively used the Packer affair to get better money for all the Pakistani cricketers.

He six times scored 1,000 runs in a season for Kent, for whom he was a constant, thrilling and buoyant match-winner.

FIRST-CLASS CAREER RECORDS

Career	M	I	NO	HS	Runs	Avge	100
1959-1982	441	703	76	196	23375	37.28	45

Ct/St	Runs	Wkts	Avge	BB	5wI	10wM
304	8776	291	30.15	6-45	5	—

TEST CAREER RECORDS

Tests	I	NO	HS	Runs	Avge	100	50
58	99	7	175	3575	38.85	11	12

Ct/St	Balls	Runs	Wkts	Avge	BB	5wI	10wM
36	3864	1502	53	28.33	5-48	2	—

CHARLES BANNERMAN

CHARLES BANNERMAN CREATED cricket history. He received the first ball bowled in a Test match (from Alfred Shaw, the master 'length' bowler); scored the first run and the first century in Test cricket; and virtually won the first Test ever played. He also made the first century for an Australian touring team in England; indeed his 133 against Leicester was the only three figure score made on that tour, when his aggregate of 726 runs was almost twice as many as the second man's. On that tour, too, he took part in the match when Spofforth and Boyle put out MCC for 19 and Australia beat them by nine wickets.

So, although his first-class playing career was cut short by illness, by the reasonable argument that a cricketer who is outstanding in his own period would be outstanding in any other, he must be accepted as a great batsman. Moreover his hundred in what is now accepted as the first Test Match – retired hurt for 165, 39 of them after a ball from Ulyett split his hand – was made

*Charles Bannerman
(1851-1930)
New South Wales and
Australia
Right-hand bat, sound
fieldsman.*

*Charles Bannerman (far
left, front row) on the
first Australian tour of
England*

out of a total of 245 in which no one else scored more than 18. It was, too, made against the best professional bowling in England and a wealth of it – Shaw, Hill, Ulyett, Southerton, Armitage, James Lillywhite and Emmett.

Born in Kent – at Woolwich – he was taught by Billy Caffyn, and described in *Scores and Biographies* as 'one of the most accomplished cricketers ever seen', Bannerman was brought to Australia 'to teach Australian batsmen to bat more enterprisingly' and coached in both Melbourne and Sydney.

Illness prevented him making the 1880 Australian tour of England, and about that time he declared his intention to return to England to play for Kent, but he never did so. Accepted as the finest batsman of his time in Australia, he hit stylishly and hard on both sides of the wicket; and, according to contemporary report, 'rarely made an uppish hit.' It was his reputation, too, that 'as a field he could not well be surpassed at long leg, middle wicket off, or at cover point, having a fine dash and quick return.' Incidentally among his list of 'firsts' may be added the fact that he was the first Australian player to score a century in New Zealand and in Canada; and the first batsman to be dropped by a fielder in a Test. Before he reached double figures he put up a simple catch off Shaw, which hit Armitage in the stomach and was grounded.

Although his early health was frail, he wore well and at the age of seventy-nine met the young Bradman. His career was, in fact, short; but for many years considerable kudos attached to those who could claim that they saw Charles Bannerman make the first hundred.

He settled in Sydney; his brother was the Sydney-born 'Alick', the legendary stonewaller. Charles settled in Australia for the rest of his life and, in 1922, the New South Wales trial match was declared his benefit and raised £490 for him; it was also the first cricket match on which commentary was broadcast.

Charles Bannerman, the first Test Match hero

FIRST-CLASS CAREER RECORDS

Career	M	I	NO	HS	Runs	Avge	100
1870-1887	44	84	6	165*	1687	21.62	1

Ct/St	Runs	Wkts	Avge	BB	5wI	10wM
20	44	0	—	—	—	—

TEST CAREER RECORDS

Tests	I	NO	HS	Runs	Avge	100	50
3	6	2	165*	239	59.75	1	—

Ct/St	Balls	Runs	Wkts	Avge	BB	5wI	10wM
—	—	—	—	—	—	—	—

WARREN BARDSLEY

WARREN BARDSLEY WAS an outstanding opening batsman for Australia; Sir Jack Hobbs described him as 'one of the best left-handers of the upright, classical school that I have ever seen.' He virtually commanded a regular place in the Australian team from the first Test of 1909 to the fifth of 1926; playing in 41 Tests and scoring 2,469 runs at an average of 40.47. The England series of 1911-12, when he had great problems with Barnes and Foster, was the only unsuccessful one of his career. Named for his birthplace in New South Wales, he was brought up in the Sydney suburb of Forest Lodge; where he went to the same school as Cotter, Kelleway and Oldfield.

A serious man, tetotaller and vegetarian, with a solemn air, he was as good as any Australian of his day on a turning pitch and had strokes all round the wicket. Shrewdly enough, he used simply to sway out of the line of bouncers. Neat on his feet, his grip on the bat was high, and he was a splendidly smooth, controlled, strong driver.

On the English tour of 1909 he became the first man to score a century in each innings of a Test; and in the Triangular Tournament of 1912 he scored more runs than anyone else on the three sides. He took up his record of success after the First World

Warren Bardsley (1882-1954) New South Wales and Australia Left-hand bat and capable outfield.

The full blade of Warren Bardsley in action against Leicestershire in May 1921

Warren Bardsley the veteran of five tours to England

War when he was rated a better batsman on English wickets than Australian. In 1921 – with Armstrong's side – he scored 2,005 runs at 54.18; in 1926, under H.L. Collins, 1,424 at 47.46. At Lord's on that tour, at the age of forty-three, he became one of the few men to carry his bat through a Test innings – for 193 not out, made in six-and-a-half hours.

As a player and selector in Sydney club cricket, he served thirty-five years (21,110 runs at 50.54). For New South Wales (83 matches) he made 6,419 at 53.04.

Remembered for his precise manner and the great green Australian cap pulled down to his ears, he seems to have been aware of his limitations. He was a steady outfield and a safe catch throughout a first-class career of twenty-four years (1903-1927) – unusually long for an Australian of his era.

Conscientious, monumentally reliable and utterly honest, he was brave, solid and respected.

FIRST-CLASS CAREER RECORDS

Career	M	I	NO	HS	Runs	Avge	100
1903-1927	250	376	35	264	17025	49.92	53

Ct/St	Runs	Wkts	Avge	BB	5wI	10wM
112	41	0	—	—	—	—

TEST CAREER RECORDS

Tests	I	NO	HS	Runs	Avge	100	50
41	66†	5	193*	2469	40.47	6	14

Ct/St	Balls	Runs	Wkts	Avge	BB	5wI	10wM
12	—	—	—	—	—	—	—

CHARLIE BARNETT

CHARLIE BARNETT WAS one of England's rare attacking opening batsmen. His father, C.S. and two uncles also played for Gloucestershire, and he himself first appeared for the county at the age of sixteen as an amateur. The next year he played more and, with growing confidence, he revealed himself to be a fine natural hitter. After he turned professional in 1929, though, he settled to an altogether more thoughtful approach and, while retaining his attacking bent, he soon became a first-class opening batsman.

High-shouldered and deep-chested, he batted with infinite gusto and from 1933 up to 1952 he was a brilliant stroke-maker, entertaining to watch, especially in his fast-scoring partnerships with Wally Hammond. His batting was the more entertaining for the fact that he was much addicted to the more exciting strokes – the cut, fine or square, and to driving. He had a special talent for driving a ball of good length or even shorter 'on the up', with

Charles John Barnett (1910-   )
Gloucestershire and England
Right-hand bat; right-arm medium pace bowler; outfielder.

Trent Bridge, 1938: Charlie Barnett in full cry during his dashing century against the Australians

immense power, by virtue of his immense strength of arm and innate timing. When he needed to defend, he did so utterly correctly; whether on the front foot or back, his bat was utterly straight. In 1934 in the Bank Holiday match with Somerset at Bath he hit 194, including 11 sixes, in just over three and three-quarter hours. The experimental lbw law and the prevalence of in-swing bowling disturbed him in 1935. By the following year, he seemed to have mastered the weakness; started to make big scores again and was chosen for the MCC team to Australia in 1936-37, when he scored 249 against Queensland at Brisbane.

Above all, he was always prepared to take a chance, even early in the innings and thus he often succeeded in wresting the initiative from the opposing bowlers. On the first day of the Trent Bridge Test against Australia in 1938 he reached 98 in the penultimate over before lunch: resignedly watched Hutton at the other end play out that over; and then reached his century off the first ball after the interval.

He was a good enough seam bowler to open the bowling for the county for many years, though he himself used to claim he merely did it 'to take the shine off for the spinners'. Certainly in his day, Tom Goddard and Sam Cook took many wickets with spin; but Barnett was a more than handy opener who took useful wickets.

Very much a West Countryman, over a career of twenty-six years he enjoyed his cricket happily and retired with dignity, leaving behind some rich memories of thrilling innings.

FIRST-CLASS CAREER RECORDS

Career	M	I	NO	HS	Runs	Avge	100
1927-1953	497	821	45	259	25389	32.71	48

Ct/St	Runs	Wkts	Avge	BB	5wI	10wM
319	12207	394	30.98	6-17	12	2

TEST CAREER RECORDS

Tests	I	NO	HS	Runs	Avge	100	50
20	35	4	129	1098	35.41	2	5

Ct/St	Balls	Runs	Wkts	Avge	BB	5wI	10wM
14	256	93	0	—	—	—	—

KEN BARRINGTON

KEN BARRINGTON WAS a most diligent, dedicated and intense cricketer. It might indeed be said, quite seriously, that he worried himself to death.

A chunky, rugged-looking man, he suffered more than most suspected from the anxieties of modern – and especially Test – cricket. A quite sterling character, who became England's sheet anchor, he was a massive compiler of runs and, in his 82 Test matches, scored 6,806 runs at 58.67: a monumental consistency. He came from Reading to Surrey at seventeen as a leg-spin bowler. On his return to the county from National Service in 1951 he worked determinedly on his batting, so effectively as to establish himself in the county side as a useful stroke-maker.

In 1955 he was picked for England against South Africa. His three innings – of 0, 34 and 18 – were patently not good enough, and they changed him as a player, if not as a man. He set out to prove 'them' wrong. To that end, although he had – as John

Kenneth Frank Barrington (1930-1981) Surrey and England Right-hand bat; right-arm leg spin bowler; generally slip field.

Ken Barrington pulls characteristically wholeheartedly

21

Woodcock once said – 'every shot in the book', and could almost juggle with a bat and ball, he set out to eliminate fun from his game and replace it with something very near impregnability. He was always a neat, controlled cutter and a skilful pusher and placer on the leg-side. Now, though, he adopted an almost exaggerated open stance – like John Langridge – to deal with the ball moving into the bat, which, of course, deprived him of the strokes between cover point and mid-off. He became, too, increasingly a back foot, and almost exclusively a bottom hand, player. He used, especially when playing back to pace, to give a little startled jump. Those who knew him well thought he was frightened of short, fast bowling, and indeed he probably was. Yet he never flinched – and that is the true courage; the courage that worried him too much. Almost desperately, too, he would cover up with pads, bat and everything – including, at need, probably, his heart.

Eventually his determined concentration led him to take seven-and-a-half hours over 137 against New Zealand. For public relations reasons, he was dropped, but only for one match; his reliability could not really be spared from the England side. In the

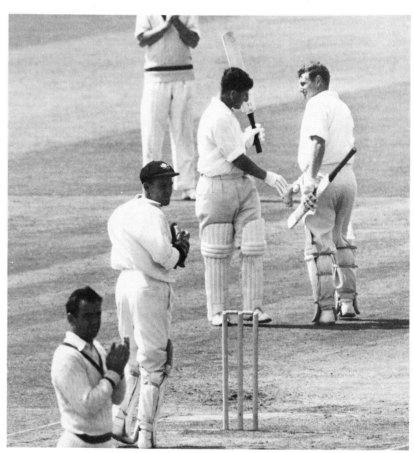

Barrington acknowledges the Australian applause as he reaches his double century at Old Trafford in July 1964

next he made 163. He had been a leg-spinner himself and he certainly played it well – he absolutely plagued Richie Benaud. Against the West Indies in the West Indies, where everything seemed against him – he accused Griffith, their fast bowler, of throwing – he scored centuries in the first two Tests of 1959-60 and another in 1967-68. In Port-of-Spain in 1968, when Griffith 'threw the lot at him' as they say, he made 143.

In Australia the pace of the pitches suited him admirably. In 1962-63 he scored 1,454 runs at 83.35, a figure at that time only exceeded for an Australian tour by Wally Hammond. In India, too, he always made runs, and was everywhere a safe slip catcher. Four times, he reached his hundred with an explosive pull for six.

He had, for all his belligerent look, and usually grim method, a splendid sense of humour; he was full of malapropisms, and a splendid mimic. Amongst his many habitual kindnesses was expertly repairing the broken-down cars of his friends – and when they were stranded, he did not mind how long he took to get them mobile.

Oh, though, he did worry; and, at thirty-eight, during a double-wicket match at Melbourne he had a thrombosis, after which, as a family man, he deemed it his duty to retire. After a few summers of charity matches in which he demonstrated his almost comic virtuosity with the bat, it was not difficult, though, to persuade him to return to the world of representative cricket, as an England Test selector, manager, assistant manager and, a voluntary, but valuable, coach to England touring teams. It was in that capacity, during the stresses of the West Indies tour of 1981 – stresses of various kinds – that he died of a heart attack in his hotel room.

Ken Barrington was a monumentally steady run-maker, an immense help to his mates on tour, and a reliable friend: in short, a good man.

FIRST-CLASS CAREER RECORDS

Career	M	I	NO	HS	Runs	Avge	100
1953-1968	533	831	136	256	31714	45.63	76

Ct/St	Runs	Wkts	Avge	BB	5wI	10wM
515	8907	273	32.62	7-40	8	—

TEST CAREER RECORDS

Tests	I	NO	HS	Runs	Avge	100	50
82	131	15	256	6806	58.67	20	35

Ct/St	Balls	Runs	Wkts	Avge	BB	5wI	10wM
58	2715	1300	29	44.82	3-4	—	—

ALLAN BORDER

*Allan Robert Border
(1955-   ) New South
Wales, Queensland,
Gloucestershire, Essex,
Australia.
Left-hand bat; slow left-
arm bowler; brilliant
fieldsman, fine thrower
and safe close catcher.*

ALLAN BORDER IS the stocky, strong, sandy-haired man who, through the recent years of trouble and depression in Australian cricket, has emerged as a staunch, reliable batsman and captain, who has won the respect of his own players and of his opponents. In the process, he has scored more runs for Australia – 7,343 – than anyone else. He has also played in most Tests – 94 – and while the statistics of this book only run to the end of the English season of 1988, he will, by such cricketing certainty as exists, play his hundredth Test at Melbourne over Christmas 1988. He is a conscientious cricketer; professional in the best sense of the word.

In 1977, at twenty-one, he played his first game for New South Wales. In the following English season, he gained experience of conditions there on the Gloucestershire staff and later in the Lancashire League. Returning home, he made his first Sheffield Shield century and only three weeks later was picked by Australia for the Third Test in the motley side enforced by the Packer defections. In the next Test he was top scorer in each innings.

Soon he was thrown in at the deep end of such a Test-playing wallow as cricketers of old simply could not have comprehended. In 1979-80 he played fifteen Tests in the space of twenty-eight weeks. In that period he set a record by reaching 150 in each innings of the same Test – Australia v Pakistan at Lahore. Almost immediately, he changed the shape of his life by marrying and going, on financially advantageous terms, to join Queensland (he took over the captaincy there in 1983). When, in 1979-80, the defectors returned, he had established his place. The West Indian fast bowlers, however, revealed a weakness in his technique against the short ball outside the off-stump. His response was highly professional: he took the utmost possible practice against that type of attack and, unlike many others, mastered it.

In 1986 he joined Essex, and they won the County Championship. In 1987 he captained The Rest of the World v MCC in the Lord's Bicentenary match, but played no county cricket. In 1988 he was second to Gooch in the Essex averages. It was in that season that he was hit by a bouncer in the match against Warwickshire, was concussed, and had his scalp stitched but, characteristically, he scored 112 on a difficult pitch in the second innings.

He plays still with basic purity of method, which prompted Sir Leonard Hutton in 1981 to say he thought him the best

RIGHT *Allan Border,
determined left-hander
with a complete repetoire
of strokes*

left-hander in the world. In that year Border was not merely top
of the Australian batting averages, but had an average twice has
high as the next man. He is now 33 years old and the mind
boggles at what he may achieve before he retires in five or more
years' time.

FIRST-CLASS CAREER RECORDS

Career	M	I	NO	HS	Runs	Avge	100
1976-1988	247	409	62	205	18810	54.20	58

Ct	Runs	Wkts	Avge	BB	5wl	10wM
240	2332	61	38.22	4-61	–	–

TEST CAREER RECORDS

Tests	I	NO	HS	Runs	Avge	100	50
94	164	27	205	7343	53.59	22	34

Ct	Balls	Runs	Wkts	Avge	BB	5wl	10wM
102	1781	699	16	43.68	3-20	–	–

IAN BOTHAM

THE FIRST MAN to score 5,000 runs and take 300 wickets in Test cricket, Ian Botham, at the start of the 1989 faced yet another challenge – to play his way back after spine surgery and go on breaking records. He had, though, already made his place in cricket history secure in 1981 by a unique all-round achievement. In that year he virtually took up a Test series between England and Australia in his bare hands and reshaped it.

He had been appointed captain of England in 1980 and lost the 1980-81 series in West Indies. He came back to England, lost the first Test with Australia, made a dull draw of the second, and resigned the captaincy which passed to Mike Brearley. Ian Botham, as a player, became a changed man, and performed the apparently impossible. In the third Test he took six for 95 in Australia's first innings of 401; scored 50 of England's inadequate 174 and when they followed-on, came in at 105 for five – still 122 behind; soon 92 behind with only three wickets standing. Then, on the brink of defeat, Botham took the Australian bowlers – including Lillee – by the scruff of the neck and made 149 not out, with 27 fours and a six. Still Australia needed only 130 to win, and seemed to be taking the game easily when Willis, in his finest Test performance, took eight for 43, and England amazingly won by 18 runs – only the second time a side has won a Test after following-on.

At Edgbaston, on an uncertain pitch, Botham made 26 – top scorer after Brearley (48) – in England's unconvincing 189. Surely enough, Australia led by 69 and England's uncertain 219 left Australia needing only 151 – the lowest innings of the match – to win. Old and Willis reduced them to 29 for three; they were 62 for three by lunch. Suddenly in the afternoon Emburey made a ball lift and Brearley immediately recalled Botham. In the next forty minutes Botham, bowling with rare fire, put out the last five Australians for one run, and England, winning by 29 runs, had again achieved the virtually impossible.

At Old Trafford, he made nought in England's 231 but took three for 28 and three slip catches to put Australia out for 130. Then Botham, coming in at 104 for five, struck a century off 86 balls, taking England to 404 and setting Australia 505 to win. This time he took useful early and late wickets. England won by 103 and, in an almost magical reversal of form, had won the rubber.

That was Botham's high peak but not an isolated one; he went on to break many records. Over six feet tall and powerfully built, he hits the ball with immense power, is a spectacular straight

Ian Terence Botham (1955-   ) Somerset and England Right-hand bat; right-arm fast-medium bowler; slip field.

driver, square cutter and hooker. In bowling, he linked the advice of Tom Cartwright to his own natural body swing, varying his length and using a bouncer and an outswinger which, in favourable conditions, was quite lethal. At slip, his speed of reaction made some improbable catches look quite simple. Again and again, he has produced match-winning performances. In 1980 he became the first player to score a century and take ten wickets in a Test. His 200 from 219 balls v India at The Oval in 1982 was the fastest Test 200 in terms of balls received, and he holds the record for most sixes in a first-class season (80 in 1985).

His cricket life has never been static. He left Somerset after the 1986 season when Richards' and Garner's contracts were not renewed, and joined Worcestershire, and if he can continue after his injury he may well set all-round figures beyond reasonable reach.

Above all, he is a brave, determined, exciting cricketer who competes to win. He has played League football, won a Somerset Junior Badminton Championship, is a keen golfer, a good shot, a fine fisherman and flies his own aeroplane. Once, as he anticipates, the surgery to his back proves successful, we shall, surely, see him back to his old greatness, though in all conscience, he has done enough already. As might be expected, the nonentities of cricket are against him – and have smeared him – without, though, damaging the image of England's greatest all-rounder of modern times.

LEFT *Another lusty blow from Ian Botham during his historic 149* against Australia at Headingley in 1981*

FIRST-CLASS CAREER RECORDS

Career	M	I	NO	HS	Runs	Avge	100
1974-1988	329	509	37	228	16422	34.79	33

Ct	Runs	Wkts	Avge	BB	5wI	10wM
303	26980	1005	26.84	8-34	53	7

TEST CAREER RECORDS

Tests	I	NO	HS	Runs	Avge	100	50
94	150	5	208	5057	34.87	14	22

Ct	Balls	Runs	Wkts	Avge	BB	5wI	10wM
109	20801	10392	373	27.86	8-34	27	4

GEOFF BOYCOTT

Geoffrey Boycott (1940-) Yorkshire, Northern Transvaal and England
Right-hand bat; right-arm medium pace bowler; outfield.

GEOFFREY BOYCOTT IS the most single-minded cricketer one can imagine: some people would say the most self-centred; others, the most perfectionist. Figures of his career are immensely impressive, not least his 8,114 runs in Tests, a total second only to Sunil Gavaskar's. What that figure might have been but for his three years of deliberate Test exile, 1974-77 (30 matches); and, again, the missed Test play of his three-year suspension for joining a mercenary team to South Africa, is amazing to contemplate. Add the fact that he was not chosen for England after that suspension ended – even though on strict playing form he was worth a place – and one is contemplating a figure which might have put him out beyond the reach of anyone else. In the English season of 1986 he scored 992 runs in all first-class matches, which ironically ended a sequence of 23 successive home seasons (1963-85) in which he had exceeded 1,000 runs. By then he had scored 151 hundreds, which placed him fifth in the

Geoffrey Boycott displays the textbook off-drive

table, behind Hobbs, Hendren, Hammond and Mead.

After carefully weighing the merits of a cricket career, Geoffrey Boycott decided in 1962 to become a Yorkshire player and was capped by the county in 1963. He is the only English batsman to average 100 runs over an entire season – and, typically, he did it twice (100.12 in 1971 and 102.53 in 1979). He takes thought over his arrangements; in 1977 he scored his 100th century – the first man to do so in a Test match, and he achieved it against Australia in front of his home crowd at Headingley. He has scored centuries against all the other first-class counties and in Tests on all current England grounds. Occasionally he has demonstrated his great virtuosity in stroke play. Long ago, though, he eliminated extravagance, explaining that he carried the main weight of England's batting – and, frequently, he did. His favourite stroke is the back-foot force to the off, which he executes perfectly and which has taken him to many landmark scores. He has a remarkable capacity to push a single off almost any ball – especially when he wants to keep the bowling – though that has cost many run-out wickets.

Geoffrey Boycott has achieved many, but by no means all, of his ambitions. He failed to attain the permanent England captaincy which he so passionately desired. Following that failure, he took himself, chagrined, out of Test cricket for three years. Then came his alternate successes and failures in his search for power in Yorkshire, however the county achieved nothing appreciable during his period – 1971 to 1978 – as captain; and suffered from his desire to be both administrator and captain. He was certainly the most discussed figure in Yorkshire cricket for two decades and he probably has never found the happiness his abilities should have produced. He will be remembered as an amazing – if not unique – compiler of runs; a man of great ambition and something near genius, as a batsman who did not achieve his entire desire.

The human face of the run machine: Geoffrey Boycott sweats it out against the Windward Islands on the 1981 England tour of West Indies

FIRST-CLASS CAREER RECORDS

Career	M	I	NO	HS	Runs	Avge	100
1962-86	609	1014	162	261*	48426	56.83	151

Ct	Runs	Wkts	Avge	BB	5wI	10wM
264	1459	45	32.42	4-14	–	–

TEST CAREER RECORDS

Tests	I	NO	HS	Runs	Avge	100	50
108	193	23	246*	8114	47.72	22	42

Ct	Balls	Runs	Wkts	Avge	BB	5wI	10wM
33	944	382	7	54.57	3-47	–	–

DON BRADMAN

*Sir Donald Bradman
(1908-   ) New South
Wales, South Australia
and Australia
Right-hand bat; occa-
sional leg-break bowler;
fine outfielder.*

DON BRADMAN WAS, at all levels, the most efficient and prolific batsman the game has ever known. Throughout his first-class career he scored centuries at a rate rather better than one innings in three. His figures were 28,067 runs at 95.14; in his 52 tests, 6,996 at 99.96. He wanted only four at The Oval in 1948 in his last innings – when Eric Hollies bowled him for nought – to have a Test average of 100. Most folk, though, would settle for 99.96.

Twice in England he scored 1,000 runs before June. No other player has done it more than once, and Bradman had only four opportunities. Those are figures unapproached in the history of the game. He occasionally bowled leg-breaks and was a fine outfield, quick and smooth in pick-up and return; though sometimes he dropped catches due to the fact that his hands were unusually small. He was an astute captain and a capable administrator. He was relatively short – 5 feet 7 inches – and, which may seem unbelievable, his eyesight was below average.

*'The Don' (Right) and Bill
Woodfull go out to the
wicket on the 1934
Australian tour of
England*

He made an undistinguished entry into Test cricket and was twelfth man for his next Test; and he did suffer that 'duck' on the somewhat sentimental occasion of his last Test appearance. In between Bradman dominated Test batting as no one else has ever done. True, some deemed him to have 'failed' in the 1932-33 series when England employed 'Bodyline' – a tactic designed specifically to combat Bradman – but even then he was top of the Australian batting with an average of 65.57.

Born in Cootamundra, the son of a farmer and carpenter, and brought up in Bowral – also in New South Wales – his first experience of batting was solitary, consisting, as is now a hackneyed story, of hitting a golf ball against a huge water tank and playing back the rebound with a cricket stump. At the age of seventeen, for Bowral, he scored 300 in a match which lasted through five Saturday afternoons.

His ability guaranteed rapid progress from his up-country club through Sydney Grade play to the New South Wales side, and the Australian team by the time he was twenty. A slight initial waver, and he was away to fame.

Physically compact, with good shoulders, Bradman was extremely nimble of feet and mind. He seemed to see and assess bowling extremely early; he used his feet to go down or back with perfect judgement. He had every stroke – and improvised others – and seemed never to relax his concentration. Excellent timing and wiry wrists invested his strokes with power; his judgement was well nigh perfect, while he was the most relentless punisher of the loose ball – and had the ability to treat even the marginally imperfect ball as 'loose'.

He captained Australia in 24 Tests; of which they won 15, drew six and lost three – two of them his first two in the captaincy, against G.O. Allen's 1936-37 side. Australia recovered to take the next three and the series – and won all five rubbers in which Bradman was involved.

He became an immense 'draw card', even to non-cricketers; huge crowds came to watch him, and grounds would almost empty when he was out. Indeed, receipts at the Sydney Cricket Ground fell dramatically when he moved to South Australia in 1935-36. He brought the same clear brain to his duties as a selector and, after he retired – when he became Australia's only cricketing knight – chairman of the Australian Cricket Board and author of several perceptive books.

Bradman remains a major figure in Australian life, and has been created a Companion of the Order of Australia, the highest honour but one that country can bestow. All in all, it is difficult to believe that cricket will ever know another such as Donald George Bradman.

Don Bradman: another staging point; he reaches his double century against England at The Oval in 1930

FIRST-CLASS CAREER RECORDS

Career	M	I	NO	HS	Runs	Avge	100
1927-1948	234	338	43	452*	28067	95.14	117

Ct/St	Runs	Wkts	Avge	BB	5wI	10wM
131/1	1367	36	37.97	3-35	—	—

TEST CAREER RECORDS

Tests	I	NO	HS	Runs	Avge	100	50
52	80	10	334	6996	99.94	29	13

Ct/St	Balls	Runs	Wkts	Avge	BB	5wI	10wM
32	160	72	2	36.00	1-8	—	—

PETER BURGE

PETER BURGE WAS a tall, strong batsman, a powerful driver — unusual for one of his height — and with something of a front-foot bias, but a highly efficient, and even dominant, hooker. He reached his peak relatively late in his career; but he played one of the finest and most important innings of modern Test cricket. He was probably handicapped as much as helped by the fact that his father was a senior administrator in Queensland cricket. On his first appearance in the state team, at twenty, he scored a valuable 54 and 46. There is little doubt, though, that he felt others thought his father's influence brought him into the Australian side for the fifth Test of 1954-55 when, with the rubber lost, the selectors tried out some younger players; and in his selection for the 1955 tour of West Indies which his father managed. He scored 177 against British Guiana but only 14 in the single Test for which he was picked; while in England in 1956, too, he could not keep his Test place. Back home, dropped off his first ball in Queensland's match with Victoria, he went on to make 210.

On his second tour of England (1961) he had grown out of his uncertainty. In the Lord's Test, when Australia were set 71 to win and Statham and Trueman reduced them to a precarious 19 for four, Burge boldly made 37 of the last 52 runs in an hour to take them to a five-wickets win. Even so, his highest score in nine

Peter John Parnell Burge (1932-   ) Queensland and Australia
Right-hand bat; useful close fieldsman.

May 1956: Peter Burge warming up against MCC; a boundary off Fred Titmus prior to his masterly century at Lord's later that summer

games for Australia against England was only 46 when he went to the last Test, at The Oval. There, however, he played the highest innings of the tour, a chanceless 181, made in seven hours, with 22 fours; altogether on the trip he marked up 1,376 at 55.04.

He returned to England for his third trip, and to the high peak of his career in 1964. Australia, by dint of a 1-1 rubber, had retained The Ashes in 1962-63. Now England gained advantage in the first and second Tests, both ruined and drawn through rain. Then, at Headingley, after making 268, England – largely the two spinners, Norman Gifford and Fred Titmus taking six wickets for 54 – had penetrated to 178 for seven, 90 ahead, when Neil Hawke came in to join Burge. At 187 Ted Dexter took the new ball, whereupon Flavell, and especially Trueman, proceeded to bowl bouncers – meat and drink to Burge, who hooked exultantly. Seven overs yielded 42 runs and the pair put on 105 for the eighth wicket in 99 minutes. So by the end of the second day Australia were 283 for eight: Burge 100 not out. Again the next morning Trueman hammered away short of a length, while Burge and Grout made 89 for the ninth wicket. By the time Trueman's 'trap' worked and the substitute, Alan Rees, took the catch at midwicket, Burge had made 160 in 315 minutes with 24 fours, and carried Australia to 389. So, when a rattled England were hustled out for 229, they needed only 111 to win. Massive batting on both sides drew the fourth and fifth Tests. In other, and simple words, Peter Burge had won the Test and the rubber with easily the highest score of the match. Burge had always said that his best batting was against England: all his four Test centuries were taken off the old enemy; the fourth of them came in 1965-66 when he saved the Melbourne Test.

For his native Queensland he made the highest score – 283 – and their record number of centuries – 24. The abiding memory is of him crashing Trueman's bouncer through the leg-side field with hooks which left the field standing, to win a Test series.

FIRST-CLASS CAREER RECORDS

Career	M	I	NO	HS	Runs	Avge	100
1952-1967	233	354	46	283	14640	47.53	38

Ct/St	Runs	Wkts	Avge	BB	5wI	10wM
166/4	129	1	129.00	1-0	—	—

TEST CAREER RECORDS

Tests	I	NO	HS	Runs	Avge	100	50
42	68	8	181	2290	38.16	4	12

Ct/St	Balls	Runs	Wkts	Avge	BB	5wI	10wM
23	—	—	—	—	—	—	—

GREG CHAPPELL

FOR MOST OF the 1970s, Greg Chappell was probably the best batsman in the world. Tall, slim and perfectly balanced, he is a stylish stroke-maker. Early in his career he was primarily an on-side player, and bowlers attacked him on and outside his off stump; by unremitting practice he corrected that tendency and became a stylish off and cover driver. Thus he emerged as a completely equipped batsman. His handicap was his physical health; he was much troubled by glandular fever, which often added to the strain of a conscientious man given to worrying.

Greg Chappell comes, of course, of a cricketing family – a fact of which they themselves may all be weary, but to an Australian it would be *lèse majesté* not to mention it. His father was an enthusiastic if not outstanding cricketer; his maternal grandfather, Vic Richardson, the Australian Test player; and, of course, his brothers Ian and Trevor have also played for Australia.

His has been a rich career. He was chosen for South Australia at eighteen and made scores of 53 and 62 in his first match. Then he went to Somerset for two valuable educative years, in the course of which he learnt the lesson many Australian batsmen find difficult – how to deal with swing bowling and its angles off 'green' pitches. He went there originally as an occasional leg-break bowler and returned to Australia a highly resourceful seam bowler, useful at any level.

He was picked for Australia under Ian's captaincy at twenty-two (in 1970) in what was the first Test ever played at Perth. When he went in, at number seven, the Australian score was 107 for five; when he was out for 108 – 326. That innings launched a majestic Test career.

On his first tour to England – still under Ian – he was top of the Australian batting after two great innings and significant in Australia drawing the series after losing the first Test. At Lord's, coming in at seven for two, he made 131 – highest score of the match – in Australia's win. They lost the fourth Test but, the two Chappells – Greg 113 and Ian 118, 201 in partnership – created their win in the fifth at The Oval.

In the Australian domestic season, 1972-73, Trevor, third brother, joined the other two in the South Australian side. Then, for the two elder brothers, to West Indies where, against the mounting fast bowling power of the home side, Australia took the rubber by 2-0: and Greg became the first Australian to score 1,000 on a tour there.

Eventually it had to happen; and, in the first Test in New Zealand, 1973-74 (Wellington) Ian Chappell made 145 and 121;

Gregory Stephen Chappell, MBE (1948-   )
South Australia,
Queensland, Somerset
and Australia
Right-hand bat; right-arm leg-break, then
medium pace bowler;
fine field (specialist slip).

and Greg 247 and 133; in the first innings they added 264 for the third wicket.

This was one of the hinge times of Greg Chappell's career; a considerable financial inducement persuaded him to move from South Australia to Queensland. Immediately afterwards, when Ian took the 1975 side to England, he walked out to the deep field during the Glamorgan match and told Greg to take over the captaincy for the rest of the game. Australia made a scrappy win of the rubber – but a win is a win. From that moment it was certain that the younger brother would take over the full office. Surely enough, he was appointed for the immediately following tour by West Indies. Another great start: in the first Test against Clive Lloyd's powerful side – at Brisbane – Greg scored 123 and 109 not out, establishing a superiority maintained by the pace of Lillee, Thomson, Walker and Gilmour, and reflected in Australia's 5-1 series win.

So he took to England a side which seemed certain to confirm Australia's world supremacy. Now, though, came the birth of the Packer – or WSC – storm; thirteen of his players had signed for Packer; and the side's morale was so crucially weakened that Mike Brearley's no-more-than-average – but brilliantly captained – side took the rubber by 3-0.

The Packer revolution guaranteed cricketers – especially those in Australia who aspired to make their living from the game – a fair living wage. It threatened to break up world cricket and, for the Australian seasons of 1977-78 and 1978-79, it sundered it. Without the supporting influence of the Chappell brothers it is doubtful if that revolution could have been sustained.

After it was over, Greg returned to the Australian captaincy and, in 1982-83, achieved his ambition to steer Australia to a win over England.

His captaincy was generally gracious; but in February 1981, at the end of play in a one-day match with New Zealand at Melbourne, when New Zealand needed six to win off the last ball, he ordered the bowler – his brother Trevor – to roll it underarm all along the ground to make a six-hit impossible. Not only was there immense anger among New Zealanders, but Australians, too, joined in the indignant protests.

He declared himself unavailable to take the 1980 team to England but returned for 1981 and captained sides against Pakistan, West Indies, New Zealand – where he did much to repair the unpleasantness – and Sri Lanka. He finished with an impressive list of Australian Test records: more runs than Sir Donald Bradman, 7,110 to 6,996; but in 87 Tests with an average of 53.86 by comparison with Sir Donald's 52 Tests and average 99.94. He had, too, beaten Bobby Simpson's record of catches

LEFT *Greg Chappell drives imperiously during his 117 against England at Perth in 1982*

Chappell taking his toll again; on his way to a hundred at Adelaide in the 1982-83 series against England

with 122; and he captained Australia 48 times. We can only wonder what his figures would have been if he had not squandered those two years of his prime on WSC.

When he retired from Test cricket in 1984, he announced he would continue to play with Queensland. A quite superb batsman and catcher, he has born his many honours modestly.

FIRST-CLASS CAREER RECORDS

Career	M	I	NO	HS	Runs	Avge	100
1966-1983	321	542	72	247*	24535	52.20	74

Ct/St	Runs	Wkts	Avge	BB	5wI	10wM
376	8717	291	29.95	7-40	5	—

TEST CAREER RECORDS

Tests	I	NO	HS	Runs	Avge	100	50
87	151	19	247*	7110	53.86	24	31

Ct/St	Balls	Runs	Wkts	Avge	BB	5wI	10wM
122	5327	1913	47	40.70	5-61	1	—

IAN CHAPPELL

IAN CHAPPELL IS the oldest of the three Chappell brothers; a brilliantly successful and abrasive captain at all levels; whose reputation is only marred by rough behaviour on the field.

He first appeared for South Australia at the age of eighteen in 1961-62 and scored his first Sheffield Shield century – against New South Wales – in 1962. He first played for Australia in the single Test v Pakistan in 1964-65, but probably was fortunate not to be chosen for the Australian team in West Indies 1964-65. However, on his first tour of England – in 1968 – he was top of the Australian batting, and a major success of the tour which Australia contrived to draw. He had a good series, too, against West Indies at home in 1968-69. In 1969-70 against South Africa he was involved in South Africa's overwhelming defeat. He remained loyal to Bill Lawry even through the following tour by England (1970-71), when he was – surely unhappily – given the captaincy for the last Test – a decision that he himself decried. He lost his first two Tests as captain; but his overall record in 30 Test captaincies was 15 wins, ten draws and five defeats. He captained South Australia often between 1970-71 to 1979-80; under him they won the Sheffield Shield twice.

Technically he was a pugnacious batsman with a great predilection for the hook which brought him many runs but also frequently caused his dismissal. At first he decided to eschew the stroke; Don Bradman persuaded him to continue with it, but to hook forward rather than backward of square. Thickly built and strong, his reputation was for aggressive driving, delicate cutting and glancing but, above all, for the pull and the hook. He had a Test batting average of 42.42 with 14 centuries.

He will, though, be chiefly remembered as the captain who took on the Australian Board of Control, fought for adequate pay and rewards for Australian cricketers: but refused – rather sadly – to accept the normal authority and standards of the game. Under him the Australian side became known for cheroot-smoking, sloppy dressing at social functions and 'sledging' – which was the abusing of opposing players. Sometimes, indeed, it seemed to his own players – and even, at times, to his friends – offensive. He inspired immense loyalty in his players, but he pleaded guilty to unlawful assault on an official during the West Indies tour of 1979: he was suspended after swearing at an umpire in Hobart and again for the same offence in Adelaide. Even after he retired from the game to become a reporter and commentator – work which he did extremely well – he was suspended for swearing on the air. It is possible to argue that Ian Chappell is one of the most

Ian Michael Chappell (1943-   ) South Australia, Lancashire and Australia
Right-hand bat, occasional leg-spin bowler, outstanding slip field.

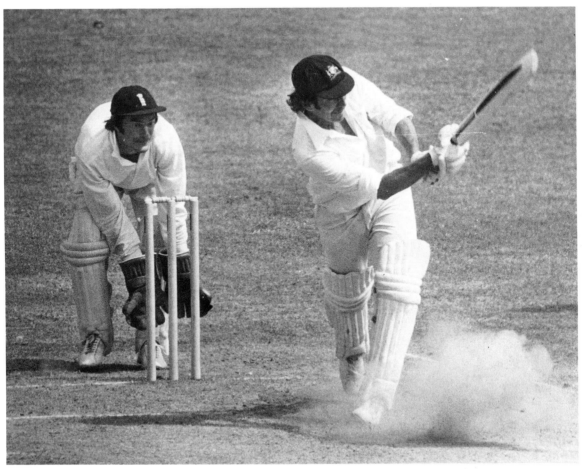

intriguing and paradoxical personalities to emerge in the modern game. It is certainly difficult to imagine a captain of recent times who is quite his equivalent.

He will be remembered as a brave batsman and bold captain, but a man unable to control his tongue or his behaviour: still, he knew the game as well as anybody; and could be great fun.

LEFT AND ABOVE *Ian Chappell, pugnacious batsman and ruthless captain: batting against England at Lord's in 1975*

FIRST-CLASS CAREER RECORDS

Career	M	I	NO	HS	Runs	Avge	100
1961-1979	262	448	41	209	19680	48.35	59

Ct/St	Runs	Wkts	Avge	BB	5wI	10wM
312/1	6614	176	37.57	5-29	2	—

TEST CAREER RECORDS

Tests	I	NO	HS	Runs	Avge	100	50
75	136	10	196	5345	42.42	14	26

Ct/St	Balls	Runs	Wkts	Avge	BB	5wI	10wM
105	2873	1316	20	65.80	2-21	—	—

DENIS COMPTON

*Denis Charles Scott
Compton, CBE
(1918-   ) Middlesex,
Holkar and England
Right-hand bat; left-
arm, finger-spin or
wrist-spin bowler; cap-
able fieldsman anywhere.*

DENIS COMPTON WAS a highly talented all-round cricketer, and
also, to some degree, a cult figure. There is no doubt that,
especially in 1947, he became a symbol of post-war euphoria;
and, with his county colleague and friend Bill Edrich, he produced
such a run of attractive and crowd-drawing successes as Lord's
had not – and has not – otherwise known in modern times. His
emergence seemed an opportune historic event. Physically
handsome, friendly and easy-going, he personified — and,
moreover appeared to make the errors of – the ordinary club
cricketer, but his genius enabled him to make those mistakes
good. For example, once in a Champion County v The Rest
match, he went down the pitch to drive Tom Goddard, slipped
and fell far out of his crease, yet contrived, while lying on the
ground, to late-cut the ball for four.

His skill was based on immense sense of the ball. For instance,
at soccer – he won a League championship medal with Arsenal

*Denis Compton proves
that even genius needs
practice*

and played for England in 14 war-time internationals – he was respected for his superb volleying of the ball, and, although he was never coached, he was basically correct and quite simply, a cricketing 'natural'. He won a place in the Middlesex team at eighteen and set a record by being the youngest player to score 1,000 runs in his first season. In 1947 – his and Edrich's carnival year – he made 3,816 runs at 90.86, with 18 centuries. When, in 1948-49, he scored 300 for MCC v. North Eastern Transvaal in Benoni, the few of us who were there realised we were watching a very exciting innings indeed, but did not appreciate then that it was the fastest 300 ever scored in a first-class fixture. Denis Compton would have resented being described as 'consistent' and he had his ups and downs – notably his unhappy Test series in Australia in 1950-51 – yet he reached his hundred centuries in 552 innings – fewer than anyone else except Don Bradman. At Capetown on the 1948-49 tour of South Africa, he bowled orthodox slow left-arm – 25 overs – to take five for 70. Normally, however, when he bowled, he trafficked in left-arm wrist spin – and he could turn the 'Chinaman' quite grotesquely: 622

National heroes: Edrich and Compton make their way through the vast crowds after England has regained the Ashes at The Oval in 1953

first-class wickets for a man who apparently refused to treat his bowling seriously is a very fair haul indeed.

After their runaway triumph of 1947 he and Bill Edrich did not enjoy the same success against Bradman's Australians of 1948: but they did share an unbroken partnership of 424 against Somerset which remains an English first-class record; and the highest for any wicket at Lord's.

Denis Compton was confirmed even further in the position of a national hero when, the same year, against the Australian fast bowling – including his friend, Keith Miller – he edged a lifting ball into his face during the Old Trafford Test. Returning almost at once to the crease, still bleeding, he went on to make 145 not out. Indeed, in that series, when England were overwhelmed, he averaged 62. Sadly though, in 1948-49 an old football injury recurred and he never again had quite the same mobility.

There were better days ahead though – with Bill Edrich at the other end – he made the winning stroke with which England won back the Ashes after twenty years. The football injury meant that eventually he had to have an operation to remove his right kneecap but, in his last Test against Australia – at The Oval in 1956 – he made 94 and 35. It was a good curtain for a cricketer who has never been forgotten.

Remembered – nay, most happily popular – in all the cricketing countries where he played, the very mention of Denis Compton's name is sufficient, even nowadays, to produce sentimental smiles on the faces of elderly ladies who were maidens when he was a young man.

FIRST-CLASS CAREER RECORDS

Career	M	I	NO	HS	Runs	Avge	100
1936-1964	516	839	88	300	38942	51.85	123

Ct/St	Runs	Wkts	Avge	BB	5wI	10wM
415	20074	622	32.27	7-36	19	3

TEST CAREER RECORDS

Tests	I	NO	HS	Runs	Avge	100	50
78	131	15	278	5807	50.06	17	28

Ct/St	Balls	Runs	Wkts	Avge	BB	5wI	10wM
49	2716‡	1410	25	56.40	5-70	1	—

BEV CONGDON

BEV CONGDON WAS a thoughtful, determined, reliable 'made' all-rounder and dogged captain, who scored more runs for New Zealand than anyone else. Lean, wiry, slightly stooping, he came from a country area and graduated through the Hawke Cup – the lesser domestic competition of New Zealand – to the Plunket Shield, first with Central Districts, then Wellington, Otago and finally Canterbury. All this time he was learning cricket, especially batting; helped by that wise cricketer and shrewd coach, Les Townsend of Derbyshire, who understood young cricketers so well. That meant a 70-mile journey, twice a week, but by then Bev had overcome the temptation of tennis for cricket.

He first made his way into Test cricket, when he was nearly twenty-seven, against Pakistan in 1964-65, purely as a batsman, but an undistinguished series cost him his place against India. In the last Test he came back: New Zealand used eight bowlers and were beaten; Congdon did not bowl. From that time he set out to guard his place with serviceable bowling. After some experiments and advice, and some five years of perfecting his technique, he was to emerge as a medium pacer – unexciting to watch but capable of swinging the ball a little each way, achieving some movement off a responsive pitch and, above all, learning to bowl a length. In England in 1965, showing signs of development as a defensive bat, he just got on as a bowler, but with no great success.

Bevan Ernest Congdon (1938-   ) Central Districts, Wellington, Otago, Canterbury and New Zealand
Right-hand bat; right-arm medium bowler; safe field anywhere.

Bev Congdon: a compact drive during his captain's innings of 175 against England at Lord's in 1973

Bev Congdon had built a secure defence, having equipped himself with fresh and controlled scoring strokes, and he finally established himself as a major Test cricketer on the New Zealand tour of West Indies in 1971-72. He made only 11 and 16 in the first Test but took three wickets; he went on to 166 not out (in a total of 348), and 82 in the second, plus three wickets. In the third Test, taking over as captain when Dowling was injured, he made 126 and took four wickets; in the fourth 61 not out and two wickets; in the fifth 11 and 58 and one wicket; and the series was creditably drawn. As a captain he was gritty and solid rather than inspirational; and, recognising that a winning position had to be worked for, he never jeopardised it. In England, his 176 at Trent Bridge and 175 at Lord's, in both founding major innings, initially against the odds, were the measure of his stature. The first was made when, having been routed in the first innings and set 479 to win, New Zealand achieved the – then – highest losing fourth innings total in Test cricket; the second when he almost established a winning position for them.

In 1973-74 he took New Zealand on what was, surprisingly enough, their first Test tour of Australia. They were beaten, but a couple of months later at Christchurch he captained them to their first win over Australia.

In the tied series with India of 1975-76 when the New Zealand captaincy passed to Glenn Turner, all Bev Congdon's four Test innings were of more than 50; at Eden Park he took five for 65. At home against Australia he made 107 not out, by far the highest New Zealand score, and in a ninth wicket stand of an hour with Dayle Hadlee, drew the match against the bowling of Dennis Lillee, Gary Gilmour, Max Walker and Kerry O'Keeffe.

He had set an impressively solid record in Tests, 3,448 runs – and 59 wickets – for New Zealand by 1978 when, at the age of forty, after a disappointing tour of England, he announced his retirement.

FIRST-CLASS CAREER RECORDS

Career	M	I	NO	HS	Runs	Avge	100
1960-1978	241	416	40	202*	13101	34.84	23

Ct/St	Runs	Wkts	Avge	BB	5wI	10wM
201	6125	204	30.02	6-42	4	—

TEST CAREER RECORDS

Tests	I	NO	HS	Runs	Avge	100	50
61	114	7	176	3448	32.22	7	19

Ct/St	Balls	Runs	Wkts	Avge	BB	5wI	10wM
44	5620	2154	59	36.50	5-65	1	—

W. G. Grace

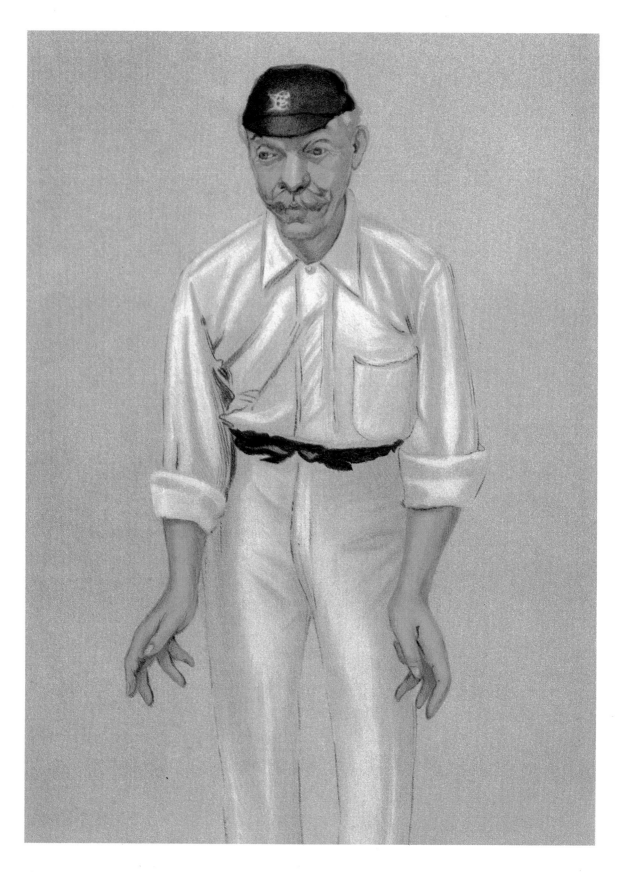

FAR LEFT: *Bobby Abel*

LEFT: *Gilbert Jessop*

Colin Cowdrey

Tom Graveney

FAR LEFT: *Norman O'Neill*

LEFT: *Graeme Pollock*

Gary Sobers

COLIN COWDREY

COLIN COWDREY WAS potentially the finest of post-war batsmen. Indeed, his batting must be spoken of in terms of superlatives. Only Sir Jack Hobbs ever played all types of bowling on all kinds of pitches with similar unhurried ease. Colin Cowdrey, though, was a batsman of moods. Where Sir Jack was cheerfully and unworriedly consistent, Colin Cowdrey could sink into pits of uncertainty when the fire ceased to burn, allowing himself to be dominated by bowlers inferior to him in skill.

Michael Colin Cowdrey, CBE (1932-   ) Oxford University, Kent and England
Right-hand bat; right-arm leg-break bowler; slip field.

It is tempting to trace the influences which made up his highly complex personality. First must come that of his father – top scorer for Europeans against the 1926-27 touring team in India – and whose enthusiasm for the game led him to give his son the initials MCC. Then India – and presumably his *ayah* – laid upon him his quiet courtesy. Charles Walford, Headmaster of Homefield Preparatory School in Surrey, was the martinet who hammered into him his purity of technique. Few cricketers are formed so early but when, in 1945, he was sent to Gover's School, Alf Gover himself wrote to Ewart Astill, the Tonbridge coach, to tell him to expect a thirteen-year-old pupil good enough for the School's first XI at once. So it proved, which led to laughably appalling breaches of school protocol, all suffered in the name of cricket; but he went to the match with Clifton at the age of thirteen, a leg-spin bowler and batting at number three. The youngest player to take part in a public schools' match at Lord's, he scored 75 – more than half his side's runs from the bat – in their first innings; 44 out of 175 in the second; while in the first Clifton innings he took three for 58; in their second, when they looked likely to win, he took the last five for 33 to win the match by two runs. This was the pattern of his success. A century as captain of the Public Schools XI against Combined Services; a season with Kent, centuries for the Free Foresters and The Gentlemen; three years an Oxford Blue, and he was chosen for Len Hutton's 1954-55 tour of Australia.

During the voyage out to Australia, his father died. Len Hutton was a comforting captain but, above all, Colin Cowdrey went on to steer himself to the success we must believe he dedicated to the father he had so briefly known. He batted usefully in the first two Tests, which went one to each side: then, at Melbourne, when Miller cut England down to 41 for four, Colin scored his first Test century to decide the match which tilted the rubber. He was then just twenty-two years old, and already a major batsman. Everything else – and it is all in the books of statistics – seemed then to follow automatically: and he did it all without the slightest

The precise certainty of Colin Cowdrey illustrated in this late cut off Bev Congdon for MCC v New Zealand at Lord's in 1965

hint of antagonism; yet, one still felt that he might have achieved more. He simply broke and set records. He played in 114 Test Matches, scored 22 Test centuries (an England record shared with G. Boycott and W.R. Hammond); with Peter May, put on 411 for the fourth wicket against the West Indies in 1957; 163 with A.C. Smith for the ninth wicket against New Zealand; took 120 catches in Tests – the England record for a fieldsman other than a wicketkeeper – and became the first batsman to score a century against every Test country except his own.

Large, steady, perfectly balanced, he was a quiet influence at the crease, or in the field, where he took so many superb, unobtrusive slip catches. Perhaps the best description of his batting is to say that, against the greatest bowlers in the world, he could look like a man playing against boys. He handled the captaincy of England with poise and a marked ability to motivate his players, but injury deprived him of the great run he should have had in that office: he was not a lucky man, but he did not complain.

He was awarded the CBE, made a member of the MCC Committee and saw two of his sons play for Kent. In April 1986 Cowdrey's appointment as MCC President for the club's bicentenary in 1987 was well-received. Quiet, kind, honest and modest – did he hide his delights as he hid his sorrows?

FIRST-CLASS CAREER RECORDS

Career	M	I	NO	HS	Runs	Avge	100
1950-1976	692	1130	134	307	42719	42.89	107

Ct/St	Runs	Wkts	Avge	BB	5wI	10wM
638	3329	65	51.21	4-22	—	—

TEST CAREER RECORDS

Tests	I	NO	HS	Runs	Avge	100	50
114	188	15	182	7624	44.06	22	38

Ct/St	Balls	Runs	Wkts	Avge	BB	5wI	10wM
120	119	104	0	—	—	—	—

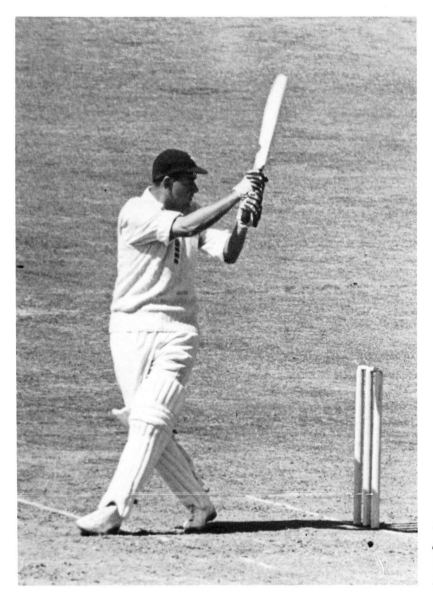

Cowdrey pulls Worrell during his 152 against West Indies at Lord's in 1957

MARTIN CROWE

*Martin David Crowe
(1962-   ) Auckland,
Central Districts,
Somerset and New
Zealand
Right-hand bat; right-
arm medium-pace
bowler.*

MARTIN CROWE IS the tall, strong, personable batsman who, before he was twenty-one, had played cricket for New Zealand and made himself a considerable reputation in English county cricket. He comes from a cricket family: his father played first-class cricket for Canterbury and Wellington, his elder brother, Jeff, for New Zealand. Even so, his advance was remarkably rapid. He first appeared for Auckland just after his seventeenth birthday, first played for New Zealand at nineteen and, at twenty-one, established himself as a conscientiously fit batsman who could bowl usefully and field brilliantly, for Somerset.

In 1984 he came to the county when Vivian Richards went on tour with West Indies. He made an atrocious start but suddenly swept through June with four centuries in consecutive matches and, altogether, 719 runs at 143.8; finished the reason with 1,870 at 55.97 in the first-class game; and also played a number of valuable and exciting innings in over-limit games. He had an outstanding season for Somerset in 1987, with a batting average of 67.79, but in 1988 he was forced to return home with a back injury, had an attack of viral fever and withdrew from New Zealand's tour of India. At about the same time he severed his connection with Somerset.

He has, however, established himself in New Zealand representative teams: and in 1986-87 he set a fresh record aggregate for a New Zealand season with 1,676 runs – with eight hundreds – and an average of 93.11. He had had some earlier experience of English conditions with what he called a 'scholarship' on the Lord's Ground Staff in 1981, League Cricket with Bradford in 1982 and, of course, the New Zealand tour to England and the World Cup in 1983.

In 1985-86, at Christchurch, he scored 137 against Australia, most of those runs coming after he had been felled by a Reid bouncer and had his chin stitched. He was, too, top scorer with 83 out of 332 when New Zealand, headily, beat West Indies to level the rubber at Christchurch in 1986-87. One of his most remarkable innings was played for Somerset against Leicestershire who were, at the time, the leaders in the Championship. Somerset were set to score 341 in a minimum 87 overs to win, and they were soon three for two wickets, only for Crowe (190) and Roebuck (128) to put on 319 in 80 overs. That was Crowe's fourth century in successive Championship matches and it included a six and 23 fours. The young man was extremely popular with colleagues and opponents in the English county game and would always be certain of a welcome back.

FIRST-CLASS CAREER RECORDS

Career	M	I	NO	HS	Runs	Avge	100
1979-1988	165	274	42	242*	13151	56.68	46

Ct	Runs	Wkts	Avge	BB	5wI	10wM
170	3685	116	31.76	5-18	4	–

TEST CAREER RECORDS

Tests	I	NO	HS	Runs	Avge	100	50
42	70	6	188	2774	43.34	9	9

Ct	Balls	Runs	Wkts	Avge	BB	5wI	10wM
46	1239	607	13	46.69	2-25	–	–

Martin Crowe, young batsman who has already confirmed his potential at the highest level

STEWART DEMPSTER

Charles Stewart Dempster (1903-1974) Wellington, Scotland, Leicestershire, Warwickshire and New Zealand. Right-hand bat; occasional wicketkeeper, slow right-arm bowler; fine cover point.

STEWART – 'STEWIE' – DEMPSTER was an exceptionally gifted cricketer – his contemporaries would say the finest batsman ever produced by New Zealand – but not a truly committed one. Indeed, in a playing career which extended over twenty-five years, he appeared in only 185 first-class matches: 40 (mainly in 1921-22, for Wellington) established him as an early choice for New Zealand; and 69, between 1935 and 1939, for Leicestershire. The entry 'Scotland' indicates a single match for the country of his family's origin in 1934 while on a business trip; and there were three for Warwickshire in 1946. Most of his other cricket was for New Zealand touring sides or Sir Julien Cahn's private XI; but chiefly he devoted his time to business.

A thickset, powerful, but not strenuous man, he played with considerable natural grace; and, especially on the non-Test tour of England, worked out his technical problems for himself – he was never coached. He emerged with an orthodox, straight-batted and handsome style, excellent timing, an intuitive player of spin, sound against pace, and strong on the leg-side.

In 1920 he went into state cricket for Wellington and played for them for two seasons, which was the basis for his international career. In his time, New Zealand used to play only two- or three-match Test rubbers (though once four), and his ten matches were spread over five series. On their 1927 tour Dempster made 1,430 runs at 44.68. In their first Test series – at home in 1929-30 – he scored their first Test century, 136, in a partnership with John Mills which put on 276 in what remains a New Zealand first wicket record; for good measure, he scored 80 not out in the second innings. He was top of their Test batting with 341 runs at 85.25. He began their 1931 tour of England – when his improvement amazed even the sternest critics – with 212 against Essex. Then, in his and New Zealand's first Test in England, at Lord's, he scored 53 and 120, with their first 'away' hundred.

His last Test was against England at Auckland in 1932-33 when, coming in when New Zealand were nought for two, he made 83 not out in a total of 156.

Joining Sir Julien Cahn's XI, he began in 1935 to play also for Leicestershire and, from 1936 to 1938, he captained them. In that period he was top of their major batsmen in every season. Close observers thought that he then batted better than ever before. Certainly he was the county's major batsman in each of those seasons and, indeed, was, each year, prominent in the national tables. Twice, too, he scored three centuries in consecutive innings – once against the 1938 Australians.

Stewie Dempster, modest and thoughtful, was undoubtedly one of the most complete batsmen of any country in his time; but he achieved, sadly, much less than his talents justified.

FIRST-CLASS CAREER RECORDS

Career	M	I	NO	HS	Runs	Avge	100
1921-1947	185	306	36	212	12145	44.98	35

Ct/St	Runs	Wkts	Avge	BB	5wI	10wM
94/2	300	8	37.50	2-4	—	—

TEST CAREER RECORDS

Tests	I	NO	HS	Runs	Avge	100	50
10	15	4	136	723	65.72	2	5

Ct/St	Balls	Runs	Wkts	Avge	BB	5wI	10wM
2	5	10	0	—	—	—	—

Stewart Dempster, dominating batsman who headed the averages in New Zealand's first Test series, against England in 1929-30

63

TED DEXTER

*Edward Ralph Dexter
(1935-   ) Cambridge
University, Sussex and
England
Right-hand bat; right-
arm fast-medium
bowler; cover field.*

TED DEXTER STOOD out as unusual in the middle of the twentieth century: he seemed to belong rather to its beginnings, in the 'Golden Age of Cricket'; or even to the days of the Regency. He was a natural and accomplished athlete and also, while he would have resented the label of intellectual, he had a sharp mind, and delighted in solving the problems of any activity to which his hungry brain persuaded him.

He might have been an outstanding as a golfer as he proved as a cricketer; he was a highly capable rugby player; he flew his family from England to Australia; was a successful journalist, capable, perceptive, and flexible enough to write to editorial satisfaction in both *The Observer* and *The Sunday Mirror*; he collaborated with Clifford Makins in two highly readable thrillers; he drove with great gusto luxury motor cars, big motor bikes and mopeds: he owned and ran a racehorse and greyhounds; and stood twice for Parliament. Once, as an undergraduate, he walked into a party, saw there a beautiful young woman, decided to marry her, did so; and they continue to live a married life which triumphantly bears scrutiny.

The point about Ted Dexter here, however, is that he was an outstanding batsman. He first emerged as a bowler; and, apparently casually he could generate a lot of speed out of his final body-swing: and, when his fielding was criticised as nonchalant, he piled into it and became highly effective in speed of pick-up and fast accuracy of return.

One day, in 1965, driving home after a day at the races, he ran out of petrol, pushed the car off the road, lost control of it and it ran away with him, smashed into a gateway, and broke his leg. So he gave up cricket – perhaps, indeed, he had lost a degree of interest in his success there, and was glad of the alibi to go away. So now he jogs with his wife in the morning and, in the President's Putter, emerges as one of the finest amateur golfers in the country. Sir Jack Hobbs in his retirement said he saw very little cricket but that he loved to walk down the road to Hove and watch an innings by Dexter.

At the time of his accident he was captain of Sussex, an office he had held since 1960. In 1961-62 in Pakistan he captained England – he did this for 30 Test Matches – and it seemed to draw the best out of him as a batsman.

RIGHT *Another fast bowler
suffers at the hands of
Ted Dexter; a
characteristic drive*

Tall, wide-shouldered and splendidly athletic, he remained rock still at the crease until he decided upon a stroke, when he launched himself with full commitment. Ted Dexter demonstrated to the cricketers of the fifties and sixties that the manner of

the century's first decade was valid: he attacked not only spinners but fast bowlers, as well – or even preferably. All this was no whim: he was soundly grounded in the game and straight in defence, but, above all, he could, and did, carry the fight to the bowlers; and the faster they were, the better he seemed to like it. It is, therefore, almost depressing that he was so often, in conscience, obliged to defend. Indeed, the annals of the game will show that Ted Dexter had his greatest Test successes in defensive innings against the might of the West Indian fast bowlers.

His class had long been apparent at University, and his 52 against New Zealand on his Test debut (1958, at twenty-three) was a handsome and impressive innings. Then, though, he was unconvincing in Australia; made 141 in New Zealand; but showed a most uncharacteristic lack of confidence against India in England. In West Indies in 1959-60, Dexter was convincing in courage, style and figures, with two centuries – one of them a considerable rescue operation, and two fine attacking innings at Port of Spain. He was useful, but no more, against South Africa in 1960 but, at Edgbaston in the following year, he hauled England up from deep distress against Australia with a solid 180 after they went in 321 behind. In 1964, he again put up mighty resistance against Australia, with 174 at Old Trafford. In the next year came the injury; retirement; but return after three years to score 203 not out against Kent – the second hundred of it at better than a run a minute.

The selectors could not resist the temptation of his unquestionable class, and called him back but, though he fought hard and did enough to indicate that he could still have been an outstanding Test player, he could not reproduce his old form numerically, so he went back into his highly active retirement. Confident, quick-witted, amusing, and never dull, Ted Dexter was the best of company, and far more thoughtful than some people appreciate.

FIRST-CLASS CAREER RECORDS

Career	M	I	NO	HS	Runs	Avge	100
1956-1968	324	567	48	205	21150	40.75	51

Ct/St	Runs	Wkts	Avge	BB	5wI	10wM
233	12539	419	29.92	7-24	9	2

TEST CAREER RECORDS

Tests	I	NO	HS	Runs	Avge	100	50
62	102	8	205	4502	47.89	9	27

Ct/St	Balls	Runs	Wkts	Avge	BB	5wI	10wM
29	5317	2306	66	34.93	4-10	—	—

BASIL D'OLIVEIRA

BASIL D'OLIVEIRA BECAME more significant than he could ever have dreamt of being when, in 1966, he walked on to the field to play for England at Lord's; and even more when, in 1969, the Queen decorated him with the OBE. Thus he gave new – and hitherto unimagined – hope to millions of the under-privileged coloured peoples of South Africa.

As long ago as 1956 he began to write earnestly from his Capetown home to England in hope of finding coaching instruction, so that he could help to teach cricket to his fellow cricketers in that Cape coloured community. It was not, though, until 1959-60, when he took part in a mixed match in the Cape, that some English professionals – Peter Walker, Alan Oakman, Jimmy Gray and Peter Sainsbury – saw him play, and could offer convincing evidence to his quality. As a result, in 1960, he came over to join Middleton in the Lancashire League on a fairly poorly paid contract. Basil D'Oliveira was then twenty-nine: and there was far to go – further, indeed, than he dreamt. His first month was one of misery. He had previously played only on matting wickets: and had never experienced anything like the sodden mud of Lancashire turf in May. Eric Price, the Lancashire slow left-arm bowler, proved his salvation with advice and encouragement. By the end of the season his average was higher than that of Garfield Sobers in the same league.

Some three years later, playing in a Sunday match with other league players against a team of English county cricketers, he scored some runs which mightily impressed Tom Graveney on the opposing side. As a result he was persuaded to join Worcestershire: he first appeared for them in 1964; and, during his qualification period, made a century against the Australians. In 1965, becoming a regular county player at the age of thirty-four he scored over 1,500 runs in the Championship. He picket up 35 wickets with his 'wobbly' medium-pace; and he took some good slip catches.

In the next year, 1966, Basil D'Oliveira found it difficult to believe that he had been picked to play for England against West Indies at Lord's. He played coolly enough but had the bitter luck to be run out in his only innings. A fortnight later, scores of 76 and 54 at Trent Bridge established him in the side, and at Headingley 88 – substantially the largest innings for England – in their defeat by the West Indies, launched him on a period of a full six years as a regular member of the England side.

Somehow, when he was quite young, Basil D'Oliveira had absorbed the knowledge to make himself a basically correct

Basil Lewis D'Oliveira, OBE (1931-   ) Worcestershire and England
Right-hand bat; right-arm medium-pace and off-break bowler; slip field.

Basil D'Oliveira driving Ian Chappell during his historic century against Australia at The Oval in 1968, the innings that indirectly ended South Africa's participation in Test cricket

batsman. Through all his cricketing life, though, those erratic wickets of his early days were reflected in his restricted – almost negligible – back-lift. Nevertheless, such was his power of wrist and forearm, that he could hit mightily; driving fast bowlers fearlessly and determinedly: for example, at Leeds in 1966, he drove a fair length ball from Wesley Hall back over his head for six. In bowling, as in batting, he led in the classic fashion with his left shoulder, and he constantly took apparently effortless catches by his high speed of reaction.

In 1968, his 158 and a second-innings seven for 50 by Derek Underwood effectively won the final Test against Australia. The next day the England side for South Africa was announced: and it did not include D'Oliveira. There were protests by MPs, MCC members resigned, and a special meeting of MCC was called to propose that D'Oliveira should, after all, be included. Then, when Tom Cartwright reported injured, Basil D'Oliveira was invited to take his place in the touring side. At this point the South African Government cancelled the tour and MCC acceded. Some intemperate remarks were made and some stupid and bigoted positions were taken up. The one person to emerge from the whole matter with credit and dignity was Basil D'Oliveira. England have not since played a Test series with South Africa.

The series with Australia of 1972 was Basil D'Oliveira's last in Test cricket. In the drawn rubber he finished third in the England averages, grinding away determinedly in a low scoring series; for the first time in a five-match rubber, no English player scored a century. Basil D'Oliveira's last innings was a gritty 43. He continued to play for Worcestershire, and to make valuable scores in difficult circumstances until, in 1979, he retired and became County Coach, enjoying – as he did most things – watching his son, Damian, playing also for Worcestershire. It is a happy life-story which he lived in highly creditable fashion, delighting by, and in, his cricket, making friends and doing honour to the game and to his people.

FIRST-CLASS CAREER RECORDS

Career	M	I	NO	HS	Runs	Avge	100
1961-1980	362	566	88	227	18919	39.57	43

Ct/St	Runs	Wkts	Avge	BB	5wI	10wM
211	15021	548	27.41	6-29	17	2

TEST CAREER RECORDS

Tests	I	NO	HS	Runs	Avge	100	50
44	70	8	158	2484	40.06	5	15

Ct/St	Balls	Runs	Wkts	Avge	BB	5wI	10wM
29	5706	1859	47	39.55	3-46	—	—

MARTIN DONNELLY

*Martin Paterson
Donnelly (1917-   )
Wellington, Canterbury,
Middlesex, Oxford
University, Warwick-
shire and New Zealand
Left-hand bat;
occasional slow left-arm
bowler; outstanding
fieldsman.*

MARTIN DONNELLY MADE a considerable reputation in an extremely restricted cricket career. In twenty-five years he played in only 131 matches and for six different teams, including a single appearance for Middlesex in 1946. Yet, when that penetrating cricket thinker, C.B. Fry, was asked if he thought any left-hander of his experience was superior to Donnelly, he said categorically: 'No, not one'. Short, neat, remarkably quick on his feet and perfectly balanced, Donnelly was master of all the strokes.

A most entertaining batsman to watch, once set he would roll out, especially, an elegant late cut and also straight and on drives, a murderous hook, and delicate placings which often unsettled bowlers. It was, too, all done with immense gusto; he played cricket solely for pleasure. He bowled, it often seemed, for sheer amusement, but he took, to his delight, a few useful wickets. In the field he compared – in some highly informed opinions – with the greatest cover-points.

At Plymouth High School, Taranaki, he was in the first XI for a most remarkable period of six seasons. At eighteen, while still at school, he was chosen for Taranaki against Errol Holmes' strong MCC bowling side; his 49 was substantially the highest score for the local team. Soon after he was included in M.L. Page's 1937 side to England, for whom he made 1,414 runs at 37.21 to finish second in their batting averages, while in the three Tests he averaged 24. Back home he went to Canterbury University College, played regularly for Canterbury and, in 1939, won the Redpath Cup for the best batting in the Plunket Shield.

Joining the New Zealand Expeditionary force as a private, he moved to the Armoured Division, fought through the Italian campaign and reached England in 1945 as a Major. Appearing for the Dominions at Lord's he scored a spectacular 133, significant in the defeat of England by 45 runs.

*Martin Donnelly,
cultured left-hander with
a brief, but brilliant
career*

Going up to Oxford he was two years a blue, top of their batting in each season, and captain in the second. In this immediate post-war period his superb batting had an immense effect on people in Oxford; indeed, it was a major entertainment in the district. He also won a Rugby blue and was capped by England. He had the classic Lord's record – now, of course, no longer possible – of scoring a century there in the University Match (142 in a total of 261) for Oxford against Cambridge; for Gentlemen v Players 162 in a bare three hours; and in a Test 206 for New Zealand in 1949.

Probably, though, the peak of his cricket was achieved on New Zealand's tour of England in 1949 when they lost only a single

match (against Oxford University!). Top of the batting with 2,287 runs at 61.81, in the four Tests – all drawn, as Wally Hadlee prophesied – he scored over 50 in four of his six innings and finished with 462 runs at 77.00. 'Too often', said *Wisden*, 'he faced the necessity of pulling round the side after a moderate start'; but concluded, however, that: 'Responsibility at no time caused him to be ultra-careful; it did make him even harder to dismiss than before.'

A few matches for Warwickshire and Martin Donnelly's first-class cricket career was over; he went into business in Australia. He is remembered as a superb – and happy – cricketer.

Donnelly survives an airborne operation by Godfrey Evans during his 206 against England at Lord's in 1949

FIRST-CLASS CAREER RECORDS

Career	M	I	NO	HS	Runs	Avge	100
1936-1960	131	221	26	208*	9250	47.43	23

Ct/St	Runs	Wkts	Avge	BB	5wI	10wM
74	1683	43	39.13	4-32	—	—

TEST CAREER RECORDS

Tests	I	NO	HS	Runs	Avge	100	50
7	12†	1	206	582	52.90	1	4

Ct/St	Balls	Runs	Wkts	Avge	BB	5wI	10wM
7	30‡	20	0	—	—	—	—

K.S. DULEEPSINHJI

Kumar Shri Duleepsinhji (1905-1959) Cambridge University, Sussex, Hindus and England Right-hand bat; occasional leg-break bowler; fine slip field.

IN THE PRINTS generally, K.S. Duleepsinhji, popularly 'Duleep', to his cricketing friends 'Smith', this nephew of Ranji was, for his sadly short career, as stylish, poised and capable as any batsman of his period. Physically slim and lissom, he was a most handsome mover on a cricket field, whether as a batsman who saw the ball early and made his frequently powerful strokes appear effortless, or as an apparently casual slip field who made quite remarkable catches. During his schooldays at Cheltenham where he was three years in the XI and captain in the last, *Wisden* picked him out as already a surprisingly mature batsman; and he was a successful leg-spin bowler (124 wickets). His precarious state of health prevented him from bowling to any extent afterwards.

So, up to Cambridge, where he was given his blue – after three matches as a Freshman – and won it in three subsequent seasons. He began the season of 1927 with 101 against Yorkshire, and 254 not out (the highest by a University player at Fenners) against Middlesex in May before an attack of pneumonia ruled him out of cricket for the rest of the summer.

He had some coaching from Aubrey Faulkner and advice from Charles Fry and Ranji; but his gifts were positive. He developed a sound defence, had convincing ability to cope with pace; and strength, particularly in cutting and glancing, but also in driving.

Following the path of his uncle Ranji, Duleep qualified by residence for Sussex in 1926, but was not fit to play for them in 1927 and was partly convalescent in 1928. However, some measure of his stature lies in the fact that, in the three seasons 1929 to 1931, he scored 7,793 runs – more than anyone else in England – at an average of 55.

He opened the season of 1930 and the new scoreboard at Hove by making 333 against Northamptonshire – still the county record – in a single day. In the same summer, again in the fashion of his uncle, with his first England cap against Australia – at Lord's – he made 173 to join those few who have made a century in their first Test innings.

Duleep captained Sussex skilfully and understandingly; and in August 1932 they were chasing Yorkshire hard for the Championship when his health broke down. He missed their last five matches, was advised not to make that winter's tour of Australia – for which he had already been chosen – and, finally, at the age of twenty-seven, had to give up cricket altogether.

By then he had played in 12 Tests (average 58), made 50 centuries, and built some splendid and memorable innings. Three times he made two centuries in a match; twice most impressively.

'Duleep', the sensitive genius whose elegant strokeplay concealed considerable power

At the time, 'Tich' Freeman, the Kent leg-spinner, was in his prolific heyday, but Duleep, making 115 and 246 for Sussex v Kent in 1929, and 125 and 103 not out in the Gentlemen v Players match of 1930, going down the wicket to drive him, or when he dropped short, leaning back and cutting, hooking or pulling, flayed him to ribbons.

After his retirement, he played one or two gentle matches in India, became Indian High Commissioner in Australia; and later, at home, Chairman of the All India Council for Sports, where he campaigned keenly for young cricketers there.

Two years after his death, a domestic inter-zonal tournament in India was as tribute to him, named 'The Duleep Trophy'.

FIRST-CLASS CAREER RECORDS

Career	M	I	NO	HS	Runs	Avge	100
1924-1932	205	333	23	333	15485	49.95	50

Ct/St	Runs	Wkts	Avge	BB	5wI	10wM
256	1345	28	48.03	4-49	—	—

TEST CAREER RECORDS

Tests	I	NO	HS	Runs	Avge	100	50
12	19	2	173	995	58.52	3	5

Ct/St	Balls	Runs	Wkts	Avge	BB	5wI	10wM
10	6	7	0	—	—	—	—

JOHN EDRICH

*John Hugh Edrich, MBE
(1937-   ) Norfolk,
Surrey and England
Left-hand bat; gully
field.*

OF ALL THE Edriches, including his four cousins who also played county cricket, John, hard, combative but philosophic left-hander, probably was the best player. Only two left-handers, Philip Mead and Frank Woolley, scored more centuries but, as with everything else he did, it was all unspectacular, thoughtful, determined and sound. He had many technical limitations, knew them, and played within them, never assuming too much; knowing, invariably, what to hit, what to play, and what to leave. He had few of the characteristics usual to left-handers, but his bat was permanently straight, he played off his pads with consummate skill and, battered as he often was, never flinched. Short, strong in the shoulders and arms and thick about the hips, he could hit like thunder through the covers when opportunity offered. Oddly, he never moved down the pitch to spin but seemed to let it come to him.

He probably, though, is best remembered for his unflinching courage and durable batting in the face of extreme fast bowling. The classic example of that, of course, was when he and Brian Close faced the West Indian fast bowlers in 1976. At Old Trafford in July of that summer John Edrich – 'young John' to distinguish him from his cousin Bill of Middlesex – took the most horrid battering. He was thirty-nine years old, and that evening he came back in after taking the biggest physical hammering anyone ever saw inflicted on a batsman. He ducked sometimes, but rarely took evasive action. That performance was, without exaggeration, heroic; though that kind of comment generally persuaded him into that broad and friendly grin, or some wrily dismissive remark.

He was twenty-one when he first came to Surrey from Norfolk and amazingly enough in only his second match – against Nottinghamshire at Trent Bridge – scored a century in each innings; and averaged 52 for the season. He played his first Test against West Indies in 1963; failed and was dropped. The next season he came back and scored a century against Australia but after several failures was dropped again.

He did not find it easy to get back into the England side but in 1965 in the third Test against New Zealand, he came back with the highest score ever made by an Englishman at Headingley: 310 not out, made in almost nine hours. Then, failing in the second half of the dual Test summer, he was left out again. Once on the boat to Australia in 1965-66, however, he seemed to make his place certain: batting at number three – though first was obviously his place – he made 32, 37 and 109, 103, 5, 1 and 85.

RIGHT *A typical forcing
shot from John Edrich on
his way to 175 against
Australia at Lord's in
1975*

On to New Zealand when he was dropped again. A cycle of his ins, outs, achievements and failures makes an, at times, sad chronicle but, by 1968 against Australia, he was ensconced; and the ultimate judgement of his efforts is his England record of 5,138 runs at 43.54, with 12 Test centuries. Fearless and safe-handed in the gulley, he was prepared to fight out any issue. He captained Surrey for five seasons without any great success, but his men would have followed him almost through the kind of fire that he accepted as normal for himself. In 1977 he was made an MBE; and Surrey, who had truly appreciated him, gave him two Testimonials. In 1981 he became a selector but after a single year gave up the office; as if it did not keep him busy enough. He was always a busy, brave, cheerful, faithful man.

FIRST-CLASS CAREER RECORDS

Career	M	I	NO	HS	Runs	Avge	100
1956-1978	564	979	104	310*	39790	45.47	103

Ct/St	Runs	Wkts	Avge	BB	5wI	10wM
311	53	0	—	—	—	—

TEST CAREER RECORDS

Tests	I	NO	HS	Runs	Avge	100	50
77	127†	9	310*	5138	43.54	12	24

Ct/St	Balls	Runs	Wkts	Avge	BB	5wI	10wM
43	30	23	0	—	—	—	—

AUBREY FAULKNER

AUBREY FAULKNER WAS one of the most thoughtful and knowledgeable of cricketers: and an outstanding match-winning all-rounder. He first emerged as a wrist spinner of good control and astute variations, including a well concealed faster ball. He soon began to work on his batting, however, and became an extremely sound player in the middle order; not particularly elegant but able to read a game well and extremely hard to get out.

In his first Test match (1905-06) his bowling played a considerable part in South Africa's first win of a match – and a rubber – against England.

He developed his batting, though, to a high standard of reliability; so that, although his overall batting average was 36.31 and, in that first series, no more than 18.42, in only 25 Tests his batting average was 40.79. In the first Test played in Johannesburg (1909-10) which South Africa won only narrowly

George Aubrey Faulkner (1881-1930) Transvaal and South Africa Right-hand bat; slow-medium leg-break and googly bowler; all-round fieldsman.

Aubrey Faulkner, outstanding all rounder, melancholy man; on the 1912 South African tour of England

by 19 runs, Faulkner scored 78 and 123, and took eight for 160. He was top of the batting in that series and in Australia in 1910-11 when he made 732 runs, until then a record aggregate for a Test series at 73.20, including 115 in the third (Adelaide) Test, the first in which South Africa ever beat Australia.

He had a distinguished record in the First World War, when he was awarded the DSO, and afterwards he set up the famous Faulkner School of Cricket, where one of his best known pupils was Ian Peebles. His powers of technical analysis and thoughtful advice, though, were of immense service to many cricketers at all levels of age and performance. He also wrote perceptively about the technique of the game. Probably the most famous innings of Faulkner's life was played in 1921 when Archie MacLaren, former England captain and selector chose 'An England XI' to play against Warwick Armstrong's Australians, who (by then, in late August) seemed certain to create a new record by going unbeaten through a tour of England. MacLaren's side was bowled out by MacDonald and Armstrong for 43. The Australians countered with 174; but then in the second innings of the English side, Aubrey Faulkner, going in first, made 153 – by far the largest innings of the match – without a chance and with a six and 20 fours, and supported by Hubert Ashton (75) he effectively won the match; and, incidentally, for something more than good measure, he took six wickets.

When the South Africans made a bad start in England in 1924 they re-called Faulkner for one Test but, at forty-three, he achieved little. His school continued to flourish but he was introspective, and prone to melancholia; and, still only forty-eight, he died tragically by his own hand of coal-gas poisoning.

FIRST-CLASS CAREER RECORDS

Career	M	I	NO	HS	Runs	Avge	100
1902-1924	118	197	23	204	6366	36.58	13

Ct/St	Runs	Wkts	Avge	BB	5wI	10wM
94	7826	449	17.42	7-26	33	8

TEST CAREER RECORDS

Tests	I	NO	HS	Runs	Avge	100	50
25	47	4	204	1754	40.79	4	8

Ct/St	Balls	Runs	Wkts	Avge	BB	5wI	10wM
20	4227	2180	82	26.58	7-84	4	—

C.B. FRY

TALL, HANDSOME, SPLENDIDLY athletic and intellectually gifted, Charles Fry was not only the most widely talented man to play first-class cricket, but probably the finest all-rounder of modern times. Well before he was thirty, and after a brilliant career at Repton, he had won Blues at Oxford for cricket, soccer, athletics (as sprinter, a long and high jumper), and missed one for rugby only through injury on the eve of the University match; he had scored a century for Oxford against Cambridge, for Gentlemen against Players and for England against Australia. At Association football he had been capped for England v Ireland and appeared (for Southampton) in the FA Cup Final. He also set a world record – which endured for twenty-one years – for the long jump. He was, too, a capable boxer, golfer, swimmer, sculler, javelin thrower and tennis player – and a brilliant conversationalist. He came down from Oxford with a first in 'Mods' and honours in Literae Humaniores.

He also wrote keenly and analytically around George Beldam's action pictures of batting, bowling and fielding. Outside sport, he won an exhibition to Wadham ahead of F.E. Smith and took a major Oxford prize for poetry; founded and edited C.B. Fry's magazine; wrote (with his wife) the novel *A Mother's Son*, became a lively journalist and produced a witty autobiography, *Life Worth Living*. Whatever engaged his wide-ranging interest he seemed able to do it well.

In his seventies he mentioned to his biographer, Denzil Batchelor, that he thought of taking up horse racing. 'What as,' asked Batchelor, 'trainer, jockey or horse?' He three times stood for parliament as a Liberal but, although on each occasion he increased the party's vote, was never elected.

Of all his achievements he was probably most proud of his forty-eight years as director in charge of the training ship *Mercury*. After the First World War he worked at Geneva as an associate of Ranji on the Indian delegation and wrote *A Key-book of the League of Nations*. It was at that time that he was offered, but refused, the throne of Albania: had he accepted it might have changed the history of Europe, indeed, of the world.

His batting was based on a strictly correct defence, from which the influence of Ranji – with whom he played for many years in the Sussex side – and his own deep thought made him a prolific scorer as a back-foot player with an on-side bias.

His concentration was intense and he had the capacity, when once in the groove, to play long sequences of high scores; for instance, once, in 1900, in consecutive innings for Sussex and in

Charles Burgess Fry (1872-1956) Oxford University, Surrey (one match), Sussex, Hampshire and England Right-hand bat; right-arm fast-medium bowler; all-round field.

OVERLEAF: *1921: C.B. Fry (Right) walks out to bat for Hampshire with George Brown. At forty-nine, Fry was asked to captain England, but declined, saying he was too old*

one Gentlemen v Players match, he made 135; 68, 72; 125, 229; 110; 96; 105.

As a bowler of fairly lively pace, he once performed the hat-trick for Oxford University against MCC and in 1895 took 57 wickets. In 1900, however, his bowling was condemned by an eleven to one vote of the county captains and, while he protested that his action was fair, he barely bowled again.

When he scored 118 and 53 and took ten wickets in the Oxford Freshmen's Match of 1892, his Blue in his first year became virtually certain; and he played also in the three subsequent years (captain in 1894). He played a single match for Surrey in 1891 on his birth qualification; joined Sussex in 1894 and remained there (captain 1904-1908) until 1908; when, on taking over T.S. *Mercury*, at Hambledon, he joined Hampshire.

Between 1899 and 1905 he six times scored more than 2,000 runs, and in 1901 over 3,000; while he five times averaged more than 70; in 1903, 81.30: in Gentlemen v Players matches (1893-1914) he averaged 44.23. He made 94 centuries, six of them in succession during 1901. His partnerships with Ranji and with Joe Vine were part of the Sussex – especially the Hove – scene for ten years.

His other commitments prevented him from ever touring Australia, though he went to South Africa and played in the three Test matches of 1895-96 there. He played against Australia in England, however; and captained England in the Triangular Tournament of 1912 in which he was unbeaten. As late as 1921, when he was forty-nine, he was invited to take over the England captaincy against Warwick Armstrong's Australians; but he refused on the grounds that he was out of practice; and he forthwith retired: a nice way to go, and in tune with the character of Charles Fry.

The remarkable C.B. Fry, whose range of sporting and intellectual prowess was immense

FIRST-CLASS CAREER RECORDS

Career	M	I	NO	HS	Runs	Avge	100
1892-1921	394	658	43	258*	30886	50.22	94

Ct/St	Runs	Wkts	Avge	BB	5wI	10wM
240	4872	166	29.34	6-78	9	2

TEST CAREER RECORDS

Tests	I	NO	HS	Runs	Avge	100	50
26	41	3	144	1223	32.18	2	7

Ct/St	Balls	Runs	Wkts	Avge	BB	5wI	10wM
17	10	3	0	—	—	—	—

SUNIL GAVASKAR

*Sunil Manohar Gavas-
kar (1949-   )
Bombay, Somerset, and
India
Right-hand batsman,
right-arm medium pace
bowler; slip field.*

SUNIL – 'SUNNY' – GAVASKAR, the Indian opening batsman, holds the world's Test records for the most appearance (125), innings (214), runs (10,122), hundreds (34), scores of 50 and over (79) and partnerships of a hundred or more (58). As a final embellishment, his last first-class appearance was in the MCC Bicentenary match in 1987 when he scored 188, his first century at Lord's.

When he equalled Don Bradman's record of 29 Test centuries, Gavaskar pointed out that he had done so in 95 matches by comparison with Bradman's 52. It may be noted, though, without claiming any greater quality in Gavaskar, that the pressure and frequency of Tests has increased, that the Indian has generally gone in first, while Bradman by no means always had to face the new ball. Gavaskar's proportion of centuries is bettered only by Bradman.

He is short – fractionally less than 5 feet 5 inches tall – but he uses the crease in masterly fashion; his quick footwork enables him to dictate length for himself. His bias is for the front of the wicket, from the covers round to mid-wicket; but, at need, he has effectively all the strokes though, like some other wise

*BELOW AND RIGHT Sunil
Gavaskar, masterly at the
wicket; dignified in
departure*

cricketers, he rarely uses the hook.

Gavaskar played his first first-class match at seventeen, but when he was chosen for the Indian tour of West Indies in 1970-71, he had played in only six first-class matches (though in them he had scored three centuries). That tour afforded him an amazing entry into Test cricket. Missing the matches in Jamaica through injury, he made his Test debut in Trinidad with 65 and 67 (there was only one higher score for India) and that was their first defeat of West Indies. He went on in the three remaining Tests to score 116, 64 not out, 1, 117 not out, 124 and 220; a tour Test record of eight innings, three times not out, 774 runs, average 154.80.

In 1980 he appeared in fifteen games for Somerset as a replacement for Viv Richards, who was on tour with West Indies: he played some fine innings before the rains came, and finished with a superb 155 not out against Yorkshire; he left both friends and admirers in the county.

He has had periods as captain of India, including an unhappy occasion against Australia at Melbourne in 1981. He had had one of his rare lean spells but had recovered to make a substantial score when he was given out lbw to Lillee. In his indignation, Gavaskar ordered his partner, Chauhan, to follow him off the field, intending, apparently, to withdraw India from the match. Happily he cooled down in time to apologise and allow play to continue (India won).

Gavaskar will always be remembered in England for his innings played when India went one down into the fourth and final Test of the 1979 series and were set 438 to win in 498 minutes. Gavaskar scored 221 – then a record for India against England – but was out to Botham when they needed 49 off 7.4 overs; they failed by nine runs and the match was drawn: Gavaskar's effort, however, remains a peak of cricket history. He was always physically resilient, and had immense concentration. Many of his records will take long to pass.

FIRST-CLASS CAREER RECORDS

Career	M	I	NO	HS	Runs	Avge	100
1966-1987	348	563	61	340	25834	51.46	81

Ct	Runs	Wkts	Avge	BB	5wI	10wM
294	1240	22	56.36	3-43	–	–

TEST CAREER RECORDS

Tests	I	NO	HS	Runs	Avge	100	50
125	214	16	236*	10122	51.12	34	45

Ct	Balls	Runs	Wkts	Avge	BB	5wI	10wM
108	380	206	1	206.0	1-34	–	–

GEORGE GIFFEN

GEORGE GIFFEN HAS been described as 'the Australian W.G. Grace' and, like W.G., he dominated his country's cricket for many years. Like him, he was physically impressive; tall, wide-shouldered and strong, with a heavy moustache and huge hands into which the ball seemed to disappear. Giffen, too, was a major all-rounder and, if his batting figures seem unimpressive, it must be remembered that, in his period, rough pitches were frequent enough to make big scores the exception.

His finest performance was epic: the occasion which indicated his quality as a cricketer when, for South Australia against Victoria, in 1891-92, he scored 271 and then proceeded to take 16 wickets for 166.

His loyalties lay in Adelaide and South Australia – whose state side he virtually carried on his shoulders throughout a long career, from 1877-1903. He was, though, something of a national property. In his first Test – against England at Melbourne in 1881-82, he and Tom Horan put on 107 for the fifth wicket in Australia's first century Test partnership. He was also a member, albeit a junior one, of the Australian team that first beat England in England – in the Test that gave rise to 'The Ashes' legend – at The Oval in 1882.

He was the first Australian to reach 1,000 runs and 100 wickets in Tests. He was, too, the first to take all ten wickets in an innings. Nine times, also, he achieved the 'double' of 100 runs and ten wickets in a match.

Technically George Giffen was a batsman in the nineteenth-century Australian mould; he had something of a stoop, was basically a sound forward defensive player but with many strokes, and was a bold, strong, but controlled driver. He bowled slow-medium off-breaks and what must have been off-cutters, plus a slower, top-spun ball which deceived many batsmen into a return catch. A game, sure-handed fieldsman anywhere, he was a member of the Australian touring teams to England in 1882, 1884, 1886, 1893 and 1896, besides refusing invitations for 1888 and 1890. It was expected that he would take the 1886 side to England, but *Wisden* observed that 'his merits as a leader were not commensurate with his merits as a player'. In cold fact, he bowled himself too much.

On his first tour he matured and, looking back, anyone must realize there was much for a young nineteenth-century cricketer from Adelaide to learn about Victorian England and its cricket: and, indeed, he insisted that he did learn much from it. His batting, partly as a matter of opportunity, developed.

George Giffen (1859-1927) South Australia and Australia Right-hand bat; right arm slow-medium bowler; all round field.

*George Giffen,
Australian father-figure:
talented batsman,
penetrative bowler*

George Giffen (far left, middle row), on the 1884 Australian tour of England

As late as 1893 he made 180 – 112 more than anyone else in the match against Gloucestershire – and punished W.G. heavily and then he took seven of the county's wickets for 11 runs before the match was washed out by rain. On the same tour, against a strong Yorkshire side, with Tunnicliffe, Peel, Ulyett, Brown, Wainwright and Hirst, he made 171 – by more than a hundred the highest score of the match; and then took five for 89. Even on his last visit, in 1896, he played a major batting part, with 80 in a partnership of 130 with Frank Iredale, in Australia's three wicket Test win, at Old Trafford.

It could still be argued that the best of his cricket was played in Australia, a fitting comment on one of that country's founding fathers of the game.

FIRST-CLASS CAREER RECORDS

Career	M	I	NO	HS	Runs	Avge	100
1877–1903	251	421	23	271	11758	29.54	18

Ct/St	Runs	Wkts	Avge	BB	5wI	10wM
195	21782	1023	21.29	10-66	95	30

TEST CAREER RECORDS

Tests	I	NO	HS	Runs	Avge	100	50
31	53	0	161	1238	23.35	1	6

Ct/St	Balls	Runs	Wkts	Avge	BB	5wI	10wM
24	6325	2791	103	27.09	7-117	7	1

GRAHAM GOOCH

Graham Alan Gooch
(1953-   ) Essex,
Western Province and
England
Right-hand bat; right-
arm medium-pace
bowler; slip field and
occasional wicketkeeper.

GRAHAM GOOCH IS a strong, six-foot, upstanding batsman with a Mexican style moustache and a forthright manner. He comes from East London, plays for Essex and, in accent, outlook, and humour reflects his origins. He did not find Test life easy at first – indeed, the particular strains of present-day cricket are great on any player, particularly a batsman.

Perhaps Gooch was brought into the England side too early; certainly Lillee and Thomson at the peak of their hostility were not the most sympathetic of reception committees. As a result, his first Test match was marked with a pair of spectacles. Twice again he fought his way in and fell back, but his determination took him through. Since then, though, his South African connections and his mixed reaction to captaincy have affected his Test selection in a way completely unconnected with his batting ability. On occasions, too, he has declared himself not available to tour overseas. He captained England, though, in the fifth West Indies Test and against Sri Lanka in 1988 and was appointed captain of the aborted tour of India 1988-89. This followed immediately upon his being top scorer on either side in the England v West Indies rubber.

The turning point of Gooch's career undoubtedly was his promotion to open the innings for England in 1978. He had trouble with the extra bounce of Australian pitches but established himself as partner to Boycott, and they might have continued together for some time if they had not joined a sponsored tour of South Africa in 1982. As a result they were both suspended from Test cricket for three years.

Recalled in 1985 to England's winning series against Australia, he had an average of 54.11 and was second in the batting for the West Indian ordeal of 1985-86, enduring much from short-pitched fast bowling and unreliable wickets.

His achievements have been considerable: with Ken McEwan he set an Essex second wicket record with a stand of 321 against Northants at Ilford in 1978. In 1979 he hit the first century ever scored in a Benson & Hedges Cup final at Lord's – a match-winning 120 against Surrey, with three sixes and eleven fours.

In his early days he aspired to be a wicketkeeper-batsman but, as he once ruefully remarked, 'It is tough enough just as a batsman'. If he has usually been at his best against pace, he showed against India that he could deal with first-class spin. He has, too, much enjoyed his bowling. His brilliant gift of mimicry in imitating other bowlers – to the great mirth of the spectators –

has tended to obscure the fact that he is a useful and intelligent medium-pace seam bowler, with the capacity to bowl the ball he wants to a specific batsman. He has faced up to his problems gamely, and it would be tragic if such a talent were ruled out by non-cricketing matters.

FIRST-CLASS CAREER RECORDS

Career	M	I	NO	HS	Runs	Avge	100
1973-1988	389	660	52	275	26745	43.98	66

Ct	Runs	Wkts	Avge	BB	5wI	10wM
380	6868	210	32.70	7-14	3	–

TEST CAREER RECORDS

Tests	I	NO	HS	Runs	Avge	100	50
68	123	4	196	4541	38.15	8	27

Ct	Balls	Runs	Wkts	Avge	BB	5wI	10wM
69	1431	550	13	42.30	2-12	–	–

Graham Gooch in belligerent mood

DAVID GOWER

David Ivon Gower (1957-   ) Leicestershire and England Left-hand bat; slow right-arm bowler; brilliant fieldsman almost anywhere

IN ENGLAND'S Headingley Test against West Indies in 1988, David Gower followed Colin Cowdrey, Geoffrey Boycott, Clive Lloyd and Sunil Gavaskar to a hundredth Test match. He did so at the age of thirty-one, which made him, by four years, the youngest cricketer to reach that figure; and he did it in ten years and fifty days. He was subsequently dropped from the fifth West Indies Test and that against Sri Lanka, though he was recalled in the selection for the winter tour.

The pressures of modern cricket are high. David Gower captained England in 26 Tests before he was superseded, and it is to be noted that his run as captain of Leicestershire was interrupted in 1988, though he was re-appointed for 1989.

He has an easy left-hander's way with a bat, but modern cricket – certainly at Test level – does not allow any batsman to be so relaxed as he sometimes appears to be. To watch him is to realize why so many liken him to Frank Woolley for, on his good days, he has the same easy grace, splendid timing and elegant flow of strokes. The cricket of the 1980s, though, has not been gentle to stroke-makers, and Gower has had to battle harder than anyone might have wished.

A certain toughening was apparent on the West Indies tour of 1986. No England batsman scored a century but Gower was top of their batting averages and confirmed his development. Crucially, he took unflinchingly all that came to him when much of the bowling was reaching the batsman between chest and

RIGHT A Champagne shampoo for David Gower after the return of the Ashes at The Oval in 1985

OPPOSITE Another smoothly timed stroke by David Gower

eyebrow height from pitches whose pace could not be guaranteed.

David Gower was born in Kent, brought up in Tanganyika, where his father was in the Colonial Service and came back to school in Hawkhurst (Kent), before the family moved to Loughborough. The son, with good educational qualifications, read law at University College, London. Then, though, after three Championship matches and six John Player games for Leicestershire, he drifted away from his studies into cricket. Mike Turner, the Leicestershire Secretary, never disguised his surprised delight at getting Gower's release from Kent and signature to forms for Leicestershire. He first played for the County at eighteen, and, at twenty-one, the Cricket Writers chose him as their 'Young Cricketer of 1978'. For some time he did not realize his potential, often playing strokes too far from his body; and some of his footwork was slack. There were, however, undeniable qualities of grace and style about his batting. In 1978 against Pakistan and New Zealand, he convinced those who watched him of both his merits and his weaknesses.

He has matured and hardened steadily. In 1983 he scored more than any other batsman of any country in the World Cup: 384 runs at 76.80.

After this beaten side returned from West Indies in 1986 Gower was superseded in the England captaincy. It is possible that he himself did not resent that, but of his qualification for a place in the side there can be no doubt. One of the most polished stroke-makers in the England team, he is an outstanding fieldsman either in the covers or close to the wicket, where he catches fearlessly.

For all his successes – and they have been considerable – he still is not completely at ease. Perhaps he is the better for being relieved of the problems of captaincy. One thing is certain: he should have many years ahead of him as one of the most felicitous batsmen in the world.

FIRST-CLASS CAREER RECORDS

Career	M	I	NO	HS	Runs	Avge	100
1975-1988	341	546	50	215	19889	40.09	40

Ct/St	Runs	Wkts	Avge	BB	5wI	10wM	
209/1	223	4	55.75	3-47	–	–	

TEST CAREER RECORDS

Tests	I	NO	HS	Runs	Avge	100	50
100	172	13	215	7000	44.02	14	35

Ct	Balls	Runs	Wkts	Avge	BB	5wI	10wM
68	36	20	1	20.00	1-1	–	–

W.G. GRACE

DR WILLIAM GILBERT GRACE was not simply a great player but was, and remains, the father figure of the game as we know it today. C.B. Fry once explained that no one would ever stand ahead of W.G. in modern cricket because he created it.

Dr Grace was not only a great batsman but a bowler of shrewd and subtle variations, a fine field, and a clever if autocratic captain. In a day when Test matches took place only rarely, and runs were often scarce, he was thirty-two before he played his first Test – which was also the first ever played in England (he scored 152) – almost fifty-one when he played his last: yet in 22 matches he scored 1,098 runs at 32.29, with two centuries; and took nine wickets (26.22). In all first-class cricket he played 43 seasons, made 54, 896 runs (39.55), including 126 centuries; in addition he played much minor cricket, in which he scored 91 more centuries. It was the judgement, too, of the astute cricket umpire and observer Bob Thoms that, if he had not been the greatest batsman, he might have been the greatest bowler. First bowling round-arm and then over-arm slow to slow-medium leg-breaks, he took 2,876 wickets (17.92).

Much of his cricket was played on dangerously rough wickets which make his figures little short of incredible. For instance, in 1871 he made 2,739 runs at an average of 78.25, all the more amazing for the fact that second in the table was Richard Daft – regarded as one of the greatest batsmen of the day – with an

Dr W.G. Grace (1848-1915) Gloucestershire and England Right-hand batsman; right arm leg-breaks; fine all-round fielder.

Hastings Festival, 1901: W.G. Grace in impish mood; J.R. Mason does not see the joke – yet: Lord Hawke watches the cricket

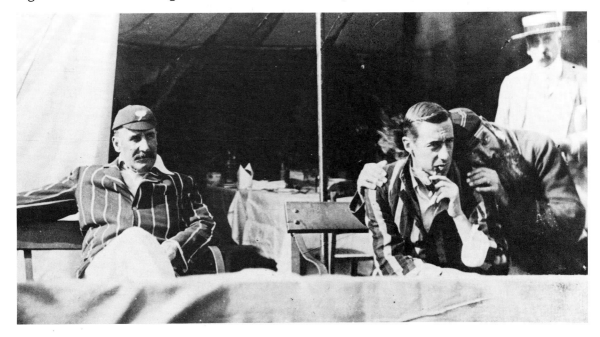

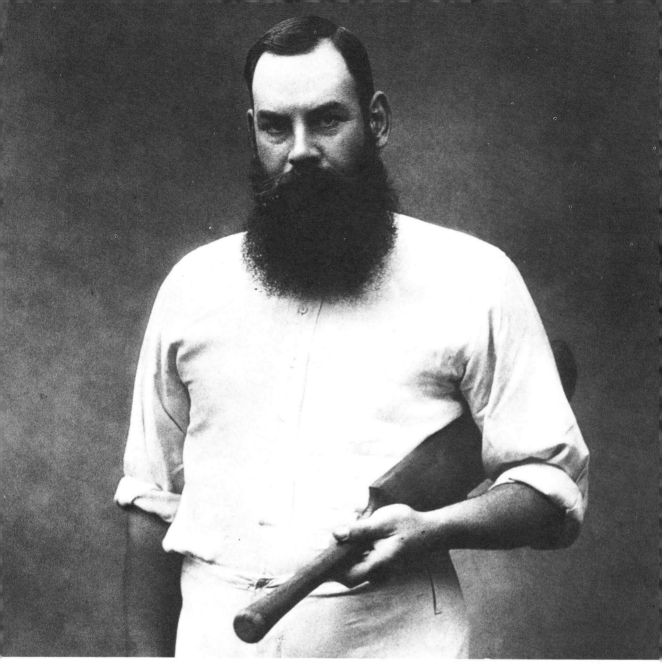

W.G. Grace, pre-eminent Victorian and sporting colossus

aggregate of 565 runs at an average of 37. Even on such pitches Grace mastered every type of bowler, including a race of furious, round-arm slingers. His technique was utterly sound: his defence all but impregnable. He had all the strokes and executed them with great power: above all, he had an air of mastery. As that master of length bowling, Alfred Shaw once expressed it: 'I puts the ball where I likes and the old man he puts it where *he* likes.' As a result, bowlers developed fresh skills to prevent him overwhelming them: they learnt to spin, swing, and bowl a length; finally they invented and introduced over-arm; and groundsmen gave them good pitches on which to practice their new skills. Bowling improved vastly. Thus Grace shaped the game: and still remained the master.

He grew up in a Gloucestershire family of country cricketers and he became the first outstanding figure in cricket as a world sport; and his two brothers played for England with him. Towering physically (he was 6 feet 2 inches tall) as well as figuratively over his contemporaries, and heavily bearded, he was an impressive figure, who both dominated and popularised the game. He was only fifteen years old, though, when he made his first appearance in an important game – 170 for South Wales against the Gentlemen of Sussex; fifty-six when he scored his last century (the 126th), 166 for London County v MCC, on his birthday in 1904. He was fifty-three when he played his last match against the Australians (Joe Darling's 1902 side, including Victor Trumper) for MCC when he scored 82 runs and took five for 29.

He set all kinds of records; had the longest continuous career in first-class cricket – 43 seasons from 1865 to 1908; was the first cricketer to complete the 'double'; to score a hundred hundreds; to aggregate 50,000 runs and to take 2,500 wickets. He took ten or more wickets in each of seven consecutive matches in 1874; and twelve times both scored a century and took ten or more wickets in the same match.

Beyond all the statistics, though, he was an immense character; a single-minded cricket enthusiast; a kind-hearted martinet; laying down the law in an uncharacteristically high piping voice. Countless stories were told about him; most of them true and none more illuminating than that of the poster outside a country cricket ground which read:

CRICKET MATCH
ADMISSION THREEPENCE
IF W.G. GRACE PLAYS ADMISSION SIXPENCE

The gates erected in his honour at Lord's say it all in their simple inscription 'W.G. GRACE, THE GREAT CRICKETER, 1848-1915'.

FIRST-CLASS CAREER RECORDS

Career	M	I	NO	HS	Runs	Avge	100
1865-1908	878	1493	105	344	54896	39.55	126

Ct/St	Runs	Wkts	Avge	BB	5wI	10wM
877	51545	2876	17.92	10-49	246	66

TEST CAREER RECORDS

Tests	I	NO	HS	Runs	Avge	100	50
22	36	2	170	1098	32.29	2	5

Ct/St	Balls	Runs	Wkts	Avge	BB	5wI	10wM
39	666	236	9	26.22	2-12	—	—

TOM GRAVENEY

Thomas William Graveney (1927-) Gloucestershire, Worcestershire, Queensland, England
Right-hand bat; occasional leg-break bowler; generally slip field.

TOM GRAVENEY, ONE of the most graceful, elegant and yet effective batsmen ever to play English cricket – brother of J.K. and uncle of David – both of whom also played for Gloucestershire – came with his family originally from Northumberland to Bristol. In Gloucestershire he was hailed as the spiritual batsman descendant of W.G. Grace and Wally Hammond. Unhappily, though, internal disagreement about captaincy in 1960 led him to leaving and going to Worcestershire where, perhaps coincidentally, he seemed to mature: certainly to become happier and more assured.

For all the felicity of his style, he contrived also to break records: he was, for instance, the first purely post-war batsman to reach 100 centuries. He is the only cricketer to score more than 10,000 runs for two different counties (Gloucestershire and Worcestershire). Another remarkable achievement was that he scored more than half his team's total in both innings of the same match – 100 out of 153, and 67 out of 107, for Gloucestershire

OPPOSITE AND RIGHT *The poise and the power: two faces of Tom Graveney as he late cuts Middlesex bowler Harry Latchman and hoists West Indian Alf Valentine for six*

against Essex in 1956. On 22 occasions he scored 1,000 runs or over in a season – two of them overseas; in seven of them, he made more than 2,000. His stand of 402 for the fourth wicket with Willie Watson for MCC against British Guiana in 1953-54 remains a record for an English touring team. The statisticians, too, have unearthed the fact that when he played his innings of 200 for Gloucestershire against Glamorgan at Newport in 1956, their score of 298 represented the lowest completed total to include a double century.

Tall, slim, and an easy mover, he could deal with every type of bowling; apparently with great ease, and to a great extent off the front foot. His relative lack of success in Tests in Australia is generally attributed to the fact that the pitches there have a height of bounce not conducive to forward play.

Some accused him of being 'casual', presumably because his style was so easy: several times, too, he was omitted from the England side in a period when he would have seemed an automatic choice. He refuted any suggestion of inadequacy in 1957 when, while the rest of the side were in obvious difficulties, he scored 258 against West Indies at Trent Bridge. Then, in 1966, he came back once more in the second Test against West Indies, and went on to score 459 runs in the rest of the series at 76.50. In 1961 he moved to Worcestershire where he spent ten successful years. He was more than forty when he made his last return to the England side with a superb hundred against West Indies at Port of Spain.

He was never a grim cricketer, and two of his performances about which he took humorous pleasure were five wickets for 28 for Gloucestershire against Derbyshire in 1953; and, improbable as his friends find it, one stumping in a first-class match. He takes a true delight in his cricket, and that fact is echoed by the evident note of pleasure as well as mature understanding, in his broadcast Test cricket commentaries.

FIRST-CLASS CAREER RECORDS

Career	M	I	NO	HS	Runs	Avge	100
1948-1971	735	1223	159	258	47793	44.91	122

Ct/St	Runs	Wkts	Avge	BB	5wI	10wM
549/1	3037	80	37.96	5-28	1	—

TEST CAREER RECORDS

Tests	I	NO	HS	Runs	Avge	100	50
79	123	13	258	4882	44.38	11	20

Ct/St	Balls	Runs	Wkts	Avge	BB	5wI	10wM
80	260	167	1	167.00	1-34	—	—

GORDON GREENIDGE

GORDON GREENIDGE IS a mighty, but controlled, striker of the ball; indeed, he probably hits it consistently as hard as any opening batsman now in the game. Born in Barbados, brought to England at the age of twelve, and sent to school in Reading, Berkshire, he might have played for either West Indies or England, and he opted for West Indies. He was introduced to Hampshire by Ray Robinson of Wantage and joined the county staff in 1968. He took his cricket immensely seriously, working hard on his fitness and his fielding. In fact he could bowl usefully and accurately at medium pace when wanted, but he developed steadily as a batsman. He was a pillar of the Hampshire innings until 1987: did not appear in 1988 when he was a member of the West Indian touring party, and did not sign a contract for the county for 1989.

In his early days he was much influenced by Barry Richards, the brilliant South African, with whom he went in first for Hampshire for eight seasons. Greenidge was not hurried into the county first team but, when others failed, he was brought in, at the age of nineteen, for the last seven matches of 1970. Even that, though, was enough for *Wisden* to decide he had made a major breakthrough. His partnership with Richards was established when, in their first five innings together, down to the end

Cuthbert Gordon Greenidge (1951-) Hampshire, Barbados and West Indies
Right-hand bat; right-arm medium-pace bowler; slip fieldsman

Gordon Greenidge square cuts with typical panache

*Greenidge celebrates his
200 at Lord's in 1984*

of that summer, they put on 40, 88, 201, 57 and 43. The partnership of West Indian and South African seemed strange to many, but it was valuable to Hampshire and none the worse for its element of competition.

In 1973, Gordon Greenidge went 'home' to Barbados, where he won a place in the island's Shell Shield side, averaged 38 in his first season, 41 in the second, and was picked for the tour of India, Sri Lanka and Pakistan. There, in his first Test, v India at Bangalore, he scored 93 and 107 and averaged 41.22 in Tests.

Life changed for him in Australia 1975-76 when, in his four Test innings, the pace bowlers put him out for 0,0,3 and 8 which cost him his place. With characteristic determination he fought his way back by revising his technique, especially his attacking strokes. He retained his immense power in driving, but his hooking and cutting became more controlled. Against England, in 1976, he played successive Test innings of 22, 23, 84, 22, 134, 101 (which made him only the second West Indian, after George Headley, to score two centuries in a Test in England) 115, 6, 0 and 85 not out. In Australia in 1979-80 he justified himself against Lillee and Co: *Wisden* said that 'He impressed steadily from an uncertain beginning and played two sterling innings in the one-day finals'. (His 80 and 98 not out in the two finals against England were the highest scores of the matches.) He had his best series against England in 1984 when he finished top of the strong West Indies batting with an average of 81.71 in Tests.

Despite a tendency to knee injury, he continues to hit the ball very hard; especially in over-limit matches, with such figures as 177 in a 60-over Gillette Cup tie; 173 in a 55-over Benson & Hedges match; and the record 163 – with ten sixes – in 40 overs of the John Player League. He remains a cricketer of zest and courage.

FIRST-CLASS CAREER RECORDS

Career	M	I	NO	HS	Runs	Avge	100
1970-1988	481	817	69	273*	34440	46.04	83

Ct	Runs	Wkts	Avge	BB	5wl	10wM
486	472	17	27.76	5-49	1	–

TEST CAREER RECORDS

Tests	I	NO	HS	Runs	Avge	100	50
87	146	14	223	6186	46.86	15	31

Ct	Balls	Runs	Wkts	Avge	BB	5wl	10wM
83	26	4	0	–	–	–	–

SYD GREGORY

Sydney Edward Gregory (1870-1929) New South Wales and Australia Right-hand bat; brilliant cover fielder.

A nonchalantly dapper Syd Gregory, veteran of a record eight tours to England, arrives for the 1912 Triangular tournament

SYD GREGORY'S 58 test appearances remained the Australian record for forty years until Ray Lindwall beat it in 1959. His 201 against England at Sydney in 1894-95 was the first double century in a Test in Australia; and it took only 270 minutes. In the course of it, he and John Blackham put on 154 for the ninth wicket, an Australian record which still endures.

He was a member of the famous Gregory family, the nephew of D.W. Gregory who captained Australia in the first Test match. The family record includes seven New South Wales cricketers, four of whom were Test players, and two Australian captains. Altogether 20 of Syd's brothers and cousins represented New South Wales at football, sailing, athletics or cricket.

Syd Gregory, who sported a waxed and curled moustache, was quite short: 5 feet 4 inches, and was known as 'Little Tich'. He was, though, jaunty and alert and made up for his lack of height by his speed on his feet, model footwork, powerful wrists and forearms. His eye was sharp and he used often to whip the ball off the middle stump, considering the runs he made showed a good return for the number of times it cost him his wicket. Although it was his nature to attack, he could be obdurate in defence and all through his career he proved resolute and capable when his side was in trouble or on difficult pitches. He was, too, a daring runner between the wickets. He had often to pay the price for that, too; but at times it completely rattled and disorganized the opposing field.

He played as much, if not more, cricket overseas than at home. He toured England a record eight times – in 1890, 1893, 1896, 1899, 1902, 1905, 1909 and – called back in emergency when a number of Australian players rejected the Board's terms and refused to go – 1912 (for the Triangular Tournament); on four of those tours he scored a thousand runs. He also toured North America, three times, South Africa and New Zealand. Gregory was surely the most travelled cricketer of his time.

FIRST-CLASS CAREER RECORDS

Career	M	I	NO	HS	Runs	Avge	100
1889-1912	368	587	55	201	15192	28.55	25

Ct/St	Runs	Wkts	Avge	BB	5wI	10wM
174	394	2	197.00	1-8	—	—

TEST CAREER RECORDS

Tests	I	NO	HS	Runs	Avge	100	50
58	100	7	201	2282	24.53	4	8

Ct/St	Balls	Runs	Wkts	Avge	BB	5wI	10wM
25	30	33	0	—	—	—	—

GEORGE GUNN

George Gunn (1879-1958) Nottinghamshire and England Right-hand bat; right-arm bowler; slip field.

GEORGE GUNN WAS a batting genius with a streak of mischief. He came of a cricketing family; the monumental William Gunn was his uncle, the all-rounder, John, his elder brother and G.V. – 'young George' – his son. Lacking the height of William or the burly solidity of John, he was a trim, neatly made man, light and quick on his feet. His career was lengthy, for he played the first-class game from 1902 to 1932 and, at the age of fifty, he, with Andrew Sandham, had an opening stand for England of 322 against Jamaica. Over twenty-two years passed between the first and the last of his 15 Tests, and probably for some twenty years he was among the two or three finest English batsmen against fast bowling.

George Gunn's was, in many ways, a strange cricketing life. He first played for Nottinghamshire at twenty-two and, within three or four years, developed into a batsman of unquestionably high class. In 1906, though, a haemorrhage of the lungs ended his season's cricket in July. He spent the next winter in New Zealand and returned in such health as to head the batting averages for Nottinghamshire in 1907, when they won the Championship outright for the first time for twenty-one years. Despite his recovery it was deemed wise to send him to Australia for the following winter with the proviso that, if needed, he would play for the MCC team touring there under A.O. Jones, his county captain. It duly fell out that Jones himself was ill and unable to play in the first Test and George Gunn, included in his place, made 119 (on his first Test appearance) and 74; top score in each innings, which ensured his place for the rest of the series. He subsequently confided to a friend that during his innings of 119 a band was playing on the ground and he was unable to concentrate on his batting because the cornet was out of tune.

In four more Test innings he made top score and finished first in the tour averages. He returned exhausted; but, as he thought wrongly, was chosen for the second Test of the 1909 series with Australia when he failed, with one and nought and was never again chosen for England in England. Even in 1921, when England, routed by the Australian pace of Gregory and MacDonald, used 30 players – more than ever before or since – he was not called up; though he was clearly the best man available against pace. In that year he was again top of the Nottinghamshire batting.

Chosen for the tour of Australia in 1911-12, he batted so consistently that, even with a highest score of only 75, he averaged 42 in Tests. Thereafter, through a long sequence of

*George Gunn,
fearless and utterly
unpredictable*

selectorial quirks he passed into the wilderness. He used to relate how, one August – could it have been 1920? – he received a letter, thrust it into his blazer pocket and did not come upon it again until the following spring. He then discovered that it had asked him if he was free to make the previous winter's tour to Australia.

When Nottinghamshire were playing at Trent Bridge, George used to lie in bed until half-past nine, when his wife brought tea up to him. One day he turned over and went to sleep again, only for his wife to come up and shake him at about a quarter past ten:

'George, you're playing.'

'Ay, but we've only a hundred and twenty – captain 'll not declare before afternoon.'

'But, George, you're eighty-two not out.'

He remained a master batsman; consistent in scoring but not in method. As the whim took him, he would stonewall, meticulously correct, for hour after hour, infuriating the spectators and laughing to himself; or, often in the same match, bat with outrageous impudence, walking down the pitch to the fastest bowlers and hitting them straight back or over the top. Ted MacDonald was his favourite victim for this treatment. If he had not at times thrown his wicket away, he must have scored far more than his 62 centuries; he was not, though, a counter of his runs.

His ability did not waver. At forty-seven he scored 100 and 109 in a match against Warwickshire. Then, warning his friends in advance that he proposed to celebrate the occasion, he marked his fiftieth birthday with an innings of 164 not out against Worcestershire, which *Wisden* said 'showed much of the supreme skill which marked his greatest days'.

A few weeks afterwards he was chosen for the MCC tour to West Indies. It was, in fact, a scondary tour – but the opposition included the fast bowling of Constantine, Griffith and Francis. In the first Test J.E.D. Sealy of West Indies at seventeen years 122 days, became the (then) youngest Test cricketer: he was not born when Gunn, who opened the England innings, had last played in a Test. George averaged 34 for the series.

He was quite delighted when he and his son, G.V., each scored a century in the same innings (v Warwickshire at Edgbaston, 1931).

George Gunn decorated the game of cricket; and sometimes cocked a snook at its establishment. English cricket, for its part, did not make the most of that most diverting man.

FIRST-CLASS CAREER RECORDS

Career	M	I	NO	HS	Runs	Avge	100
1902-1932	643	1061	82	220	35208	35.96	62

Ct/St	Runs	Wkts	Avge	BB	5wI	10wM
473	2355	66	35.68	5-50	1	—

TEST CAREER RECORDS

Tests	I	NO	HS	Runs	Avge	100	50
15	29	1	122*	1120	40.00	2	7

Ct/St	Balls	Runs	Wkts	Avge	BB	5wI	10wM
15	12	8	0	—	—	—	—

WALLY HAMMOND

WALLY HAMMOND WAS among the half-dozen finest cricketers of all history. Above average height, powerfully but proportionately built, he moved with a superbly athletic, balanced assurance. As a batsman he developed from the dashingly spectacular young striker of the ball, a vivid hooker and cutter, to the majestic craftsman who mastered all the best Test bowling in the world. Eschewing the hook, he played largely off the back foot, through the great V from cover-point round to midwicket with such concentration and control that he amassed mighty scores. For instance, in Chapman's 1928-29 side to Australia, his Test innings were 44, 28; 251, 200; 32 (run out); 119, 177; and, the rubber well won, 38, 16. Against New Zealand in 1932-33, he made the fastest Test triple century, in 287 minutes in the course of 336 in 318 minutes with ten sixes (also a record).

With a perfect, sideways-on action, he bowled fast-medium with shrewd control and late swing; but, at will, he could increase his speed menacingly, wresting considerable pace from the pitch (he took 83 Test wickets). In his early days, he was a most brilliant outfield, but soon his ability dictated that he moved to slip, where he had no superior in the world. In 1928, when he made 78 catches, he took ten in the Gloucestershire-Surrey match at Cheltenham: both records for a fieldsman other than a

Walter Reginald Hammond (1903-1965) Gloucestershire and England Right-hand bat; fast-medium bowler; slip field.

Wally Hammond walks out to bat at Trent Bridge in 1930; the black armband is a mark of respect for Sir Frederick Toone, the England team manager who had died three days earlier

Wally Hammond, in relaxed mood, tossing up with Queensland skipper Don Tallon on the 1946 MCC tour to Australia

wicketkeeper. In the first Test of the 1927-28 tour of South Africa, when he frequently opened the bowling, he took five for 36; for Gloucestershire v Worcestershire in 1928; nine for 23.

Born in Dover and the son of a regular soldier, he spent his childhood in China and Malta; when the family returned to England he went to school in Gloucestershire – because he did not want to play for Kent, Lord Harris high-handedly had him banned from Gloucestershire for two qualifying years. In the winter tour of 1925-26, he picked up a bug which almost killed him: mercifully it cost him only the season of 1926; the Second World War meant another six years gone. What Wally Hammond might have done with two more youthful, one growing-up and six mature years, gives great pause for thought. As it was, he scored 50,551 runs; 7,249 in Tests; add nine years at such a performance rate and the others would have been groping after him.

In all cricket he scored 167 centuries, bettered only by Jack Hobbs and Patsy Hendren. In 85 Tests he scored 22 centuries; a figure equalled by Boycott in 108; and Cowdrey in 114.

Memory recalls, beyond dimming, the Lord's Test of 1938. Ernie McCormick cut loose on the first morning and had reduced England to 20 for two when Hammond came in; soon it was 31 for three. Hammond, with backing from Eddie Paynter (99) and Leslie Ames (83), made 240 in six dominant hours, hammering McCormick mercilessly.

This was a great man; but his end in Test cricket was sad. He had already become an amateur when he captained the English side to Australia for the tour of 1946-47 at a difficult time in his personal life. Although he had fair success in other games, his top score in four Tests – he was unfit for the fifth – was 37. He came back home and retired from the game. That last tour cannot, though, reduce the stature of one of the unforgettable giants of all cricket; Wally Hammond was precisely that. Memory will recall him moving smoothly, easily, out to the crease, exuding infectious confidence; and standing upright, destroying famous bowlers.

FIRST-CLASS CAREER RECORDS

Career	M	I	NO	HS	Runs	Avge	100
1920-1951	634	1005	104	336*	50551	56.10	167

Ct/St	Runs	Wkts	Avge	BB	5wI	10wM
819/3	22391	732	30.58	9-23	22	3

TEST CAREER RECORDS

Tests	I	NO	HS	Runs	Avge	100	50
85	140	16	336*	7249	58.45	22	24

Ct/St	Balls	Runs	Wkts	Avge	BB	5wI	10wM
110	7969	3138	83	37.80	5-36	2	—

HANIF MOHAMMAD

Hanif Mohammad (1934-) Bahawalpur, P.I.A., and Pakistan Right-hand batsman; could keep wicket at Test level; somewhat unusually, though not particularly effectively both a right- and left-arm bowler; neat close field.

CRICKET NICKNAMES ARE not always apt, but the tag of 'the little Master' was most appropriately attached to this middle of five brothers, four of whom played for Pakistan.

Hanif was justifiably a national idol. When a knee injury put him out after the first Test against West Indies at Karachi in 1958-59, he had appeared in the first 24 Test Matches played by Pakistan. Short – barely 5 feet 6 inches tall – and freshly boyish-looking, he was a batsman of immense talent. He was capable of quite brilliant attacking strokes, especially on the leg-side. Indeed, Brian Statham, who rarely employed the weapon, will surely never forget bowling the young man two fierce bouncers, each of which was immaculately and powerfully hooked for six.

He had most of the strokes, but Hanif was most desperately concerned for the standing and honour of Pakistan, and most of his historic innings – and many of them were indeed historic – were of a defensive character. Thus he played both the longest and the highest innings of all first-class cricket. The latter was, of course, his 499 for Karachi against Bahawalpur in 1958-59. Originally an opening batsman of impeccable technique, he moved down to number four; but, in his last (and 55th) Test – against New Zealand at Karachi in 1969-70 – he went in first with

Free to enjoy batting: Hanif hits out for a Rest of the World XI against an England XI at Lord's, 1965

his brother Sadiq, while a third brother, Mushtaq, was at number four. It was only the third instance of three brothers playing in the same Test (the others were the Graces and the Hearnes). A fourth brother, Wazir, played in 20 Tests and a fifth, Raees, was twelfth man in an official Test.

Although the family originated in Junagadh in India, it is clear that Hanif was the first great Pakistani batsman. It is intriguing to conjecture how much more successful – statistically at least – he might have been in an established team, in which he did not need to be so deeply involved with the prestige of a rising cricket power. It is important that the outstanding contemporaries of other countries never questioned his title to greatness.

FIRST-CLASS CAREER RECORDS

Career	M	I	NO	HS	Runs	Avge	100
1951-1975	238	370	44	499	17059	52.32	55

Ct/St	Runs	Wkts	Avge	BB	5wI	10wM
178/12	1515	53	28.58	3-4	—	—

TEST CAREER RECORDS

Tests	I	NO	HS	Runs	Avge	100	50
55	97	8	337	3915	43.98	12	15

Ct/St	Balls	Runs	Wkts	Avge	BB	5wI	10wM
40	206	95	1	95.00	1-1	—	—

Cricket as ballet; Hanif bows, Bannerjee pirouettes

NEIL HARVEY

*Robert Neil Harvey
(1928-   ) Victoria,
New South Wales and
Australia
Left-hand bat;
occasional slow right-
arm off-break bowler;
and brilliant outfield.*

THE OVERWHELMING IMPRESSION of Neil Harvey as he came out to bat – a little below average height, trim, fresh-looking, with dark wavy hair and a brisk approach – was that of a young man who firmly believed he was going to enjoy the innings ahead. He was one of four brothers, all of whom played for Victoria, and one – Mervyn, as well as Neil – also for Australia.

He made brilliant beginnings everywhere, and then fell little below them. He made a century in his first club match; another on his first appearance for Victoria; another in his second Test (v India 1947), and also when he first toured against England (Headingley 1948, as the youngest member of the Australian team).

He was the most brilliant stroke-maker. Technically it used to be said by some bowlers that he was vulnerable outside his off stump: certainly he was out there more often than on the other side of the wicket; on the other hand, that was where they always bowled at him. He did, in fact, as they said, 'always give the bowler a chance out there' but, on the credit side, he could point to the fact that between 1948 and 1963, he scored more runs in Tests than any other Australian except Don Bradman – also the only man ahead of him in Test centuries and average.

Harvey was the youngest Australian ever to make a Test century (v India at Melbourne in 1948). There will long be arguments as to who was the best of all Australian outfieldsmen – Alan Davidson or Neil Harvey. Both were raised on baseball, and Harvey retained the habit of clapping his hands around the ball above his head in baseball fashion. He was fast in covering, retrieving and returning; a fieldsman whose enthusiasm shone through all he did; and he was a virtually infallible catcher. His major reputation, though, will rest upon his batting, as an unusually graceful left-hander. Always hungry for runs, he was an utterly murderous destroyer of the bad ball. Strong in driving and cutting – his square cut went with the speed of light – he hooked explosively. His footwork was immaculate and, against spin bowling, at times almost terrifyingly fast as he went down the pitch to punch it away on either side of the wicket.

He played for Victoria for most of his Australian domestic career but ended with four years with New South Wales. For more than a dozen years he was a permanent member of the Australian side, popular with his fellow players and spectators. Neil Harvey was, indeed, an engaging person who obviously enjoyed his cricket and gave immense pleasure to all who watched him – one of the most attractive personalities in the history of the game.

Harvey playing a typical cover drive

Neil Harvey on the 1956 tour of England

FIRST-CLASS CAREER RECORDS

Career	M	I	NO	HS	Runs	Avge	100
1946-1962	306	461	35	231*	21699	50.93	67

Ct/St	Runs	Wkts	Avge	BB	5wI	10wM
228	1106	30	36.86	4-8	—	—

TEST CAREER RECORDS

Tests	I	NO	HS	Runs	Avge	100	50
79	137†	10	205	6149	48.41	21	24

Ct/St	Balls	Runs	Wkts	Avge	BB	5wI	10wM
64	414	120	3	40.00	1-8	—	—

LINDSAY HASSETT

LINDSAY HASSETT WAS without question a great batsman. He had, however, so far as most spectators were concerned, two completely separate career-characters. The overall judgement must be that he was extremely effective: he never had a poor Test series, and when he retired he had made more runs – and more centuries overall – than any other Australian batsman apart from Bradman.

He first won his place in the Victorian side at nineteen in the 1932-33 season. Before the war he was a brilliant, adroit, attacking player; although he was only 5 feet 6 inches tall he had not only the short player's strokes, like the hook and the cut, but he could step up to drive – and to drive on the 'up' – or to pull. Above all, his footwork was well nigh perfect, and carried him easily throughout his career to the ball wherever he wanted to play it. From 1946 onwards, though, after his war-time absence, he seemed to lose confidence in his attacking play. His defence, however, became almost flawless, though never dull. Returning to post-war cricket and his first Test of that 1946-47 season, he made 128 in six-and-a-half hours against England at Brisbane, putting on 276 for the third wicket with Bradman. In those days one regarded him as almost a miniaturist of batting. He could simply saunter into position and deal with any type of bowling unruffled, calm and controlled: his batting was almost witty. As a man he had an impish sense of humour and as a captain he was shrewd, considerate and highly skilful.

When he first came to England in 1938 he scored 1,589 runs at 54.79; on the second occasion in 1948, as vice-captain to Bradman, 1,563 at 74.42; and in 1953, when he was captain, 1,236 at 44.14. Like all Australian batsmen at that time he was overshadowed by Bradman, but was calmly, almost amusingly, capable of the long innings. His humour enabled him to enjoy the frustrations of bowlers who pattered impotently against his defensive bat.

Against India in 1947-48, when he made his highest Test score of 198 not out at Adelaide, he averaged 110.66; even at that he was second to Bradman. His 138 at Trent Bridge in 1948 was a minor defensive masterpiece. Then he took over from Bradman, captained the side in South Africa, scored two centuries, and averaged 67.00. At Adelaide, against South Africa in 1952-53, he and his fellow Victorian, Colin McDonald, put on 275 for the second wicket. Now, at the side's need, he went in first and, against England in 1953, despite all the side's problems, he was top of the batting with 365 runs at 36.50. In the Sheffield Shield

Arthur Lindsay Hassett, MBE (1913-   ) Victoria and Australia Right-hand bat; only occasional right-arm medium bowler.

he was massively successful, and in Test cricket averaged 46.56. He was well-liked throughout the game except by those who lacked a sense of humour; and he was understandingly helpful to young cricketers. As a young man he was not only a good cricketer but a fine tennis player. In his retirement to the coast, he was philosophically delighted by fishing.

FIRST-CLASS CAREER RECORDS

Career	M	I	NO	HS	Runs	Avge	100
1932-1953	216	322	32	232	16890	58.24	59

Ct/St	Runs	Wkts	Avge	BB	5wI	10wM
170	703	18	39.05	2-10	—	—

TEST CAREER RECORDS

Tests	I	NO	HS	Runs	Avge	100	50
43	69	3	198*	3073	46.56	10	11

Ct/St	Balls	Runs	Wkts	Avge	BB	5wI	10wM
30	111	78	0	—	—	—	—

Old Trafford, 1953: Godfrey Evans and Trevor Bailey look on frustrated as Lindsay Hassett indulges in a typically creative stroke

TOM HAYWARD

TOM HAYWARD WAS the second batsman – after Dr W.G. Grace – to reach 100 hundreds; and second also of the three great Surrey opening batsmen – Bobby Abel and Jack Hobbs were the other two. He was considered the best professional batsman of the era 1895 to 1908. He came from a family of outstanding cricketers; the Haywards had played for Surrey before they moved from Mitcham to Cambridge where they settled and played. In the mould of the Victorian model professional, correct, calm, sound in defence, capable of controlled attack, considered and informed, he was the typical senior professional, his advice sought by captains at all levels of the game. For 20 seasons in succession he scored over 1,000 runs, including 2,000 eight times and 3,000 twice. Eight times he carried his bat through an innings. In 1900 he reached 1,000 runs on the last day of May; while, in 1906, when Surrey batted second on a difficult pitch in their match with Gloucestershire, their score at the end of the day was 127 for three wickets, of which Hayward had scored a chanceless 100 not out: their only double figure innings.

Hayward was essentially a dominant batsman; tall, strong, raw-boned and serious; three times he scored two centuries in a match; made seven scores of over 200, and another of over 300; while for Surrey, he and Jack Hobbs 40 times put on 100 for the first wicket; ten times more than 200. Tom Hayward had brought the young Hobbs from his native Cambridge to The Oval in 1903; and once in 1907 they opened with partnerships of 100 or more in both innings of two consecutive matches.

For some time Hayward was justly considered as an all-rounder. On a responsive pitch, his lively off-breaks could be difficult to play and he made an extremely dangerous combination with Tom Richardson. At Leicester in 1897, the two bowled unchanged gainst Leicestershire, twice bowling them out for 35; Tom Hayward made top score of the match – 26 – and Surrey won by an innings and 94 in the single day. In 1899 he twice did the hat-trick; he bowled little after 1904, but altogether he took 481 first-class wickets. he had trouble with the 'new fangled' googly bowling: he was growing heavy on his feet and slow in the field.

Hayward did not attempt to take up the game again after the First World War. He went home to coach in Cambridge and later in the Parks at Oxford, but he always returned to Cambridge when the University season was over. There the great Tom Hayward was an impressive sight for the young to point out, with his heavy moustache, stiff butterfly collar, brown boots, walking stick and bowler hat – and the aura of history about him.

Thomas Walter Hayward (1871-1939) Cambridgeshire, Surrey and England Right-hand bat; right-arm fast-medium bowler; steady fieldsman at mid-off or mid-on.

Tom Hayward, whose aggregate of 3,518 runs in a season (1906) remained a record for forty-one years until Denis Compton and Bill Edrich broke it in 1947

FIRST-CLASS CAREER RECORDS

Career	M	I	NO	HS	Runs	Avge	100
1893-1914	712	1138	96	315*	43551	41.79	104

Ct/St	Runs	Wkts	Avge	BB	5wI	10wM
492	11042	481	22.95	8-89	19	2

TEST CAREER RECORDS

Tests	I	NO	HS	Runs	Avge	100	50
35	60	2	137	1999	34.46	3	12

Ct/St	Balls	Runs	Wkts	Avge	BB	5wI	10wM
19	887	514	14	36.71	4-22	—	—

VIJAY HAZARE

VIJAY HAZARE, WHOSE brother, son and two nephews also played for Baroda, was a talented all-round cricketer. A Roman Catholic, a captain in the state army of Baroda, and an expert tiger-hunter, he was of only average height and lean, but wirily strong and determined. His stance was ugly but his timing was good, his movement quick, and he struck the ball well; he had most of the strokes, but was at his strongest in the hook and in cutting.

His bowling was unusual in its range; at between medium and a shade faster, he bowled inswing, outswing and cut the ball both ways. However, coached by Clarrie Grimmett when young, he bowled at medium pace a full, four-finger flipped leg-break which, in favourable conditions, was extremely difficult to play; though he often erred in bowling it short.

Vijay Samuel Hazare (1915-   ) Maharashtra, Central India, Baroda, and India
India
Right-hand bat; right-arm medium to fast-medium bowler; close field.

Vijay Hazare, determined batsman and courteous captain

He made his first deep impression at the age of twenty-four with two huge scores: 316 for Maharashtra against Baroda in 1939-40, and an even more surprising 309 not out (in a total of 387!) for the Rest against Hindus some four years later. In 1946-47, immediately after he had returned from a successful and influential tour of England, he shared with Gul Mahomed in a fourth wicket stand of 577 for Baroda against Holkar in the Ranji Trophy final. That remains a world record partnership for any wicket in any class of cricket; and, by way of something more than mere good measure, he took six for 85 in the first innings of Holkar.

He was a regular and important member of Indian Test teams from 1946 to 1953 (30 Tests) and captaining them in 14 Tests. Indeed, he had a Test average as high as 47.75 when, after an unhappy series in West Indies (1952-53), he was peremptorily dropped as both captain and player. He remains one of India's major post-war players.

FIRST-CLASS CAREER RECORDS

Career	M	I	NO	HS	Runs	Avge	100
1934-1966	238	367	45	309	18635	57.87	60

Ct/St	Runs	Wkts	Avge	BB	5wI	10wM
166	14501	592	24.49	8-90	27	3

TEST CAREER RECORDS

Tests	I	NO	HS	Runs	Avge	100	50
30	52	6	164*	2192	47.65	7	9

Ct/St	Balls	Runs	Wkts	Avge	BB	5wI	10wM
11	2840	1220	20	61.00	4-29	—	—

Basil D'Oliveira

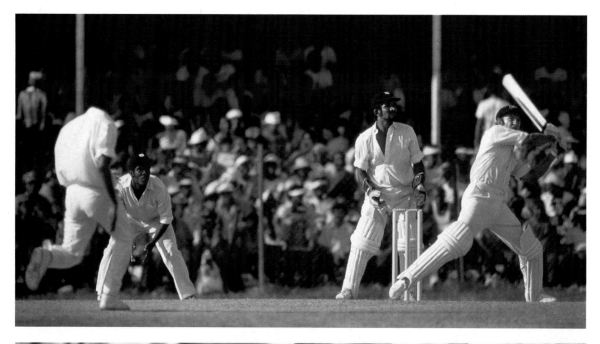

TOP: *Doug Walters*   ABOVE: *Javed Miandad*

Barry Richards

ABOVE: *Geoff Boycott*

FAR LEFT: *Glenn Turner*

LEFT: *Sunil Gavaskar*

Gundappa Viswanath

GEORGE HEADLEY

THE GENERAL ENTHUSIASM for cricket among the people of the West Indies made it virtually certain that they would eventually produce a great player. George Headley was their first great batsman; and 'great' is the appropriate word; but few would have expected such a player from such roots as his. He was born in Panama and at ten brought to his mother's home-island of Jamaica, which was at that time physically so distant from the other islands as to have little cricketing contact with them. Indeed, but for the delay in the receipt of his American visa, George Headley would have gone to the USA to train in dentistry instead of remaining to play for Jamaica in two matches of 1927-28 against the Hon. Lionel Tennyson's (quite strong) team of English cricketers. The young Headley, still only eighteen, quite self-taught, demonstrated against an attack of E.W. – 'Nobby' – Clark, fast left arm of Northants, Maurice Allom, fast-medium, both English Test players, Garnett Lee, Derbyshire leg-spinner and Trevor Arnott, Glamorgan fast-medium, that he was already a competent batsman. His innings of 211 was described by *Wisden* as: 'of many strokes, and with only one chance, a hard

George Alphonso Headley (1909-1983) Jamaica and West Indies Right-hand bat; right-arm leg-break bowler; good general – and sometimes acrobatic – field.

Headley sweeps against Surrey in 1939

George Headley, nicknamed 'the black Bradman' by all but the West Indians, to whom 'The Don' was merely 'the white Headley'

one early in his innings'; in the second match he scored 71. Only the often peculiar politics of West Indian cricket of the time can explain why that was not enough to put him on the boat for England and West Indies' first Test series in 1928.

When Freddie Gough-Calthorpe took the first English Test Team there in 1929-30, though, Headley was picked for the first Test in West Indies, in which he scored 21 and 176; he followed that in the remaining three Tests with 8, 39, 114, 112, 10 and 223 (703 at 87.88). For years he was called the 'Atlas' of West Indian cricket because he carried their batting on his shoulders. Up to the start of the Second World War he had not missed a Test played by

West Indies for ten years. In that period he scored 2,135 runs (ten centuries) at an average of 60.83, and had never failed in a series. His performance was recognized by his appointment as captain of West Indies for the first Test of 1947-48 – the first black man to hold that office – when he made 29 and seven not out; but a back condition prevented him from playing again in the series. He was recalled for the first Test of 1953-54 (at the age of forty-four) and made 16 and one before the same injury again incapacitated him.

George Headley was, perhaps, more completely a back-foot player than any other great batsman. He based his technique on complete safety but he had so many strokes that he was never a slow scorer. Perfectly balanced, smooth and quick on his feet and so utterly sure of his stroke that Sir Leonard Hutton considered he had never seen a batsman play the ball later; while Clarrie Grimmett thought him the finest on-side player he had ever seen.

George Headley was effectively the founder of modern West Indian batting; and no Test-playing country ever had a batsman who carried so much responsibility with such prolific assurance and grace.

FIRST-CLASS CAREER RECORDS

Career	M	I	NO	HS	Runs	Avge	100
1927-1954	103	164	22	344*	9921	69.86	33

Ct/St	Runs	Wkts	Avge	BB	5wI	10wM
76	1842	51	36.11	5-33	1	—

TEST CAREER RECORDS

Tests	I	NO	HS	Runs	Avge	100	50
22	40	4	270*	2190	60.83	10	5

Ct/St	Balls	Runs	Wkts	Avge	BB	5wI	10wM
14	398	230	0	—	—	—	—

PATSY HENDREN

*Elias Henry Hendren
(1889-1962) Middlesex
and England
Right-hand bat; right-
arm slow bowler; fine
outfield.*

'PATSY' HENDREN WAS one of the most prolific run scorers, and one of the friendliest, most humorous and companionable of cricketers of his time – which was roughly the inter-war period. Only Sir Jack Hobbs scored more than his 170 centuries; only Sir Jack and Frank Woolley bettered his career aggregate of 57,611 runs; only Wally Hammond and Sir Don Bradman played more than his 22 innings of 200 or more. He was immensely popular with his fellow players, and with crowds, wherever he went. It was obvious why he was called Patsy for, quite apart from his Irish ancestry, he had a comically Irish face, with button nose, laughing eyes, and a perky little bottom that suggested a creator's afterthought; and he could clown magnificently. In West Indies, above all, he was loved, not merely for his 205 not out – his highest Test score, made at Port of Spain in 1929-30 – but for his comic common touch. Indeed, it is not truly possible to recall a visiting cricketer better liked in the Caribbean.

Stocky, strong and quick on his feet to attack spin bowling, he was also a master against high pace; in fact arguably the finest hooker England has produced. He moved right inside the line of the ball, and then placed his hook with the control he wished, but rarely more than a little fine of square. Fearless against fast bowling, it was only partly a joke – for he had twice been hit by bouncers – when he appeared for a Lord's Test against West Indies wearing a strange helmet-cap with three peaks.

He was taken on to the Middlesex staff at sixteen, and first appeared in the county side at eighteen (1907) though he did not bat. Before the First World War, though, he was largely played for his magnificent fielding in the deep (he made 755 catches in his career). When he returned to the county game in 1919 he was thirty, and his rich talent was manifest.

*Patsy Hendren, whose
cricket sparkled with
Cockney courage and
comedy*

Unhappily, though, when picked in representative matches, he became desperately nervous, especially at the start of his innings. The apparently comic, relieved scamper for his first run was not simply a joke. Once he overcame that problem (insofar as he ever did) – which he probably began to do against South Africa in 1924 – he became a more or less regular middle order batsman choice for England. 'More or less' because there were at least ten strong challengers for the batting places.

One light, but revealing, memory is of Patsy at the height of his powers, signing autographs for a long queue of small boys, when another – lesser – player passed, saying 'Don't you get fed up with that, Patsy?' 'Yes' he replied, smiling, 'but I shall be a damned sight more fed up when nobody wants it.'

Hendren punishing Kent at Lord's in 1920

Patsy had many friends, and he cherished them; he much relished a partnership of 375 against Hampshire at Southampton in 1934, not merely because it was a world record for the third wicket – as it was at the time – but especially because it was made with his friend, Jack Hearne.

In 1937, to his pleasure, the young Denis Compton and Bill Edrich both joined him in the Middlesex side. Patsy had had a good run – every season from 1920 to 1929 he scored 2,000 runs; in 1928, 3,311 at 70.44. He had a rather useful season in 1937, too, with 1,809 at 39.33, with five hundreds; but he decided to go with, to his mirth, nought in his last innings. Why? 'While you still ask me that – I'm not waiting till you ask me why not.' He came back for one match, for an England XI, in 1938. He had by then become coach at Harrow; and took a similar post with Sussex in 1942. Middlesex made him a life member, and he served on their committee for some years. He became, too, county scorer – in which office he was as good company as ever – until, in 1960, fading health compelled him to give up. He missed that intensely. He died in 1962; and still, all over the world, he is recalled with an affectionate smile.

FIRST-CLASS CAREER RECORDS

Career	M	I	NO	HS	Runs	Avge	100
1907-1938	833	1300	166	301*	57611	50.80	170

Ct/St	Runs	Wkts	Avge	BB	5wI	10wM
755	2574	48	53.62	5-43	1	—

TEST CAREER RECORDS

Tests	I	NO	HS	Runs	Avge	100	50
51	83	9	205*	3525	47.63	7	21

Ct/St	Balls	Runs	Wkts	Avge	BB	5wI	10wM
33	47	31	1	31.00	1-27	—	—

CLEM HILL

Clement Hill (1877-1945) South Australia and Australia Left-hand bat; occasional slow bowler; fine outfield.

HIS CONTEMPORARIES WERE convinced that Clem Hill was the finest left hander in the world. His batting instinct was to attack; he had a strong leg side bias, coupled with the ability to pull with surprising certainty even from outside the off stump through midwicket; but was also a fine straight and off driver and a neat and controlled cutter. He was, though, preponderantly a fine example of the Australian fighting batsman and, at his side's need, could maintain obdurate defence for long periods.

Short and powerfully built, he had an ugly stance, slightly stooping and with hands low on the bat handle, but he was quick on his feet and as a fine a player of fast bowling as any of his time. Consistently successful, he was Australia's bulwark in many a crisis. He had, though, an unenviable reputation for being out in the nineties; he was dismissed at 96, 97, 98 and 99 (the last three in consecutive innings in Australia 1901-02) in Tests against England.

His was a cricketing family; the father, J.H., was the first man to score a century on Adelaide Oval, and, Clem was one of his eight sons (there were also eight daughters): six of whom played cricket for South Australia. At sixteen Clem made 360 retired, until then the highest score recorded in Australia, in an inter-college match in Adelaide. Until then the young man had kept wicket; but was then advised not to risk such damage to his hands. At eighteen he led the South Australian batting averages for 1895-96; and, although not originally selected for the 1896 tour of England, an innings of 206 against New South Wales caused an effective public demand for his inclusion.

His first Test century came only little more than a year later; and an historic one it was. In the first innings of the fourth Test of 1897-98 in Australia he was joined by Hugh Trumble at 58 for six. Together they put on 165 (still the Australian record for the seventh wicket against England) which substantially won the match for Australia. His 188 remains the highest score in an England-Australia Test by a batsman under twenty-one; no one else in the match scored more than 64. Made without a chance, it was long regarded historically as his finest Test innings.

A powerful striker of the ball, in 1904-05, for Australia against New Zealand at Wellington, he took 26-6, 6, 6, 4, 4-off an over from K.M. Ollivier.

He was top of the Test averages in England in 1899, when his 135 at Lord's was instrumental in winning the only Test of the series to yield a result and which retained the Ashes for Australia. Incidentaly, in the same innings, Victor Trumper made the same

Mr. Clem. Hill

Clem Hill, cool-headed at the crease; once, at least, hot-tempered away from it

score, 135. Those two were, of course, the great Australian batsmen of the period, and their Test records are remarkably similar:

Tests
C. Hill
  (1896–1911–12)
| 49 | 89 | 2 | 191 | 3412 | 39.21 |
V.T. Trumper
  (1899–1911–12)
| 48 | 89 | 8 | 214 | 3163 | 39.04 |

The apparent discrepancy between the appearance of two men who were for their entire careers automatic choices is explained by the fact that while Hill entered Test cricket first, he refused the England tours of 1909 and 1912.

Clem Hill was a great fieldsman in the deep and a mighty thrower. In 1902 at Old Trafford he ran from long leg to square leg to take the spectacular catch that dismissed Dick Lilley, virtually won the match for Australia by three runs, and decided the rubber.

He was a man of high principle; and refused to make the England tours of 1909 because he mistrusted the Board's terms; he also refused that of 1912, when he was one of six who would not tour unless they could elect their own manager. His disagreement with Percy McAlister, a fellow selector, over the team choice of the Australian Team in 1911 led to a terrific fist-fight between the two which was reported by *The Australian*, though no winner was ever declared. Even without those two England tours, Clem Hill remained the most prolific Australian Test batsman until the days of Ponsford and Bradman.

He holds the unique record of scoring a Test century at Bramall Lane, in 1902, during the only Test ever played on that ground, which is no longer used for cricket.

FIRST-CLASS CAREER RECORDS

Career	M	I	NO	HS	Runs	Avge	100
1892-1924	252	416	21	365*	17213	43.57	45

Ct/St	Runs	Wkts	Avge	BB	5wI	10wM
168/1	323	10	32.30	2-6	—	—

TEST CAREER RECORDS

Tests	I	NO	HS	Runs	Avge	100	50
49	89†	2	191	3412	39.21	7	19

Ct/St	Balls	Runs	Wkts	Avge	BB	5wI	10wM
33	—	—	—	—	—	—	—

JACK HOBBS

THIS WAS THE man his contemporaries christened 'The Master', while Percy Fender, who saw much of his play, and was a shrewd judge of cricket, called him 'the greatest batsman the world has ever known'. He was, too, of outstanding character, with a natural dignity – charming, kind, honest and modest, a God-fearing man with a splendid sense of humour.

His cricket career was one of immense success; he scored more runs than anyone else (61,237); more centuries (197) – plus another 47 in minor matches – and more seasonal totals of 2,000 or more (17). He shared 166 partnerships of 100 or more, most of them with Andrew Sandham (66), 40 with Tom Hayward (four of them in a single week), and 26 with Herbert Sutcliffe. Although his career was spread over twenty-nine years, he missed four to the Great War, most of another to illness and played in only twelve matches in each of the last two.

Sir John Berry Hobbs (1882-1963) Cambridgeshire, Surrey and England Right-hand bat; right-arm fast-medium bowler; specialist cover point.

1935, at the age of fifty-three Hobbs' perfectly balanced cover-drive shows why he was called 'The Master'

He was, though, by no means a creature of statistics, which had little meaning for him. The eldest of six children of a poor household, he had virtually no coaching, yet he grew up to be an almost flawless batsman. By luck, Tom Hayward saw him playing in their native Cambridge and recommended Surrey to give him a trial. All the rest was the result of his own ability and effort. He satisfied the county at his trial and in 1905, after his period of residence, to qualify at the age of twenty-two was put in the first team. In his first match, against the Gentlemen of England captained by W.G. Grace, he scored 88; in his second, against Essex, 155 – and was instantly awarded his county cap.

From then his great career fell into two distinct periods separated by the Great War. Up to the outbreak of war he was sheerly brilliant, a batsman of immense skill and attacking bent, quick as a cat about the crease; never beaten for pace, he read spin like an open book. He had glorious wrists, a rare ability to identify the flight and pitch of the ball early, and superb footwork. He mastered every type of bowling he faced, from the initial South African deployment of googly bowling, to leg theory. Even the finest bowlers frequently found it difficult to bowl at him. After that war, when he was thirty-six, he entered upon the second phase of his eminence. Ripeness, indeed, was all; he scored another 132 centuries and eight times averaged more than 60 for a season or a tour (in 1928, 82).

Inclining increasingly towards the back foot, he seemed to move infallibly and without hurry into the right position for every ball. He continued, too, to take quick singles by dint of his judgement, and quick mental response. He would check a stroke with surprising control, sending the ball slowly to a fieldsman when, if he had played it with full power, it would have reached the man too soon to allow a run.

Andrew Sandham, who saw more of him from the opposite end than anyone else, thought him: 'the finest batsman in my experience on all sorts of wickets, especially the bad ones. He would knock up fifty in no time at all and the bowlers would often turn to me as if to say "did you see that?" He was brilliant.' That sharp cricketing brain, Wilfred Rhodes (he and Hobbs scored 323 for the first wicket against Australia at Melbourne in 1911-12, which is still the English record) said: 'He was the greatest batsman of my time,' and perhaps more significantly: 'He could have had thousands more runs but he was often content to throw his wicket away when he had reached his hundred and give someone else a chance.'

OPPOSITE *Jack Hobbs: perfect professional and ultimate gentleman*

Neither runs nor records mattered too much to him, but he said once: 'If Sandy was going well, we had plenty of batting to come and I would give one of my old bowler mates a chance; but if

Sandy and Tom (Shepherd) and Andy (Ducat) got out, then I had to earn my money from Surrey and get some runs.'

Essentially he made batting seem easy; often it was not until the spectator perceived the difficulty his partner – however good a player – was having that he recognised the extent of Sir Jack's genius. Much of his quality is captured in an anecdote of George Duckworth's: 'When he was fifty-one, he promised to come up and play in my benefit match in 1934; and, despite bitterly cold weather, he hit the last first-class century of his career. He told me he did it to keep warm'.

In his younger county days he was reckoned an extremely capable relief bowler (he took 107 wickets at 25.00); and from a rather slack fieldsman, he made himself, by unremitting practise, one of the finest cover points in the world, with a fast, low, deadly return. Indeed, on the 1911-12 tour of Australia he ran out 15 batsmen.

He aged with dignity, kindliness, generosity and unfailing good humour. He was made an honorary member of Surrey, where he served on the committee until his death; and of MCC. In 1953 he was knighted for services to cricket, the first professional so honoured. Characteristically, he insisted on answering every one of his hundreds of letters of congratulations in his own rather laboured hand; the task took him many days. With great tenderness, and completely unaided, he nursed Lady Hobbs – his beloved Ada – through the last eight disordered years of her life. When she died, his affectionate duty discharged, he seemed simply to relax and, within a few months, slid into death himself. He remains a fine legend as both cricketer and man.

FIRST-CLASS CAREER RECORDS

Career	M	I	NO	HS	Runs	Avge	100
1905-1934	825	1315	106	316*	61237	50.65	197

Ct/St	Runs	Wkts	Avge	BB	5wI	10wM
334	2676	107	25.00	7-56	3	—

TEST CAREER RECORDS

Tests	I	NO	HS	Runs	Avge	100	50
61	102	7	211	5410	56.94	15	28

Ct/St	Balls	Runs	Wkts	Avge	BB	5wI	10wM
17	376	165	1	165.00	1-19	—	—

CONRAD HUNTE

LIKE MOST WEST Indian batsmen, Conrad Hunte was a natural stroke-maker and attacking batsman. He was, however, also a man of considerable humility and consideration. He thoughtfully conceived it his duty to become the sheet-anchor batsman the West Indies side of his time so seriously needed. The measure of both his dedication and his success lies in the fact that, in all first-class cricket his average was 43.92, but in Test matches 45.06: few batsmen have such a statistical justification of their Test match dedication. The main strength of his batting lay on the leg-side, hitting through mid-wicket, hooking or glancing. He could, though, also drive through the off-side quite handsomely. His slow-medium cutters were occasionally useful, and he took some splendid catches close to the bat.

Conrad Hunte made his first appearance for Barbados in

Conrad Cleophas Hunte (1932-) Barbados and West Indies Right-hand bat; right-arm medium-pace bowler; sound all-round fieldsman.

A swashbuckling square cut from Conrad Hunte

Conrad Hunte

1950-51. Through an unfortunate misunderstanding with the West Indies Board, he missed the England tour of 1957, and at that time came near to joining Kent. In fact he was much missed because both Asgarali and Ganteaume had an unhappy time. He became a teacher and a civil servant in Barbados. It was seven years before he was chosen for a Test; then, in his first series, against Pakistan in 1957-58, he scored 622 runs at 77.75. In the third Test of that series he made 260 – his highest Test score – when he and Garfield Sobers put on 446, a West Indian record, for the second wicket. He batted consistently through the Australian tour of 1960-61, in England in 1963 (when he scored more runs than anyone else), and against Australia in 1964-65, when he was quite monumentally steady.

He settled in England as a league pro and coach while he continued University studies. He was a kindly man, and when once, at Adelaide in 1960-61, Kanhai ran him out, Hunte, seeing Kanhai's distress, went over, spoke a few words of comfort to him. Then, thrown deep into thought, walked off the ground and straight through an exit gate into the crowd!

He became attached to Moral Rearmament in Australia after seeing a film of the life of Dr Mary Bethune, the Negro educator, and thereafter, began then to devote part of his cricket earnings to their funds; finally he became a full-time worker in that cause.

FIRST-CLASS CAREER RECORDS

Career	M	I	NO	HS	Runs	Avge	100
1950-1966	132	222	19	263	8916	43.92	16

Ct/St	Runs	Wkts	Avge	BB	5wI	10wM
68/1	644	17	37.88	3-5	—	—

TEST CAREER RECORDS

Tests	I	NO	HS	Runs	Avge	100	50
44	78	6	260	3245	45.06	8	13

Ct/St	Balls	Runs	Wkts	Avge	BB	5wI	10wM
16	270	110	2	55.00	1-17	—	—

LEN HUTTON

LEONARD HUTTON MADE his mark at the top level of cricket when he was relatively young, and sustained it for many years. In 1938, at the age of twenty-two, he made the then record Test score – 364 – for England against Australia at The Oval. In 1952 he became the first professional of modern times to captain an England Test side and, for good measure, he won the Ashes in England and, even after heavy defeat in the first Test of the series, retained them in Australia in 1954-55. Altogether he captained England in 23 Tests, of which they won 11, lost only four and never lost a rubber: an impressive record. It is the more so for the fact that so much of it was achieved in the face of handicaps. He was never robust. The young man who made his mark in 1938 with a record score took 13 hours to make it: and it is an abiding memory that at every interval during that innings, as he came in to the pavilion, he looked a little paler and a little more drawn: but he had set out to create his career and he succeeded. Moreover, a war-time injury necessitated an operation leaving his left arm shorter than the

Sir Leonard Hutton, (1916-   ) Yorkshire and England Right-hand bat; right-arm leg-spin bowler; generally close field.

Len Hutton congratulated by Australia's Bill Brown after breaking Don Bradman's world test record during his historic 364 at The Oval in 1938

right. Some critics formed the opinion that this rendered him vulnerable to the off-break, but, after a little while to understand and acclimatise to the problem, he refuted that suggestion. He was effectively the first of modern batsmen to play spin bowling from the crease and possibly that, rather than any physical handicap, rendered him, initially, at least, vulnerable to off-spin. Secondly, many readers of today may not appreciate the extent to which, even thirty years ago, snobbish prejudice in Britain made the new professional captain extremely uneasy. Indeed, it is difficult to resist the conclusion that Sir Leonard retired from the captaincy

Hutton takes the attack to the spinners

primarily as a result of accumulated nervous strain.

The England batting of his time was not strong: Hutton and Denis Compton were its mainstays; and he laboured, almost throughout his career in the captaincy, under the need to shore up an unreliable batting side.

There is no clearer indication of his value to an England side than the fact that, in 1950-51, when Australia beat the side under F.R. Brown by four to one, Hutton's average was 88.83, 50 more than that of the next English batsman; and, for that matter, 45 in front of the leading Australian. He could play the most handsome strokes, for he had immense natural talent, and his cover driving in particular was quite admirable. He was, though, a pragmatist; he put efficiency first; he was, too, modest; he probably bowled himself too little, for his leg-breaks could be extremely valuable; and he had a remarkably safe pair of hands at short-leg.

He was unobtrusive in his captaincy, although he had all the subtleties, a deep knowledge of the game, an instinctive, if slightly avuncular, affection for his players, and an immense willingness to understand their problems and help to solve them. Thus, his handling and guidance of Frank Tyson in Australia in 1954-55 was an essential part of that player's, and the team's, success. He used to remember wrily that he scored nought and one in his first Test match: in his second, though, he scored a century – a fact he did not use to cap the first remark. He hold the record for the number of runs made in a single month – 1,294 in June 1949; and he used, in referring to that, to point out that it included three consecutive ducks. In his rather dry way he was a humorous man, who compelled affection and respect. Since those days he has become a successful businessman, and has developed his golf in the stockbroker belt, as fine a 'reader' of a match as any, and the most relishable of company.

FIRST-CLASS CAREER RECORDS

Career	M	I	NO	HS	Runs	Avge	100
1934-1960	513	814	91	364	40140	55.51	129

Ct/St	Runs	Wkts	Avge	BB	5wI	10wM
400	5090	173	29.42	6-76	4	1

TEST CAREER RECORDS

Tests	I	NO	HS	Runs	Avge	100	50
79	138	15	364	6971	56.67	19	33

Ct/St	Balls	Runs	Wkts	Avge	BB	5wI	10wM
57	260	232	3	77.33	1-2	—	—

ARCHIE JACKSON

Archibald Jackson (1909-1933) New South Wales and Australia Right-hand bat; outfield.

Archie Jackson

ARCHIE JACKSON WAS the tragic hero figure of Australian cricket; he was dead at twenty-three, but already he had established himself as a great batsman. Greatness is a matter of quality, not of statistics; yet even the figures of his brief career are impressive. Although he did not live to anything like cricketing maturity, in all cricket he scored 4,383 runs at 45.65; and in his eight Tests, 474 at 47.40.

Scottish born – Rutherglen, on the edge of Glasgow – he was taken to Australia by his parents, who had very little money, and who settled in Balmain, Sydney. A sad consequence of their poverty was the boy's poor physique and general ill health. Even as a lad in short pants he gave evidence of immense promise as a creative stroke-maker, and Dr Evatt – cricket student and later deputy Prime Minister – and Arthur Mailey, captain of Balmain, in their different ways helped him to establish himself in the club.

A few weeks after his seventeenth birthday he took a firm place in the New South Wales side and, in that first season, made 500 runs (with two centuries) at an average of 50. In the next season – 1927-28 – he became the youngest man to score two centuries in a match, with 131 and 122 against South Australia.

A year later, after a 'blooding' trip to New Zealand, he opened the innings with Bill Woodfull in his first Test match – the fourth of the 1928-29 series with England – and became the youngest man to score a century on his entry into Anglo-Australian Tests. His innings grew healthily, from the nervousness of a nineteen year old in an awe-inspiring situation – 250 minutes to 100 – and then the full, rich flowering of his batsmanship which brought the next 60 in an hour. In the final Test he made a stylish 46, and ensured his choice for Woodfull's 1930 tour of England with 182 – the highest score he ever made – in the Test trial.

England did not see the best of him; he made a polished 73 in the decisive stand with Don Bradman at The Oval, in the fifth Test, which won the Ashes for Australia. Yet he simply had neither the strength nor the stamina to play to his potential, for the cruel disease which was soon to kill him was already tightening its grip. On his return to Australia he had a haemorrhage before the match with Queensland; sent to a sanatorium by the Australian Board of Control, he could not endure the boredom and discharged himself, but one collapse followed another. He was engaged to his fiancée, Phyllis Thomas, on what proved to be his deathbed. English and Australian players from the fourth Test came to his hospital to visit him. On 16 February 1933 he asked the Test score; and on the day that England regained the Ashes, Archie

*Studied elegance: Archie
Jackson at practice*

Jackson died from tuberculosis of both lungs. He was taken back
for burial to Sydney where his pall bearers in the Field of Mars
Cemetery were Bill Woodfull, Don Bradman, Bert Oldfield, Vic
Richardson, Alan Kippax and Bill Ponsford.

FIRST-CLASS CAREER RECORDS

Career	M	I	NO	HS	Runs	Avge	100
1926-1930	70	107	11	182	4383	45.65	11

Ct/St	Runs	Wkts	Avge	BB	5wI	10wM
26	49	0	—	—	—	—

TEST CAREER RECORDS

Tests	I	NO	HS	Runs	Avge	100	50
8	11	1	164	474	47.40	1	2

Ct/St	Balls	Runs	Wkts	Avge	BB	5wI	10wM
7	—	—	—	—	—	—	—

JAVED MIANDAD

Javed Miandad Khan (1957-   ) Karachi, Sind, Habib Bank, Sussex, Glamorgan and Pakistan
Right-hand bat; leg-spin bowler; cover fieldsman.

JAVED IS A QUITE outstanding, aggressive, stroke-making batsman. A precocious cricketer, he first came into first-class cricket (for Karachi Whites) at sixteen-and-a-half, while, a few months later, he scored 311 for them (v National Bank). Such was his promise even then, that Sussex hurried to recruit him. While he was still qualifying for the county and barely eighteen, he struck 227 runs of such quality against Hampshire Second XI that experienced players who saw the innings were amazed by his brilliance.

At nineteen he became only the second player to score a century in his first Test innings for Pakistan; less than a month later he became their youngest to score a double century in a Test. Before he was twenty-two he had scored six centuries for Pakistan. At twenty-two he was made captain of his country, almost certainly too soon, for he is an extremely volatile personality. Indeed, in 1981-82 in Australia, he was involved in a fiery scene with Dennis Lillee. When, subsequently, he was replaced as captain by Imran Khan, he had a poor 1982 tour of England. Then, at Lahore, he played a dogged out-of-character innings of 138 to round off Pakistan's 3-0 win in the rubber against Australia.

He has rarely given the impression of one over-concerned with record-breaking. Yet he has already, at the age of thirty-one, made most Test appearances for Pakistan (92); most runs (6,621); and most hundreds (17); he has now captained them in nineteen Tests.

When in 1980 Sussex found their list of overseas players too long, Javed moved to Glamorgan with instant – county record-breaking – but all too brief success. The economics of the county's overseas talent sometimes meant that he was left out in favour of a bowler. It should not be forgotten, however, that in the 1975 Prudential World Cup, against a strong West Indies side, Miandad bowled his 22 overs of leg-spin for an economical 42 runs. He is, too, a fast – indeed, spectacular – fielder in the covers. If he can steer clear of injury he may end his career with quite remarkable figures. For the moment he is one of the most interesting and exciting players in the world to watch.

FIRST-CLASS CAREER RECORDS

Career	M	I	NO	HS	Runs	Avge	100
1973-1988	355	562	88	311	25400	53.58	72

Ct/St	Runs	Wkts	Avge	BB	5wI	10wM
303/3	6395	191	33.48	7-39	6	–

A typical straight drive by Javed Miandad, the youngest scorer of a Test Match double century

TEST CAREER RECORDS

Tests	I	NO	HS	Runs	Avge	100	50
92	141	18	280*	6621	53.82	17	35

Ct/St	Balls	Runs	Wkts	Avge	BB	5wI	10wM
79/1	1470	682	17	40.11	3-74	–	–

GILBERT JESSOP

*Gilbert Laird Jessop
(1874-1955)
Gloucestershire,
Cambridge University,
London County and
England
Right-hand bat; fast
right-arm bowler;
outstanding field at cover
point or deep field.*

EVEN IN THE vastly rich variety of what has been – justly – called the 'Golden Age' of cricket, Gilbert Jessop was unique. No one else consistently took such risks, and scored so fast, with such success; his fielding and throwing at cover point or short mid-off have never been surpassed for speed and accuracy. He was also considered good enough to open the bowling for England. Now you have the picture of a fine all-round cricketer. 'Jessopus' was also the most exciting batsman of his – or any other – day to watch.

Arthur Haygarth's monumental *Scores and Biographies* records such performances: 286 out of 355 made in 175 minutes; 233 out of 318 in 150 minutes; 234 out of 346 in 155 minutes. For Gloucestershire v Hampshire at Bristol in 1909, he made 161 and 128; the 161 out of 199 was made in 95 minutes, in the course of which he struck Charlie Llewellyn, an appreciable Test bowler, for 61 off four overs. The 129 came out of 170 in 98 minutes when he made 100 while his partner, Langdon, scored eight. Others like 101 out of 118 in 40 minutes (v Yorkshire, 1897) are in character, and he thrice scored 50 in 20 minutes. There are over two closely printed pages of such performances. Of course, he could not sustain such scoring in Test matches. Once, however, against Australia at The Oval in 1902, he lifted his scoring rate to that exalted level. In the second innings of that Test he went in when England, needing 273 to win on a worn pitch, were 48 for five. In 75 minutes, against high-class bowling, Jessop made 104, leaving Hirst and Rhodes to see England home.

Short, broad-shouldered, long-armed and immensely strong, with steely wrists and a fine sense of timing, because of his stance he was nicknamed 'The Croucher'. It is important – even crucial – that he was no mere slogger; for instance, despite the spectacular power of his driving, a large proportion of his runs were scored behind the wicket. He cut and glanced brilliantly.

He was often out through trying to score too quickly at the start of his innings or, as the wise men of his time averred, through taking unjustified risks against good bowling. That, though, was his batting nature. An amazing aspect of his batting is that he sustained it for twenty years. He played for Gloucestershire from 1894 to 1914, and was captain from 1900 to 1912, was four years a Cambridge Blue, where he was captain in 1899. His health broke down during the First World War, and he could not play afterwards. During those twenty years, though, he scored 26,698 runs – including 53 centuries – at 32.63; made a thousand runs in a season 14 times; with 2,000 in 1900 – when he also took 104 wickets – and in 1901. Most convincing are the

*Gilbert Jessop,
unquenchable exponent
of attacking batting*

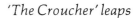

figures that show that his centuries were scored at an average rate of 82.70 runs an hour, and his five double centuries at barely less than 100.

We have not looked upon his like before or since.

FIRST-CLASS CAREER RECORDS

Career	M	I	NO	HS	Runs	Avge	100
1894-1914	493	855	37	286	26698	32.63	53

Ct/St	Runs	Wkts	Avge	BB	5wI	10wM
463	19904	873	22.79	8-29	42	4

TEST CAREER RECORDS

Tests	I	NO	HS	Runs	Avge	100	50
18	26	0	104	569	21.88	1	3

Ct/St	Balls	Runs	Wkts	Avge	BB	5wI	10wM
11	742	354	10	35.40	4-68	—	—

ALVIN KALLICHARRAN

Alvin Isaac Kallicharran (1949-) Guyana, Warwickshire, Queensland, Transvaal, Orange Free State and West Indies
Left-hand bat; slow right-arm bowler; outfield.

DESPITE HIS LACK of height – he is 5 feet 4 inches tall – 'Kalli' is a brilliant, entertaining and masterly batsman. One of eleven children, he comes from Port Mourant, the small town in Berbice County on the east coast of Guyana which also produced Basil Butcher, Rohan Kanhai and Joe Solomon. In 1966-67, at seventeen, he became the youngest cricketer to play for Guyana. He scored a century in each of his first two Test innings – both against New Zealand in 1971-72 – and in 1982, for Warwickshire against Leicestershire, he and Geoff Humpage shared a fourth wicket stand record of 470 for all English counties.

His cricket career has not been without its hitches. In 1973-74 against England, in the first Test at Port of Spain, he had made 142 when, after Julien played the last ball of the day on to the pitch, Kallicharran walked off without grounding his bat and Tony Greig threw down the wicket. On appeal to umpire Sang

Alvin Kallicharran in action ...

152

... and repose

Hue, he was given out, but in an acrimonious atmosphere Sang Hue diplomatically allowed his – perfectly correct – decision to be overruled next day; but Kalli was out for 158. He himself felt that he had rarely batted better. He did, however, play quite memorably when he made 91 – out of 289 – in the attempt to win the third Test of 1972-73 against Australia. Others will feel that his finest performance was against India in 1974-75, with an amazing 124 out of 289 – 64 of the last 77 added when the pitch turned evil, and Venkatraghavan made the ball talk.

He signed for Mr Packer, then discovered that his contract with a Queensland radio station did not allow him to join that operation. In an amazing *volte face*, he became captain of West Indies for nine Tests, when Clive Lloyd withdrew. His weakness has never been technical, but it may be physical; he seemed to tire under pressure of play. When in 1981 he was dropped after an unsuccessful series in Pakistan he accepted a £20,000 contract to coach and play for Transvaal in South Africa. He enjoyed enormous batting success for them, but he was banned from playing for West Indies. In the following season, though, he joined a team of West Indians touring there. He still, however, bats well – sometimes quite brilliantly – for Warwickshire.

FIRST-CLASS CAREER RECORDS

Career	M	I	NO	HS	Runs	Avge	100
1966-1985	448	739	77	243*	29771	44.97	78

Ct/St	Runs	Wkts	Avge	BB	5wl	10wM
286	3443	75	45.90	5-45	1	—

TEST CAREER RECORDS

Tests	I	NO	HS	Runs	Avge	100	50
66	109†	10	187	4399	44.43	12	21

Ct/St	Balls	Runs	Wkts	Avge	BB	5wl	10wM
51	406	158	4	39.50	2-16	—	—

ROHAN KANHAI

ROHAN KANHAI, AS a batsman, has provided a quite remarkable blend of brilliant improvisation and consistency. Almost anyone who ever watched him will recall the remarkable stroke by which he would pick up a full-length ball and swing it to leg with a violent lunge which swung him of his feet and the ball out of the ground. He is only 5 feet 7 inches tall but wirily strong, with whippy wrists and an immense striking power.

His grandparents came from India to Berbice, a small village in Guyana (then British Guiana) with a strong cricketing tradition. It was not easy, though, to advance from the lower to the higher levels of play there; and Kanhai used to recall with some amusement that there were so many candidates for a major trial there that four cricketers from Berbice had to draw lots for two places. Kanhai was unlucky, but while he watched the next day's practice, one of the 'lucky' players sprained his ankle and Kanhai

Rohan Babulal Kanhai (1935-   ) Guyana (British Guiana), Trinidad, Warwickshire, Western Australia, Tasmania and West Indies
Right-hand bat; right-arm medium-pace bowler; all-round fieldsman; occasional wicketkeeper.

Kanhai's famous 'falling' hook

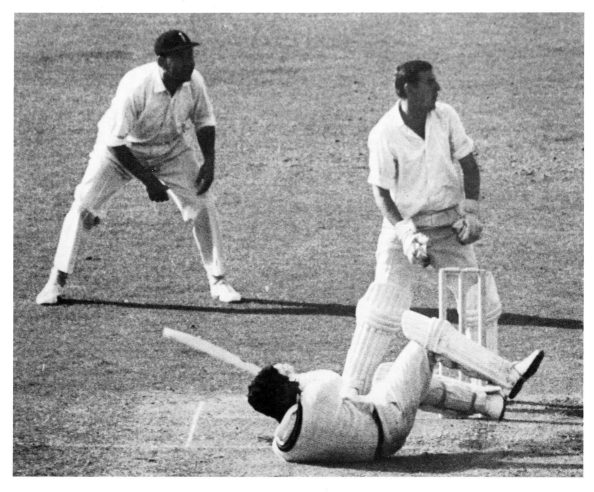

was called in to replace him. He won a regular place in the British Guiana side following scores of 51 and 27 against the Australian touring team.

Afterwards, on tour with West Indies in Australia in 1960-61, he pulled a hamstring and the team's medical officer forbade him to play. After a night of pain and misery he went to his captain – Frank Worrell and offered to turn out. Worrell decided to risk it; Kanhai made 84 (out of 181) and established his team place. His remarkable sequence of 61 consecutive Test matches was broken when he had to return to Birmingham from the West Indies home series with England for a cartilage operation.

He has an impressive Test average of 47.53; and he has played domestic cricket in four countries; but much of his best batting has been for Warwickshire. In 1968 he (253) and 'Billy' Ibadulla set a then county record of 402 in a stand for the fourth wicket against Nottinghamshire, and in 1974 he (213 not out) and John Jameson set a world record of 465 unbroken for the second wicket against Gloucestershire. As a batsman Kanhai combined an entertaining quality with reliability to an unusual degree.

OPPOSITE *Kanhai the orthodox: a classical cover drive*

FIRST-CLASS CAREER RECORDS

Career	M	I	NO	HS	Runs	Avge	100
1954-1981	416	669	82	256	28774	49.01	83

Ct/St	Runs	Wkts	Avge	BB	5wI	10wM
318/7	1008	18	56.00	2-5	—	—

TEST CAREER RECORDS

Tests	I	NO	HS	Runs	Avge	100	50
79	137	6	256	6227	47.53	15	28

Ct/St	Balls	Runs	Wkts	Avge	BB	5wI	10wM
50	183	85	0	—	—	—	—

BILL LAWRY

William Morris Lawry (1937-   ) Victoria and Australia
Left-hand bat; capable outfield.

BILL LAWRY WAS a tall, lanky, dour, watchful left-hander, and a better player than he looked. He was picked for Victoria at only eighteen, but then lost his place for almost two seasons until an innings of 266 against New South Wales took him into Benaud's side to England in 1961, as a virtual unknown. He was an awkward-looking batsman, and many English bowlers watching him for the first time mistook his late leaving of the ball as 'playing and missing'. In the event, with 57 in his first Test and 130 out of 238 in his second, he established himself and finished top of the batting with 2,109 at 61.18 for the tour, 420 at 52.50 in Tests; and was instrumental in winning the series.

He was fearless against pace, as he showed against Trueman and Statham on an ugly pitch at Lord's; his hooking became quite imperious, and he gradually extended his stroke play beyond his former leg-side limitations. Indeed, he was generally at his best against England (with 2,233 runs at 48.54). In the home series of 1965-66 he scored more runs than anyone else on either side (592 at 84.57), and three times stood effectively between England and a winning position.

He made such an impression on that tour that on his return he was made captain of Victoria and retained the post for ten years; and in 1968 was made captain of Australia. He survived as captain of the Australian side trounced in South Africa in 1970; and won in India, but when he lost the Ashes in 1970-71 he was replaced – the first Australian captain to be dropped during a series – by Ian Chappell.

His figures argue better than such peremptory treatment. It may well have been his attitude rather than his ability which brought about his downfall, for he was certainly the most difficult Australian batsman of his day to dismiss. His highest Test score was 210, made at Bridgetown, Barbados, against a West Indian attack as impressive as Wesley Hall, Charlie Griffith, Garfield Sobers and Lance Gibbs. He and Bobby Simpson put on 382 in Australia's highest first-wicket partnership, and the only instance of both opening batsmen scoring double centuries. He played a major part, too, in Australia's home series against West Indies in 1968-69, which Australia took by 3-1 after losing the first, in what Henry Blofeld called 'A major shift in the balance of world cricket'. On the India tour of 1969-70, Lawry, a non-smoker and non-drinker, with little time for social functions, was not happy. Although Australia won the series, the manager could hardly help but submit an unfavourable report; Lawry's dismissal followed during the next home rubber.

Although not an attractive batsman, Bill Lawry was a great fighter, and a splendid resister in a corner. His nickname was 'Phant' or 'The Phantom' because of his enthusiasm for that comic strip character. When he left cricket, he concentrated on his lifelong hobby of pigeon-fancying. All over the world, though, fast bowlers remembered him with immense respect.

FIRST-CLASS CAREER RECORDS

Career	M	I	NO	HS	Runs	Avge	100
1955-1971	249	417	49	266	18734	50.90	50

Ct/St	Runs	Wkts	Avge	BB	5wI	10wM
121	188	5	37.60	1-3	—	—

TEST CAREER RECORDS

Tests	I	NO	HS	Runs	Avge	100	50
67	123†	12	210	5234	47.15	13	27

Ct/St	Balls	Runs	Wkts	Avge	BB	5wI	10wM
30	14‡	6	0	—	—	—	—

Bill Lawry hooks firmly

MAURICE LEYLAND

*Maurice Leyland
(1900-1967) Yorkshire
and England
Left-hand bat; left-arm
wrist-spin bowler; out-
field.*

MAURICE LEYLAND WAS the very picture of a Yorkshire cricketer: county cap at an angle on his fair hair, fresh-faced, with a firm jaw and an engaging grin, stocky, wide-shouldered and broad-beamed, with muscular arms, broad and sturdy legs – and he was as firm as he looked. Not a particularly prepossessing-looking batsman, he took a fairly high grip on the bat and loved to attack; when he batted, he had something of the look of a hammerman. But, at bottom, his defence was technically sound, and absolutely resolute in character; a great man in a corner and against the odds, he loved a cricketing battle and rescued many an innings in his time, and his good humour never failed.

It is tempting to read some statistics as revealing their subject; Maurice Leyland's average in all cricket was 40.50; for Yorkshire, 41.05; in all Tests 46.06, against Australia 56.84. He made 80 first-class centuries, 62 of them for Yorkshire; nine in Tests, seven of them against Australia. He shared in three of Yorkshire's record partnerships: with Wilfred Barber for the second wicket (346); with Herbert Sutcliffe for the third (323), and with Emmott Robinson for the sixth (276).

He played his first game for Yorkshire in 1920 and his last, against MCC in the Scarborough Festival of 1946 (though he appeared in odd representative first-class matches until 1948). After he ceased to play, Yorkshire did not want to lose him and made him the county coach until the onset of his terminal illness in 1963.

He did not play for England until he was twenty-eight; on Chapman's 1928-29 tour of Australia, he was brought in for the fifth (Melbourne) Test; made 137 and 53 not out, and remained a steady choice for a decade (51 Tests). Indeed, when in 1938 he was omitted for the first four Tests, he was brought back at The Oval and scored 187; and his second wicket partnership of 382 with Len Hutton set a record for England-Australia Tests. At Brisbane, on G.O. Allen's 1936-37 tour, when McCormick knocked down the first three wickets to leave England 20 for three, Maurice Leyland made a dogged 126, crucial in England's win.

Yorkshire in his time were well-equipped with left-arm spin; Maurice used to bowl the left-arm, wrist-spin off-break and its complementary googly which, like so much of his cricket, he learned from his father, Ted Leyland, for years a respected pro and groundsman in Yorkshire, Lancashire and Warwickshire league cricket. He was not always as accurate as Yorkshire cricket demands, but he was good enough to take 466 wickets at 29.29 as

OPPOSITE *Maurice Leyland
hitting with characteris-
tic power*

Leyland relaxing on his way to Australia with the MCC in 1932

a change bowler. That particular type of delivery is known as 'The Chinaman', and when someone asked Maurice, who was generally credited with its christening, why it was called a Chinaman he replied, with disarming simplicity: 'Well, what else would you call it?'

He was faster than he looked in the deep field; tidy and safe-handed and, in his time, made 245 catches.

Honest, friendly, a great team man and a game opponent, Maurice Leyland was popular, and is remembered wherever he played cricket.

FIRST-CLASS CAREER RECORDS

Career	M	I	NO	HS	Runs	Avge	100
1920-1947	685	932	101	263	33659	40.50	80

Ct/St	Runs	Wkts	Avge	BB	5wI	10wM
246	13651	466	29.29	8-63	11	1

TEST CAREER RECORDS

Tests	I	NO	HS	Runs	Avge	100	50
41	65†	5	187	2764	46.06	9	10

Ct/St	Balls	Runs	Wkts	Avge	BB	5wI	10wM
13	1103‡	585	6	97.50	3-91	—	—

CLIVE LLOYD

CLIVE LLOYD WAS a memorable sight on any cricket field. He compelled immense attention first by his fielding at cover-point, where he was acrobatic and almost miraculously effective. About 6 feet 5 inches tall and relaxed looking, he batted skilfully – if not always happily at the start of an innings – striking the ball with quite remarkable power. The average batsman uses a 2lb.2oz or 2lb.3oz. bat but Lloyd's weighs 3lbs. and he adds three rubber handle grips. In conjunction with his great height and long arms this results in a quite terrifying leverage, and from time to time he has hit the ball great distances.

His father died when he was at school, and he combined being the bread-winner of the family with establishing himself as a

Clive Hubert Lloyd (1944-   ) Guyana (British Guiana), Lancashire, and West Indies
Left-hand bat; right-arm leg-break, then medium-pace bowler; great cover-point and later slip field.

Clive Lloyd: as crowds love him …

163

… as bowlers prefer him

cricketer. He ensured his place in the Guyana (then British Guiana) side with an innings of 194 against Jamaica, but he was unlucky – yet another victim of West Indian island politics – to be left out of the 1966 team to England. He joined Lancashire in 1968 and, importantly, was appointed captain of West Indies in 1974-75; and of Lancashire in 1981. Captaincy never affected his batting, and his consistency was astonishing. In fact, he holds the record for the most Test innings before a first nought – 58 – from December 1966 until February 1974.

He equalled Jessop's record of a double century in two hours (West Indians v Glamorgan 1976) when he reached his first hundred in 80 minutes and made the second in another 40. His performances in over-limit matches both as a fieldsman and batsman have been quite amazing, but his towering achievement has been as a captain: he took West Indies into 74 Tests, of which they won 36 and lost 12, while of his 18 rubbers they lost only two (v Australia 1975-76) and – which will surprise many – v New Zealand in 1979-80. His records include most Tests as a captain; most wins as a captain, most successive wins (11) and most consecutive matches without defeat (26). Only Colin Cowdrey played more than his 110 Tests; only Gavaskar, Boycott, Sobers and Cowdrey scored more Test runs than his 7,515.

In effect he picked up after a gap of years from Frank Worrell, stabilizing West Indies cricket in discipline and dignity.

FIRST-CLASS CAREER RECORDS

Career	M	I	NO	HS	Runs	Avge	100
1963-1985	483	722	95	242*	30885	49.25	78

Ct/St	Runs	Wkts	Avge	BB	5wI	10wM
377	4104	114	36.00	4-48	—	—

TEST CAREER RECORDS

Tests	I	NO	HS	Runs	Avge	100	50
110	175†	14	242*	7515	46.67	19	39

Ct/St	Balls	Runs	Wkts	Avge	BB	5wI	10wM
90	1716	622	10	62.20	2-13	—	—

CHARLIE MACARTNEY

Charles George Macartney (1886-1958) New South Wales, Otago and Australia Right-hand bat; left-arm slow bowler; capable field, notably at mid-off.

CHARLIE MACARTNEY, WHOM Australians of his generation for good and obvious reasons called 'the Governor General', was one of the most commanding, vivid and exciting batsmen of this century. At first he was an all-rounder whose primary ability was finger spin, a bowler of accurate length and a well-hidden faster ball; that phase lasted virtually until 1914. After the First World War – that is to say, after he was thirty-two, he suddenly emerged as a major batsman of immense attacking skill, and a sheer destroyer of even the best bowling.

Physically he was of the ideal cricketing build – virtually the prototype of the great Australian batsman – a little under average height, wide-shouldered, strong in the arms and wrists and fast on his feet. His quick eyes, steady regard and a square, all but pugilistic jaw, coupled with the imperious quality of his batting, explained his nickname.

As a bowler, he took an unusually long run for a spinner, but he believed that it steadied him – not that he ever seemed to need any sedative as a batsman. Many think the best of his cricket was played in England. On the tour of 1909 he took 71 wickets at 17.46, while his batting figures were no better than 638 at 19.33. In the Tests he had 16 wickets – more than anyone else except Cotter, who had 17 – at 16.12; and 148 runs at 18.50.

In the Triangular Tournament of 1912 – not a happy competition for Australia – his batting future was hinted at, like the tip of an iceberg, at Lord's when he made 99. It was the highest score for Australia in the series, before he tried to hit a full toss from Frank Foster for six and edged it to the wicketkeeper. He bowled little and indifferently (six wickets at 23.66).

After the First World War he was troubled by illness and was able to appear in only two Tests on England's 1920-21 tour, but headed the Australian batting with 86.66. So to England with Warwick Armstrong's Gregory-and-MacDonald-equipped winning side of 1921. There Macartney achieved the most unusual feat of being the only batsman on either side to score a Test century: 115 at Leeds. *Wisden* described it as: 'painstaking – such a restrained innings that he was at the wicket for three hours and ten minutes'. He made more runs than any other Australian in the Tests that season – 300 at 42.85 – and, in all matches – 2,335 at 58.37 – while bowling little.

His other – perhaps, indeed, the most outstanding performance of the tour – long remembered in those parts – was performed against Nottinghamshire at Trent Bridge on 25 June. On the first morning, on a desperately 'plumb' pitch, 'Titch' Richmond

Charlie Macartney, imperious batsman with a flair for improvisation

bowled Bardsley for nought; and Macartney himself was dropped at slip when he had made nine. He then proceeded to score 345 against five Test bowlers, in under four hours, with four sixes and 47 fours: this is still the record number of runs scored in a day's play.

Macartney on his way to a hundred before lunch on the first day of the 1921 Headingley Test

He appeared in only two of the three Tests the side played in South Africa on the way home, in which he was top of the averages with 493 runs at 70.42.

He was unable to play in any of the home Tests of 1924-25 because of his recurrent illness. In 1926, however, he made his last tour to England, and probably achieved his greatest triumph. In May he made a glorious 148 in two-and-a-half hours against Essex. The first Test was virtually washed out, but against Lancashire he played what was, by common consent, as brilliant an innings as even he had ever produced, when he made 160 out of 303 in three-and-three-quarter hours. He followed it up by taking four wickets for 15 runs. His fortieth birthday fell on the Sunday of the Lord's Test and, on the Tuesday, he made 133 not out. Leeds was his crowning triumph of the tour, when he became only the second batsman (Victor Trumper was the first and Sir Donald Bradman the third) to score a century before lunch in a Test against England. Bardsley was caught for nought in Tate's first over, and off the fifth ball Arthur Carr dropped Macartney at slip. So far from being disturbed by his escape, Macartney attacked the bowling from the outset to such an extent that he outpaced his partner when he made 51 out of 64, 100 out of 131, and altogether 151 in three hours. He followed it with his third century in consecutive Tests, 109 made in three hours. By way of valediction, in his last innings in England he made 100 in less than two-and-a-half hours against an England XI at Blackpool.

Those who saw the century at Leeds still swear that Charlie Macartney was the most exciting of all Test batsmen.

FIRST-CLASS CAREER RECORDS

Career	M	I	NO	HS	Runs	Avge	100
1905-1935	249	360	32	345	15019	45.78	49

Ct/St	Runs	Wkts	Avge	BB	5wI	10wM
102	8781	419	20.95	7-58	17	1

TEST CAREER RECORDS

Tests	I	NO	HS	Runs	Avge	100	50
35	55	4	170	2131	41.78	7	9

Ct/St	Balls	Runs	Wkts	Avge	BB	5wI	10wM
17	3561‡	1240	45	27.55	7-58	2	1

A.C. MACLAREN

ARCHIE MACLAREN WAS an outstanding batsman for many years but was – and is – remembered chiefly for two achievements. For Lancashire against Somerset at Taunton in 1895, he scored 424 (in seven hours 50 minutes, with a six and 62 fours). It was then the highest score made in a first-class match, beating W.G.'s 344 of 1876, and endured until Ponsford's 429 of 1922-23, but remains the record for English cricket.

Then twenty-six years later, at the age of forty-nine, he selected and captained the first team to defeat Warwick Armstrong's side of 1921 in England. As a batsman, he refused to be tied down; masterly on bad wickets, he played forward or back with equal facility and while he commanded all the strokes, his especial glory was his regal off and straight driving.

Tall, handsome – even patrician – in appearance and autocratic in manner, he made an early mark when he won his colours for Harrow at fifteen and scored 55 and 67 against Eton. He continued in the side, and at eighteen, also against Eton, made 76 out of a total of 133, batting with a maturity which surprised

Archibald Campbell MacLaren (1871-1944) Lancashire and England Right-hand bat; right-arm fast bowler (rarely); slip field.

A.C. MacLaren, patrician batsman and despotic captain

169

A.C. MacLaren

many informed observers. In the same year he was invited to play for his native county – Lancashire – and in his first innings for them (and in first-class cricket) he scored 108. In 1894, at twenty-two, he was made captain of the county, and held that post for all but two seasons until 1907.

When W.G. Grace retired from the England captaincy in 1899, Archie MacLaren – who had not yet played a first-class match that season – was invited to succeed him. In his first match in office – against Australia at Lord's – England followed on but, on a most difficult pitch, MacLaren made 88 not out, the highest score of the match for his side. Taking out the team of 1901-02, his 116 at Sydney made him the first man to score four centuries in Test cricket, and the last England captain to make a hundred in Australia for fifty-seven years (until P.B.H. May, 1958-59).

He was always less happy in England, where the damper weather adversely affected his lumbago, than in Australia where he toured three times – twice under Andrew Stoddart and once with his own side. On those visits he scored 2,769 runs at an average of over 50, and was regarded there as probably the finest batsman in the world.

As a captain, while no one doubted his tactical acumen, he seemed unable to motivate – or perhaps even to convince – the players under him. He captained England in 22 Tests – all against Australia – of which four were won, 11 lost, and seven drawn.

Materially his career was unsuccessful. In 1902 he agreed to join Hampshire, but financial arrangements for an appointment there were never agreed. In 1921 Lancashire engaged him as their county coach. Then, in the winter of 1922, he took an MCC team to New Zealand where the man who had come into first-class cricket with a century, went out of it, at the age of fifty-one, with an innings of 200 not out. In the course of it he so injured a knee that he could play no more; but the point had been made – with a characteristically lordly gesture.

FIRST-CLASS CAREER RECORDS

Career	M	I	NO	HS	Runs	Avge	100
1890-1922	424	703	52	424	22237	34.15	47

Ct/St	Runs	Wkts	Avge	BB	5wI	10wM
452	267	1	267.00	1-44	—	—

TEST CAREER RECORDS

Tests	I	NO	HS	Runs	Avge	100	50
35	61	4	140	1931	33.87	5	8

Ct/St	Balls	Runs	Wkts	Avge	BB	5wI	10wM
29	—	—	—	—	—	—	—

MAJID KHAN

MAJID, A HIGHLY civilized, personable, independent and proud character, was born to cricket. His father, Dr Jahangir Khan, was a pace bowler, Cambridge Blue and Indian Test player; his brother Asad also a Cambridge Blue; while his cousins, Imran Khan and Javed Burki, both captained Pakistan. On his initial appearance in the first-class game, at fifteen, he made 111 not out and took six wickets for 67 for Lahore against the Khairpur Division. Soon afterwards, in a remarkable performance, after Punjab University, playing Karachi, stood at five for four wickets, Majid scored 286 to win the match. He played Test cricket at eighteen years twenty-six days first as a pace bowler but, after his action was questioned, he turned mainly to batting.

Majid Jahangir Khan (1946-   ) Lahore, P.I.A., Punjab, Rawlpindi Cambridge University, Glamorgan, Queensland and Pakistan Right-hand bat; right-arm fast-medium bowler then slow off-spinner, superb close catcher.

His home form was considerable and he was chosen for the tour of England in 1967. He failed abjectly in the Test matches, but in the match against Glamorgan at Cardiff he scored 147 not out in 89 minutes with 13 sixes; five of them coming in one over from Roger Davis. Small wonder that public acclaim in Wales brought him to the county, where he had two good seasons before he went up to Cambridge, whom he led to their first win over Oxford for fourteen years.

Returning to Wales, he captained Glamorgan from 1973 until he resigned in 1976. Queensland took him to Australia and he made two centuries for them before he seemed to lose interest. He scored a run of Test centuries against Australia, West Indies and New Zealand but, by an odd coincidence, only played two innings against Australia in Pakistan – when he scored 89 and 110 not out. He remains one of the few players ever to score a century before lunch on the first day of a Test Match (v New Zealand at Karachi, 1976). He helped Glamorgan to the Championship of 1969 but left the county after ten years. In 1982 he passed Hanif's record as leading Pakistani run-scorer; but he was soon overtaken by both Zaheer and Javed Miandad. Surprisingly, for a highly intelligent and gifted captain, he only led his country three times – against England in 1972-73 when all the Tests were drawn.

A player of unquestionable charisma, Majid played a series of great innings at all levels and scored eight Test centuries. Still, though, for all his brilliance, it must be doubted if he quite realized his full potential. On the other hand, he made many good friends, and his memory is cherished round the international cricketing circuit. There was an air of relaxation about his approach to the game that made Majid a particularly attractive batsman for any spectator.

FIRST-CLASS CAREER RECORDS

Career	M	I	NO	HS	Runs	Avge	100
1961-1984	410	700	62	241	27444	43.01	73

Ct/St	Runs	Wkts	Avge	BB	5wI	10wM
408	7197	224	32.12	6-67	4	—

TEST CAREER RECORDS

Tests	I	NO	HS	Runs	Avge	100	50
63	106	5	167	3931	38.92	8	19

Ct/St	Balls	Runs	Wkts	Avge	BB	5wI	10wM
70	3584	1456	27	53.92	4-45	—	—

The easy authority of Majid Khan; he brought a 'Golden Age' grace to 1970s cricket

VIJAY MANJREKAR

VIJAY MANJREKAR, LIKE so many major Indian batsmen of his time, was related to a well-known player: his uncle was D.D. Hindlekar, the wicketkeeper-batsman of the 1935-1946 period. Manjrekar is included here primarily as a batsman of fine gifts who was consistently outstanding against fast bowling at a time, roughly from 1952 to 1964, when that was his country's main weakness. Although short, he was nimble, a good positional player and an especially fine cutter and hooker.

He entered the first-class game at eighteen, played his first Test

Vijay Lakshman Manjrekar (1931-1983) Bombay, Bengal, Andhra Pradesh, Uttar Pradesh, Rajasthan, Maharashtra and India
Right-hand bat; off-break bowler; versatile field who could keep wicket.

The versatile Vijay Manjrekar, capable of gritty defence or fluent attack

– against England at Eden Gardens, Calcutta – at twenty; and came to England as the youngest member of Hazare's side of 1952. That was the season when Trueman so murderously routed the Indian batting, and in the first Test of the series – only the third of his career – Manjrekar came in at 42 for three. He thereupon proceeded to score 133 – the first century of his career – and to put on 222, which is still the Indian Test record for the fourth wicket, with Vijay Hazare.

Although increasing weight became a trial to him, he retained his speed about the crease and in India's next series, in West Indies, he scored 118 in a second wicket partnership of 237 – then an Indian record – with Pankaj Roy. His two most successful series were both in India; he made 386 runs at 77.20 against New Zealand in 1955-56, and 586 at 83.71 in 1961-62 when India won their first rubber against England. In 1964-65 his two innings of 59 and 39 were of critical value in India's narrow first Test win against Australia. His last Test innings, before some twist of Indian cricket politics took him out of the representative game for ever, was of 102 not out against New Zealand.

Most unusually, Vijay Manjrekar played for six different sides in the Ranji Trophy. He died at the early age of fifty-two when visiting Madras for a sporting gathering. He leaves behind a reputation for courage and for rising to the challenging occasion.

FIRST-CLASS CAREER RECORDS

Career	M	I	NO	HS	Runs	Avge	100
1949-1967	198	295	38	283	12832	49.92	38

Ct/St	Runs	Wkts	Avge	BB	5wI	10wM
72/6	657	20	32.85	4-21	—	—

TEST CAREER RECORDS

Tests	I	NO	HS	Runs	Avge	100	50
55	92	10	189*	3208	39.12	7	15

Ct/St	Balls	Runs	Wkts	Avge	BB	5wI	10wM
19/2	204	44	1	44.00	1-16	—	—

PETER MAY

PETER MAY HAS been described as the best post-war English batsman. He was already outstanding as quite a young boy when he was coached by Bob Relf at his preparatory school in Reading; and later by George Geary at Charterhouse. There he played his way into the school team at fourteen and, against Harrow, scored the only century for Charterhouse that season. Three more years in the school team, captain in the last, he played for the Public Schools at Lord's at fifteen and, during school holidays, turned out for Berkshire.

When he was seventeen, he played an innings of 146 for Public Schools against Combined Services which impressed everyone who watched it. At eighteen he joined the Royal Navy and had some experience in both the Navy and Combined Services sides, so that, in 1949, he finished third – behind Joe Hardstaff and Len Hutton – in the first-class averages (63.18). In 1951, still only twenty-one, he made his first Test appearance – against South Africa at Leeds – and scored a century, and at the end of the season was top of the averages with 2,339 runs at 68.79.

He was less spectacularly successful in 1952 but, in the following season, it was generally accepted that the Australians under Lindsay Hassett, set out to play him out of the England side: it was a major compliment – and effective. Lindwall was appointed to do the job and, in the first innings of the touring side's match with Surrey – in May – he bowled Peter May an over which no one who saw it will ever forget. Moving the ball both ways at high speed and to a perfect length, he beat the bat on both sides and eventually had him caught at the wicket by Don Tallon, for nought. In the second innings Ron Archer bowled him for one.

Nevertheless May had already done enough to be included in the first Test match, when he was again caught at the wicket, but this time off Jack Hill for nine. That cost him his place in the next three Tests, after which, in Surrey's second match with the touring side, he scored an uncharacteristically subdued 56. This brought him back into the team for the final Test at The Oval. There he scored a valuable 39 and 37; England under Len Hutton won the Test by eight wickets, and so took the Ashes for the first time for twenty years.

Six feet tall, raw-boned, wide-shouldered and immensely strong, Peter May was a natural ball-games player; he captained Cambridge at soccer and won a Blue for fives. The purists used to argue that his backlift was crooked, but his bat came down in a perfectly straight pendulum – which was the effective fact: and

Peter Barker Howard May (1929-   ) Cambridge University, Surrey, England Right-hand bat; close field.

he seemed to have no identifiable weakness. He was boldly resistant when England were in trouble; and for a conscious amateur, was extremely professional. He rarely allowed himself the pleasure of cutting loose; though, for MCC against an Australian XI at Sydney 1958-59, he scored his second hundred between lunch and tea on the third day, with an absolute welter of attacking strokes. Strokes, he had them all, from slip round to fine leg, and excelled in what has been described as the most difficult of all to play – the on-drive.

Probably his greatest performance was at Edgbaston against West Indies in 1957 when Ramadhin threatened to run through the England batting as he had done in 1950. In the first innings he took seven for 49, in the second he had taken two wickets when Colin Cowdrey joined Peter May. That night Bill Bowes had suggested that Ramadhin ought to be played as an off-spinner. Acting on that counsel, the two made 411 together: England's highest stand for any wicket and the world Test record for the fourth. Ramadhin's was the more depressing statistic: he bowled more balls – 588 – than anyone else had ever done in a first-class innings. Historically, his teeth were drawn – he was never so effective again, and England took the series which they had threatened to lose. May's 285 not out remains the highest score made by an England Test captain in office.

May captained England in 41 Tests: up to then a record, and won 20 of them. He also lost 10, most of which could not be avoided. As a captain he was considered polite, but absolutely ruthless. It might also be said that he was unimaginative and inflexible. He also captained Surrey for five years. During the England tour of West Indies in 1959-60, he became ill and withdrew before the end, and this led to his retirement from the first-class game. He subsequently became Chairman of the TCCB Cricket Committee, President of MCC, and, in 1982, Chairman of Selectors.

OPPOSITE *Peter May, splendid strokemaker and determined captain*

FIRST-CLASS CAREER RECORDS

Career	M	I	NO	HS	Runs	Avge	100
1948-1963	388	618	77	285*	27592	51.00	85

Ct/St	Runs	Wkts	Avge	BB	5wI	10wM
282	49	0	—	—	—	—

TEST CAREER RECORDS

Tests	I	NO	HS	Runs	Avge	100	50
66	106	9	285*	4537	46.77	13	22

Ct/St	Balls	Runs	Wkts	Avge	BB	5wI	10wM
42	—	—	—	—	—	—	—

STAN McCABE

Stanley Joseph McCabe (1910-1968) New South Wales and Australia Right-hand bat; right-arm medium-fast bowler; sound all-round fieldsman.

STAN McCABE HAD nearly all the virtues that could reasonably be asked of a batsman. The adjective that first springs to mind for him is 'gallant'; but, quite objectively, he was technically sound, brave, enterprising, entertaining, brilliant in stroke-play, yet a shrewd judge of batting risks; a splendid team man, who rose to the major challenge; a pleasing personality; a capable all-round field and, to cap it all, was good enough to open the bowling for his country.

Stan McCabe in 1934, the year he scored over 2,000 runs including eight centuries in England

McCabe was always going to be a fine player. Outstanding as a schoolboy, at eighteen he had the unusual distinction of being picked for his State – New South Wales – while still a country player; and at nineteen he was taken on the 1930 tour of England. There he batted in that order of all the talents which read Woodfull, Ponsford, Bradman, Kippax, Jackson, McCabe; and, in such company, averaged 35 in Tests. Crucially – and this is the ultimate measure of his eminence – almost alone among his Australian contemporaries he was not overshadowed by Don Bradman.

It is odd that so consistent a batsman – he averaged 48.21 in Tests, 49.39 in all first-class cricket – should be remembered cheifly for three innings. Perhaps the explanation is that, while he habitually played well, on those three occasions he excelled even himself (and, incidentally, 'The Don' as well).

In the so-called 'Bodyline' series of 1932-33 (when he averaged 42.77) he made 187 – more than half the side's first innings total of 360 – against the pace attack of Larwood, Voce and Allen. The second of the epic performances was the 189 not out of 274 for two against South Africa in 1935. The third, and perhaps the greatest, was the mighty effort at Trent Bridge in 1938 when, in face of an England score of 658, he made 232 in a total of 411 in less than four hours. That was the occasion when Bradman called the rest of the Australian side out of the dressing room to watch and, when he came in, said to him: 'If I could play an innings like that, Stan, I would be a proud man.' No one who watched it will ever forget it.

For all his brilliance Stan McCabe was a modest man, and as immensely popular as he was respected. He did not return to the first-class game after the Second World War, when he became a sports goods dealer in Sydney, where he was most congenial company, especially in the Cricketers' Club. He was killed, tragically, in a cliff fall.

FIRST-CLASS CAREER RECORDS

Career	M	I	NO	HS	Runs	Avge	100
1928-1941	182	262	20	240	11951	49.38	29

Ct/St	Runs	Wkts	Avge	BB	5wI	10wM
139	5362	159	33.72	5-36	1	—

TEST CAREER RECORDS

Tests	I	NO	HS	Runs	Avge	100	50
39	62	5	232	2748	48.21	6	13

Ct/St	Balls	Runs	Wkts	Avge	BB	5wI	10wM
41	3746	1543	36	42.86	4-13	—	—

PHIL MEAD

*Charles Philip Mead
(1887-1958) Hampshire
and England
Left-hand bat; slow left-
arm bowler; slip field.*

PHILIP MEAD WAS a massively competent and consistent left-hander, who scored 55,061 runs – more than anyone else except Sir Jack Hobbs, Frank Woolley and Patsy Hendren. His 48,892 for Hampshire, though, is the greatest aggregate by anyone for a single club in the history of the game.

An unforgettable figure, his style was not graceful: for years, at number four for Hampshire, he came out at a slightly pin-toed toddle; he had drooping shoulders, deep chest, wide-hips and powerful, bowed legs; and his deeply lined face was always solemn.

His batting was based on an all but impregnable defence, on which he built a wide range of controlled strokes; and his temperament was absolutely imperturbable. He rarely lifted the ball and, because of his unhurried air of deliberation, there was a tendency to describe him as slow, which overlooked the fact that without appearing to hurry he had a quite remarkable ability to take a single off almost any ball. His placing was so consummately skilful that he constantly scored boundaries merely, it seemed, by steering his strokes – especially cuts and glances – through gaps in the field. In fact he scored at an average rate of 40 runs an hour.

For instance, in 1929, for the MCC Australian side against Lord Hawke's XI whose bowlers were 'Gubby' Allen, Nigel Haig, Alan Peach, Vallance Jupp and Wilfred Rhodes, he scored 233 in a few minutes over five hours; and *Wisden* records such other innings as 180 in three and a half hours, 213 in four and a quarter, 110 in two and a quarter.

In addition to all the bits and pieces of pushing the score along, he hit his cover drives gloriously; and was so strong playing later and wider that opposing captains had often to post two third men to him.

He had one odd mannerism; before every ball he received throughout his career, he stood, bat pointing upwards, and, turning towards square-leg, touched his cap peak four times; next, he grounded his bat, tapped it four times in the crease and, finally, took four small, shuffling steps up to it. If an impatient bowler attempted to bowl before he had completed the ritual, he simply held up his hand, stopped him, and went through the entire performance again. He wore out many cap peaks.

Philip Mead was born in Battersea and, at sixteen, was taken on the Surrey staff as a promising slow left-arm bowler. Feeling that he was ignored there, he signed for Hampshire, who were given permission to play him against the touring Australian side of

1905 during his two-year qualification period. He was eighteen, and his innings of 41 not out against Cotter – then probably the fastest bowler in the world – established his ability against high pace. In the following season, in his second match as a qualified Hampshire player – against Yorkshire – he created something of a cricketing sensation by scoring 60 and 109. From that day on his place in the team remained secure for thirty years.

Phil Mead in 1927

Phil Mead, master run-getter, much neglected by his country

Altogether, he scored 153 centuries; made 1,000 runs in each of 27 seasons (including his last, 1936, when he was 49 and the county did not re-engage him). In nine of those seasons he made over 2,000; in two more, 3,000; twice he was top of the first-class batting averages, three times second, four times third.

In 1921, when the Australian fast bowlers routed the English batting, Mead, brought in for the fourth Test, made 78 and, in the fifth, 182 not out, which for seventeen years remained the highest by an Englishman against Australia in England. He played in only 17 Tests between 1911 and 1928; all against Australia or South Africa; and, in his last – in Australia 1928-29 – he made 73, top score of the innings, and was dropped for the remaining four games of the series. In general, Frank Woolley, who played in 64 Tests, was preferred to Mead on the grounds that 'he bowls' or 'he is a better-looking batsman'; yet Mead's Test average was 49 compared with Woolley's 36.

He was, though, a wrily philosophic man, Philip; one who got on with the job. He took, altogether, 277 wickets; and, at slip, to the surprise of many who thought him slow, few made more than his 671 catches. When Hampshire did not re-engage him, he went and played for Suffolk – with fair success – second in the overall Minor Counties averages with a figure of 71 in 1939.

Four years later he was blind; and used to sit in the dressing room at Bournemouth, welcome, wise and never boastful. In that interim period, though, one of the most significant comments of all about his cricket was made by a good, regular county cricketer. Philip had been asked to play in a war-time charity match on a pitch only made the day before. As he struggled against lifters and shooters on his way to the highest score of the match, that younger professional said drily: 'Look at the old man; old enough to be my father, damned nearly blind and batting better from memory than I shall ever do.'

FIRST-CLASS CAREER RECORDS

Career	M	I	NO	HS	Runs	Avge	100
1905-1936	814	1340	185	280*	55061	47.67	153

Ct/St	Runs	Wkts	Avge	BB	5wI	10wM	
671	9613	277	34.70	7-18	5	—	

TEST CAREER RECORDS

Tests	I	NO	HS	Runs	Avge	100	50
17	26†	2	182*	1185	49.37	4	3

Ct/St	Balls	Runs	Wkts	Avge	BB	5wI	10wM
4	—	—	—	—	—	—	—

ALAN MELVILLE

ALAN MELVILLE WAS one of the most stylish and pleasing batsmen of his period – 1928 to 1948 – an intelligent captain and altogether a most personable cricketer; yet his entire playing career was bedevilled – and eventually ended – by illness and injury. His talent was apparent while he was still at Michaelhouse School in Natal; he was five years in the eleven, three as captain and, during the last two, chosen for Natal.

Melville's second game for the province was also a trial for the 1929 South African team to England, for which he was wanted. His father, however, decided that he ought to continue his studies with a view to going on to Oxford. So he remained at home; but he sustained fractures of three vertebrae in the small of his back, an injury which troubled him, in varying degrees, throughout his playing days.

He went up to Oxford in 1930, however, where 132 not out and eight for 72 in the Freshmen's match took him into the University side and led to the first of his three Blues. He was captain in 1931, after D.N. Moore fell ill; and in 1932, when he barely recovered from a broken collar bone in time to play in the University match. The presence of Ian Peebles, an England Test spinner, precluded his bowling in his first year; and of 'Tuppy' Owen-Smith in the next two meant that Melville's leg-spin was barely used for the University. Throughout his career he was criticised for bowling himself too little and indeed, in 1932, he performed the hat-trick against Leveson-Gower's XI and was top of the Oxford bowling averages; and in 1933, took five for 17 for Sussex against Gloucestershire.

In 1932, he began to play also for Sussex and captained them in 1934 (when he was operated on for appendicitis) and 1935; the county finished second and seventh in those two seasons.

In this period, surely, only his South African origin prevented him being chosen for England. Despite the apparent fragility of his limbs, he was a splendid player of fast bowling. Tall (six feet two) and slim, he used his height most effectively, and was a magnificent hooker and cutter as well as an apparently languid – but, through his fine timing, powerful – driver.

In both his years as captain of Sussex he was top of their batting averages and, in 1935, of their bowling as well (12 wickets). Delightful to watch, he played many memorable innings for the county; notably 101 in 90 minutes against Larwood and Voce; but, perhaps even more impressive, was his 114 (in two-and-a-half hours) against the West Indian fast bowling at its most hostile in 1933.

Alan Melville (1910-1983) Natal, Transvaal, Oxford University, Sussex and South Africa Right-hand bat; leg-break bowler.

In 1936 he returned to South Africa where he became captain of the Wanderers Club, then of Transvaal and, in 1938-39, of South Africa. A leg injury seemed to have ruled him out of the series but he played in the fourth Test and, opening with his old Oxford colleague, Peter van der Bijl, he shared a stand of 108; while, injured again in the fifth – the 'Marathon' – Test he hobbled in to make his first Test century.

An injury sustained on war service which revived the old back trouble forced him to wear a steel jacket, and it was thought that his cricket was ended. Intensive physical exercises brought him back, the South African selectors unhesitatingly nominated him as their captain for the 1947 tour of England. Early in the tour he broke a bone in his left hand and suffered a severe thigh strain. Nevertheless, he scored a century in each innings of the first Test; and another in the second which – in conjunction with that of 1939 – made him the only man to score centuries in four consecutive Test innings against England. The strain of the tour so told on him, though, that his performance fell away. Never robust, he lost over two stones in weight on the tour; returned utterly exhausted and retired from the game. He played two useful if laboured innings against George Mann's 1948-49 side and then finally left the active side of the game he had graced to become a wise and kindly selector.

OPPOSITE *Alan Melville: quick foot movement and typical concentration*

FIRST-CLASS CAREER RECORDS

Career	M	I	NO	HS	Runs	Avge	100
1928-1948	190	295	15	189	10598	37.85	25

Ct/St	Runs	Wkts	Avge	BB	5wI	10wM
156	3959	132	29.99	5-17	7	—

TEST CAREER RECORDS

Tests	I	NO	HS	Runs	Avge	100	50
11	19	2	189	894	52.58	4	3

Ct/St	Balls	Runs	Wkts	Avge	BB	5wI	10wM
8	—	—	—	—	—	—	—

VIJAY MERCHANT

Vijay Madhavji Merchant (1911-   ) Hindus, Bombay, and India Right-hand bat; occasional right-arm medium-pace bowler; generally an outfieldsman.

VIJAY MERCHANT WAS India's first major Test match batsman. At eighteen he was picked for the Hindus in the Quadrangular Tournament, but for private reasons he did not accept the invitation to play in the national trials of 1932. During the 1933 tour of Douglas Jardine's MCC team, however, he scored 19 not out and 67 not out against them. In the course of his second

High efficiency: Vijay Merchant

186

innings, Maurice Nichols, the Essex fast bowler, hit him under the chin with a lifter; an English doctor on the ground stitched him up. He resumed his innings for another three hours, and that played him into the Indian side until, in 1952, the recurrence of an old shoulder injury led to his retirement from all active cricket.

A most courteous and modest man, Vijay Merchant was a bare 5 feet 7 inches in height, and his movements seemed soft but heavy-footed. He was, however, perfect in footwork, had a sharp eye, and, especially off the back foot, he was a heavy scorer; he cut square and late, hooked with utter safety and drove off his legs skilfully. He was, too, an absolutely infallible punisher of the loose ball, putting it away for four as certainly as anyone except, perhaps, Don Bradman. He was essentially a man who played the ball off the pitch, enabled to do that by his immense speed of reaction. He was, above all, an innings-builder, patient, of immense concentration, unhurried, unworried and absolutely determined to play his cricket positively and under complete mental control. A man of immense honesty and truth, he was always, and essentially, a patient and thoughtful cricketer.

In England in 1946 he was at his peak, with 2,585 runs at 74.53 and with seven centuries. In Tests he had 245 at 49, with 128 in the rain-spoiled Oval Test as his best score. In his last Test – against England at Delhi in 1951-52 – he made 154, putting on 211 for the third wicket with Vijay Hazare, then an Indian record for any wicket against England. Those two were comrades, partners and rivals as India's two best Test batsmen of that period.

Merchant first made his mark in England, however, in partnership with the tall left-hander, Mushtaq Ali. As a pair they built up a considerable reputation in 1936. Merchant later became a highly responsible writer on Indian cricket, Chairman of Test Selectors, an Honorary Member of MCC, and one of the most respected figures throughout the world of cricket.

FIRST-CLASS CAREER RECORDS

Career	M	I	NO	HS	Runs	Avge	100
1929-1951	146	229	43	359*	13248	71.22	44

Ct/St	Runs	Wkts	Avge	BB	5wI	10wM
115	2072	65	31.87	5-73	1	—

TEST CAREER RECORDS

Tests	I	NO	HS	Runs	Avge	100	50
10	18	0	154	859	47.72	3	3

Ct/St	Balls	Runs	Wkts	Avge	BB	5wI	10wM
7	54	40	0	—	—	—	—

COLIN MILBURN

*Colin Milburn
(1941-   ) North-
amptonshire, Western
Australia and England
Right-hand bat; right-
arm medium-pace
bowler; short-leg field.*

ON 23 MAY 1969, Colin Milburn, 27 years old, lost the sight of his left eye in a motor car accident. Huge of muscle, chest, body and heart, he had come like a great gush of north-eastern fresh air into some over-serious English and, indeed, world cricket. He was 5 feet 9 inches tall and, at the time of his accident, had reduced his weight to a little over 16 stone. He was a simple and straightforward cricketer, blessed with a sharp eye, good timing and immense muscle; and he made many friends, not only among those who knew him well but among those who, only seeing him from the spectators' seats, recognized him as one able to reduce cricket to its heartiest, but most effective, basics.

He came from Burnopfield in north Durham where, at thirteen, he opened the batting and the bowling for a local club: and, at eighteen, in the only innings he ever played for the Minor County of Durham, he made 101 against the Indian tourists.

Milburn signed for Northamptonshire in 1960 and in that qualifying season scored 1,153 runs for the Second XI. In 1961, opening the innings against Middlesex Second XI, he scored 201 not out in a total of 256; and twice in following weeks he scored two centuries in a match. In the first team he made 63 out of 125 against Surrey but was sent back to the Second XI for correction of his vulnerability to off-spin. In July 1962 he came back; scored his first first-class century against Cambridge University and then, in the same month, played what he still believes to be his best county innings, on a green wicket at Buxton against the powerful Derbyshire seam attack. He made 102 out of a total of 182; for the rest of the batting, Mick Norman made 58; no one else more than five. In 1963 Milburn scored 48 and 123 (with seven sixes and 14 fours) against Yorkshire; 100 and 88 against West Indies. His most murderous innings was in 1965 when with seven sixes and 15 fours, he struck 152 not out against Gloucestershire. With M.J.K. Smith's MCC team in East Africa he hit a local leg-spinner for six off each of the first five balls of an over and was caught on the boundary from the sixth.

His first Test came in 1966, against West Indies. Run out for nought in the first innings, he made 94 in the second. Then on to Lord's where he was lbw to Hall for six and then made 126 not out. Such was the mood of the selectors, however, that seven and 12 in the third Test, 29 and 42 in the fourth, did not preserve him for the fifth. Neither, it seemed, could they decide whether to open with him or to bat him first wicket down. There was long a tendency to under-rate him; presumably because of his shape; but he was no crude slogger: he picked the ball to hit and then did

*Milburn hooks; short leg
wisely takes evasive
action*

so very hard indeed. The majority of his sixes were struck straight-batted between mid-off and wide mid-wicket; and he hooked with great certainty. Even though he reduced his weight, he had trouble in maintaining his useful medium-pace bowling through back trouble; and, although he was not a speedy fieldsman, in 1964 he took 43 catches – a Northamptonshire record – at forward short leg.

He spent the early part of the 1968-69 winter playing for Western Australia, for whom, in an amazing innings of 243 against Queensland, he made 181 in two hours between lunch and tea. He went on to join the England team in Pakistan, and in his last Test innings made 139 at Karachi. He returned to the season of 1969 with 158 against Leicestershire, but a few days later came his horrid accident. Nevertheless, and blind in one eye, he came back in 1973 and played 43 innings over the next two seasons but, with a top score of 57, and unable to bowl, he grinned and turned it in. What a grand man; what guts; what humour; what resilience; some say he is much missed but, in fact, he is still around and, although not playing, he is still splendid company.

FIRST-CLASS CAREER RECORDS

Career	M	I	NO	HS	Runs	Avge	100
1960-1974	255	435	34	243	13262	33.07	23

Ct/St	Runs	Wkts	Avge	BB	5wl	10wM
224	3171	99	32.03	6-59	1	—

TEST CAREER RECORDS

Tests	I	NO	HS	Runs	Avge	100	50
9	16	2	139	654	46.71	2	2

Ct/St	Balls	Runs	Wkts	Avge	BB	5wl	10wM
7	—	—	—	—	—	—	—

KEITH MILLER

KEITH MILLER, QUITE the most exciting figure in world cricket for a decade after the Second World War, was a splendidly athletic, extrovert, generous, spectacular, unpredictable all-rounder: a giant of his time. He first appeared for Victoria in 1937-38 and made 181 against Tasmania in his first match (he moved to New South Wales for 1947-48). He flew with the RAF from British bases during the Second World War. He once brought his Mosquito into a Norfolk airfield with its starboard engine in flames and crash-landed it with no more damage than the loss of its tail!

In the post-war celebrations he made 185 in 165 minutes for the Dominions XI at Lord's: the pavilion had rarely experienced such a barrage. A glorious driver, he could, too, cut late and precisely. His batting was no doubt impaired by the tendency of his captains to use him as a key bowler, and also by the injuries he sustained when bowling. He preferred to play forward: he pulled and swept powerfully, and once began the day's play in a Test with a six. In the West Indies in 1955 he was second in the averages with a figure of 73.16. Of his 41 centuries, seven were of 200 or more, with a highest score in Tests of 147 (Jamaica 1954-55).

He needed competition: in Australia's game with Essex in 1948, runs seemed to him so cheap that he deliberately removed his bat from the line of his first ball and was bowled. He was not always happy on wet wickets, but he averaged 36.97 in his 87 Tests, in which he also took 170 wickets at 22.97: add his 38 catches – many of them almost impossibly acrobatic – and you have a picture of a dynamic cricketer.

Six feet tall, superbly muscled and supple, he bowled at immense speed which often did not necessarily bear any relation

Keith Ross Miller, MBE (1919-   ) Victoria, New South Wales, Nottinghamshire and Australia
Right-hand bat; right-arm fast bowler; versatile fieldsman.

Keith Miller, batting against Sussex in 1956, glides a ball neatly through the leg side

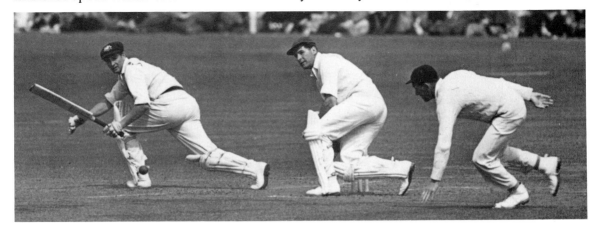

to the pace or length of his approach. He amused himself and teased crowds by bowling bouncers: but his skill was beyond question. His bowling partnership with Ray Lindwall in 1948 in England became legendary.

For some years he captained New South Wales; sometimes idiosyncratically, often surprisingly, invariably he motivated his men; and there was often a touch of genius about his leadership. When eventually he retired after the 1956-57 series, it was usually assumed that he did so because he resented – and with very good reason – the appointment of Ian Johnson as captain of the 1956 side to England.

In England, in 1959, he was invited to play for Nottinghamshire – turned out against Cambridge University and scored 62 and 102 not out which, although he was then forty years old, was shown in the record books as: 'Century on first appearance for County'. An addict of classical music and horse-racing, he once led the players off the field during a Sheffield Shield match so that they might listen to the broadcast of the Melbourne Cup. He had friends everywhere; and admirers, not simply for his achievements – impressive enough in themselves – but, above all, for the compelling quality of his cricket. He played in the first post-war Test Match (Australia v New Zealand) at Wellington in 1945-46 and for a full ten years strode the fields of the world in convivial rivalry.

Journalist, columnist, commentator, author of several books with his friend and biographer, R.S. Whitington, he was, too, a considerable Australian Rules footballer, known for his long kicking, is an honorary member of MCC, and was made an MBE for services to cricket.

Anyone given his choice of a player to win a match off the last ball – by a six, a wicket, or a catch – could only pick one man, Keith Ross Miller.

FIRST-CLASS CAREER RECORDS

Career	M	I	NO	HS	Runs	Avge	100
1937-1959	226	326	36	281*	14183	48.90	41

Ct/St	Runs	Wkts	Avge	BB	5wI	10wM
136	11087	497	22.30	7-12	16	1

TEST CAREER RECORDS

Tests	I	NO	HS	Runs	Avge	100	50
55	87	7	147	2958	36.97	7	13

Ct/St	Balls	Runs	Wkts	Avge	BB	5wI	10wM
38	10461	3906	170	22.97	7-60	7	1

BRUCE MITCHELL

A SKILFUL, POISED batsman, Bruce Mitchell, with an extremely correct technique, became an outstandingly sound and reliable defensive player. He was one of those rare players whose average in Tests was higher than in all cricket. Coached by Herbie Taylor and a most studious pupil, he first won his place in the Transvaal side as an accurate slow off-break bowler. Indeed, in his first Currie Cup match – against Border, in 1926 – at the age of seventeen, he had figures of five for 23 and six for 72. Even at school, though, he had been a major run scorer and so rapid and convincing was his advance as a batsman that he bowled relatively little afterwards. This may have been in order to husband his strength – for he was never physically robust – and in any event his batting spoke for itself. Technically Bruce Mitchell made the best use of his height (about 5 feet 10 inches) to get over the ball, played very straight and, assured even against the highest pace, conveyed overwhelmingly the impression of having time to spare for his strokes.

At twenty, although he had only minimal experience of turf pitches, he was included in 'Nummy' Deane's side to England. It is said that he himself was not certain whether he had been chosen as a batsman or a bowler. In the opening match – against Worcestershire – he was sent in at number seven, and scored 83.

Thereafter Deane moved him steadily up the order; he constantly justified his promotion and, indeed, he was made opening batsman in the first Test. At the start he batted six cautious hours for 88; and, in the second innings, scored 61 not out. From that time, for another 41 Tests in twenty years, he was a regular member of the South African team.

He was mentally and temperamentally well-suited to the role of sheet anchor; for his concentration was complete. Indeed, during the last Test of 1947, at the Oval – when he scored two centuries in the match and was on the field for all but eight minutes of the game – he was under instructions to close one end; which he did to the extent of batting all through the last day for 188 runs. The game might well have gone either way; and, with a chance to win, when the sixth wicket fell, Melville sent in a bat swinger in 'Tufty' Mann ahead of Athol Rowan and, when he was out, followed with Lindsay Tuckett. The scoring became more brisk and at one point when Mitchell hit a four and the two batsmen checked in midwicket, he looked in disbelief at Tuckett: 'Lindsay,' he said 'but where's "Tufty"?' Mann had been out half an hour earlier; but such was Mitchell's absorption that he had not registered the fact.

Bruce Mitchell (1909-) Transvaal and South Africa Right-hand batsman; off-break bowler; specialist slip field.

In 1935 when he was – not for the only time – out clear at the top of the South African Test batting, came his much cherished 164 not out in a second innings score of 278 for seven declared which effectively gave them their first Test win and their first rubber in England. It was, too, their first series win for twenty-eight years – since before Mitchell had played in a Test. That remained more important to him than the fact that he scored more runs in Tests than any other South African.

FIRST-CLASS CAREER RECORDS

Career	M	I	NO	HS	Runs	Avge	100
1925-1949	173	281	30	195	11395	45.39	30

Ct/St	Runs	Wkts	Avge	BB	5wI	10wM
228	6382	249	25.63	6-33	15	2

Bruce Mitchell hits another boundary on his way to 120 in South Africa's first innings (he scored 189 in the second) against England at The Oval in 1947

TEST CAREER RECORDS

Tests	I	NO	HS	Runs	Avge	100	50
42	80	9	189*	3471	48.88	8	21

Ct/St	Balls	Runs	Wkts	Avge	BB	5wI	10wM
56	2519	1380	27	51.11	5-87	1	—

ARTHUR MORRIS

ARTHUR MORRIS WAS one of the best-liked cricketers of his generation – or, indeed, of any other. He was wise enough to realise that, even for a Test player, cricket was by no means the be-all and end-all of existence. A charming, philosophical, relaxed person, he was arguably the best left-hander of his time. Originally in Grade cricket, a slow left-arm bowler who went in last, he became a batsman who virtually never bowled.

He first appeared for New South Wales at the age of eighteen in 1940-41 and, in his debut match, scored 148 and 111 – the first recorded instance of a man making two centuries on his first appearance in the first-class game. Perhaps one of the best examples of his mental approach lies in the story of Keith Miller bowling him a bouncer and being hooked for four. Miller, at the time only twenty, proceeded to bowl him a full over of bouncers which cost him 24 runs – the most runs he ever yielded from a single over.

Then Arthur Morris went away from cricket for six years' service with the Australian Army in New Guinea. He returned in time for the 1946-47 season, and in his first game scored 27 and 98 for New South Wales against Queensland. He settled back into cricket at once, and enjoyed it. Scoring 115 for an Australian XI against MCC, and 81 not out for New South Wales against the tourists, he ensured his Test place. He duly made 21 and 155 in the third Test; 122 and 124 not out in the fourth. At about this time it was almost impossible to bowl at him.

He came to England in 1948 and enjoyed the visit in every possible way. He always cherished the fact that he scored a century in his first innings in each of four different countries. There is, of course, a theory among bowlers that left-handers are vulnerable to off-spin. Arthur Morris was not. In 1948 he hit Jim Laker out of the England Test side; and Tom Goddard of Gloucestershire, certain that he could defeat him, was hammered quite mercilessly. Goddard characteristically persisted: Morris scored 102 before lunch; 231 by tea. On the other hand, he was undoubtedly vulnerable to the in-swinger pitching on his leg stump, constantly nicking it to leg slip, a weakness which Alec Bedser exploited. Morris's two outstanding innings of the 1948 tour were 182 in the Leeds Test and 196 at The Oval; he was top of the Test batting in that series with 696 runs at 87.

There was controversy in Australia as to whether Morris or his friend Keith Miller should captain the New South Wales side (in fact they did so 26 times each). The selectors preferred Morris as Lindsay Hassett's vice-captain, but they lost the two Tests in

Arthur Robert Morris, MBE (1922-   ) New South Wales and Australia
Left-hand bat; just occasional left-arm wrist spinner.

which he captained them. While he was in England he met and became engaged to the delightful Valerie Hudson and, in 1955, he retired from the game to care for her in her early fatal illness.

As a footnote to his career, at the age of forty-one he was invited back to play for the Commonwealth side in India in 1963, when he batted so brilliantly at Bombay that Norman O'Neill called the rest of the side to the dressing room balcony to watch his splendid display, and the spectators rose to him in acclaim. Only Bradman of all Australian batsmen has ever scored more than his eight centuries against England; in all he made 46. Since 1965 he has held the prestigious post of membership of the Sydney Cricket Ground Trust. Throughout his career he has commanded respect and liking as cricketer and man. This may well stem from the basis of his approach, which was: 'Cricket is only a game and one to be enjoyed'.

OPPOSITE *Arthur Morris, who came to a splendid maturity in England in 1948*

FIRST-CLASS CAREER RECORDS

Career	M	I	NO	HS	Runs	Avge	100
1940-1963	162	250	15	290	12614	53.67	46

Ct/St	Runs	Wkts	Avge	BB	5wI	10wM
73	592	12	49.33	3-36	—	—

TEST CAREER RECORDS

Tests	I	NO	HS	Runs	Avge	100	50
46	79†	3	206	3533	46.48	12	12

Ct/St	Balls	Runs	Wkts	Avge	BB	5wI	10wM
15	111‡	50	2	25.00	1-5	—	—

BILL MURDOCH

William Lloyd Murdoch (1854-1911) New South Wales, Sussex, London County, Australia and England
Right-hand bat; occasional wicket keeper.

BILLY MURDOCH WAS the first Australian to match the ability of the best English batsmen. In the first Test Match played in England he scored 153 not out, which was one more than his friend and rival, W.G. Grace, who was out. He was also a capable wicketkeeper but eventually gave way to Blackham in Australian representative teams. He virtually did not bowl; but was a thoughtful and wise captain. He toured England with the Australian sides of 1878, 1880, 1882, 1884 and 1890, captaining them on the last four, when he was also top of their batting averages. He subsequently (1893 to 1899) played for, and captained, Sussex. During that period he went in W.W. Read's side to South Africa (1891-92) where he appeared for England in

W. L. Murdoch.

Billy Murdoch on the 1884 Australian tour of England

198

the only Test played and scored twelve in his single innings. From 1901 to 1904 he played with London County under W.G. Grace.

A merry man with a rosy, smiling face and an original mind and turn of humour, he was popular with players and spectators in both countries. Short, round and stocky, he was handicapped technically by his limited reach, but compensated for it by his quick footwork and willingness to go down the wicket to attack. He was at his best as an off-side player who cut and drove attractively and profitably. At need, though, he defended safely and correctly.

In 18 Tests for Australia he scored 896 runs at 32.00. He was the first player of any country to score a double century in a Test – 211 against England at The Oval in 1884. In all cricket he averaged 26.86 for 16,953 runs, with a top score of 321 for New South Wales against Victoria, which long remained the record in inter state cricket.

He died of a heart attack while watching Australia play South Africa at Melbourne; his body was embalmed and brought to England for burial.

FIRST-CLASS CAREER RECORDS

Career	M	I	NO	HS	Runs	Avge	100
1875-1904	391	679	48	321	16953	26.86	19

Ct/St	Runs	Wkts	Avge	BB	5wI	10wM
218/25	430	10	43.00	2-11	—	—

TEST CAREER RECORDS

Tests	I	NO	HS	Runs	Avge	100	50
19	34	5	211	908	31.31	2	1

Ct/St	Balls	Runs	Wkts	Avge	BB	5wI	10wM
13/1	—	—	—	—	—	—	—

MUSHTAQ MOHAMMAD

Mushtaq Mohammad (1943-   ) P.I.A., Karachi, Northamptonshire, Staffordshire, Pakistan Right-hand bat; leg spin and googly bowler; all-round fieldsman.

MUSHTAQ WAS THE original infant prodigy of cricket. The fourth in age of the five brothers – Wazir, Raees and Hanif were all older, Sadiq younger – he was virtually born into cricket. The family's

Mushtaq the full blooded aggressor; but he was capable of epic innings of concentration as well

documents were lost when they migrated from India to Pakistan after partition. When they were found, they showed him to have been the youngest man to appear in first-class cricket at thirteen years and forty-one days; the youngest (at sixteen years and seventy days) to appear in a Test and, at seventeen years and eighty-two days the youngest to score a Test century (101 v India, fifth Test, 12 February 1961).

It is dangerously easy and desperately mistaken to allow Mushtaq's cherubic expression, habitual broad smile and predilection for bowling leg-breaks to convey an impression of a light-hearted approach to the game. He is, and always has been, a fiercely competitive cricketer. That quality, linked to his great defensive ability – similar to Hanif's – enabled him to save the match, and the rubber, against India at Delhi in 1961 and made him, at eighteen, the first player in history to score two Test centuries before the age of twenty.

His characteristic twirl of the bat before he takes guard is one of the few indulgences he allows himself; otherwise his batting is utterly serious. Quick on his feet and powerful – although only 5 feet 7 inches tall, he weighs more than 12 stone – he is at his best against fast bowling. An entertaining and a stylish player through the covers, he is a murderous leg-side run-scorer when he moves inside to glide, steer or, above all, to hook with quite savage power. Add the fact that he has, too, always been a masterly player on bad wickets, and you have the skills of one of the best and most consistent of modern batsmen.

In 1976 he took over the captaincy of Northamptonshire when they had their most successful season in their history, winning the Gillette Cup – their first major honour – and runners-up in the County Championship. But in the following year there were dissensions in the club and, after 14 seasons (15,961 runs at 39.12; and 551 wickets at 24) he left the county and joined Staffordshire in the Minor Counties – with a world of experience.

FIRST-CLASS CAREER RECORDS

Career	M	I	NO	HS	Runs	Avge	100
1956-1985	502	843	104	303*	31091	42.07	72

Ct/St	Runs	Wkts	Avge	BB	5wI	10wM
347	22790	936	24.34	7-18	39	2

TEST CAREER RECORDS

Tests	I	NO	HS	Runs	Avge	100	50
57	100	7	201	3643	39.17	10	19

Ct/St	Balls	Runs	Wkts	Avge	BB	5wI	10wM
42	5260	2309	79	29.22	5-28	3	—

NAWAB OF PATAUDI Jnr

Nawab of Pataudi junior, later Mohammed Mansur Ali Khan (1941-   ) Sussex, Oxford University, Delhi, Hyderabad, India Right-hand bat; occasional right-arm medium-pace bowler; all-round fieldsman.

THE YOUNG AND extremely personable 'Tiger' Pataudi was the son of that Nawab of Pataudi who played for England in three matches from 1932 to 1934; and captained India in England in 1946. The elder Pataudi died in 1952 when his son was only eleven, but the younger man idolised his father. On paternal advice the young boy went to Winchester, where his talent as a batsman was instantly recognized; in fact, he beat D.R. Jardine's batting record for a school season there, and was highly regarded as a captain. His school coach, George Cox, persuaded him to qualify for Sussex and he played usefully for them in six county matches in 1958. He went up to Oxford in 1960, where he was the first Indian to captain either University when he was appointed to that office for 1961. Before the University match, however, he lost the sight of his right eye as a result of a motor accident.

The rest of his career is a story of triumph over adversity. Within a month he was batting again, learning to re-focus, altering his stance, experimenting with spectacles and contact lenses. To crystallize the story of his success: he returned to captain Oxford in 1963, and to play in 46 Tests for India – 40 of them as captain – and to captain Sussex in 1966. He took over the captaincy of India in the West Indies in 1961-62 when Nari Contractor was injured. He had, though, little batting success then, nor in India in 1963-64; his use of his right eye varied in a fashion that he could neither control nor foresee. Against Australia in 1964-65, though, he scored 270 runs at 67.50. He had a good series against New Zealand in India, when he scored two centuries; and he twice captained India to defeat them.

He took only one team to England – in 1967 – and, although India were beaten, he stood out as a batsman; he made 74 and 148 at Headingley and averaged 44.83; immediately afterwards he was top of their Test averages with 56.50 against Australia. After his title was taken from him he played against England in 1972-73 though not as captain. But taking up the office again, against West Indies in 1974-75, he was injured fielding in the first Test, never found form, and dropped out of the Test scene.

Nevertheless, and despite his appalling handicap, he has a Test average of 34.91, including six centuries. In 40 Test matches as captain he won nine of them – a better record than any other Indian captain. He was, too, a relishable human being. Above all, in a period when Indian cricket was tending towards the pedestrian, he set a constant example of attacking the opposing bowlers with aggressive strokes. He was completely without self-pity; and, in every way, a popular cricketer.

FIRST-CLASS CAREER RECORDS

Career	M	I	NO	HS	Runs	Avge	100
1957-1975	310	499	41	203*	15425	33.67	33

Ct/St	Runs	Wkts	Avge	BB	5wI	10wM
208	776	10	77.60	1-0	—	—

TEST CAREER RECORDS

Tests	I	NO	HS	Runs	Avge	100	50
46	83	3	203*	2793	34.91	6	16

Ct/St	Balls	Runs	Wkts	Avge	BB	5wI	10wM
27	132	88	1	88.00	1-10	—	—

The Nawab of Pataudi hits out for Oxford University against Surrey at The Oval in 1961

DUDLEY NOURSE

Arthur Dudley Nourse (1910-1981) Natal and South Africa Right-hand bat; capable close field.

DUDLEY NOURSE WAS the son of the redoubtable 'Dave' Nourse, who in 1895 went to South Africa as a nineteen-year-old trumpeter with the West Riding Regiment and stayed to become the father figure of the game in that country. In a remarkably long cricketing career of forty years he scored more runs than anyone else in South African domestic cricket. A left-hand bat, left-arm swing bowler and huge-handed slip, he was an immensely competitive all-rounder. In their joint span, he and Dudley between them played in 79 out of 100 Tests for South Africa.

The old man told his son to go out as he had done and learn the game for himself. Dudley did just that. Indeed, he was twenty-two years old before his father saw him bat; that was when the younger man scored 105 in a friendly match for Natal against Western Province – for whom his father was then playing – and bowling. Dudley Nourse, like the other four major South African batsmen of his period – Bruce Mitchell, 'Tuppy'

Dudley Nourse batting against Kent in 1951

Owen-Smith, Alan Melville and Eric Rowan – lost crucial years of batting experience to the Second World War.

Crucially, he was another of those rare batsmen who had a better average in Test cricket than in all play. Dudley Nourse was a four-square, firm-jawed man, powerful, and predominantly a back-foot player who hit the ball massively hard, notably in cutting, especially square; hooking or driving. Stoically unworried by pace, he was not, though, an unsubtle batsman. In the second Test of 1935-36, against Australia, with the spin of Grimmett and O'Reilly, he scored 231 in 289 minutes. Again, in 1948-49, when 'Roly' Jenkins threatened to unsettle the South African batting, Nourse, 'reading' him perfectly, scored heavily (536 runs at 76.57).

He first played for Natal at the age of twenty; and went in Herby Wade's 1935 side to England where, though he scored well in county matches, he made an unconvincing start in Test cricket and lost his place, but he regained it before the end of the series and was to hold it beyond dispute for sixteen years.

In the following South African season, though, when Australia toured there and won overwhelmingly Nourse was easily the outstanding home batsman (518 runs at 57.55). In 1938-39 he was again the leading South African batsman; and, in the 'timeless' Test against England, he curbed his normal attacking tendency to score 103 in more than six hours. He came to England again as vice-captain to Alan Melville in 1947, when only Denis Compton – in his great year – scored more than his 621 (at 69.00) in Tests. Nourse succeeded Melville as captain, and the appointment did not affect his performances. Indeed in the first – Trent Bridge – Test of 1951, batting with a fractured thumb pinned, and in constant pain, he made 208, which proved the foundation of South Africa's first win for sixteen years. In the next year he withdrew from active play but, in his retirement, became a Test selector and tour manager.

The imperturbable Dudley Nourse, South African captain on MCC's 1938-39 tour

FIRST-CLASS CAREER RECORDS

Career	M	I	NO	HS	Runs	Avge	100
1931-1952	175	269	27	260*	12472	51.53	41

Ct/St	Runs	Wkts	Avge	BB	5wI	10wM
135	124	0	—	—	—	—

TEST CAREER RECORDS

Tests	I	NO	HS	Runs	Avge	100	50
34	62	7	231	2960	53.81	9	14

Ct/St	Balls	Runs	Wkts	Avge	BB	5wI	10wM
12	20	9	0	—	—	—	—

NORMAN O'NEILL

Norman Clifford O'Neill (1937-) New South Wales and Australia Right-hand bat; right-arm leg-break or medium-pace bowler; brilliant cover field.

NORMAN O'NEILL WAS one of the most exciting of all post-war batsmen. Six feet tall, well-built, strong and virilely handsome in appearance, he was a splendid stroke-maker, especially off the back foot. Strong in driving, fast on his feet to attack spinners, he was a most compelling batsman to watch. A cover fieldsman outstanding in every way, O'Neill had a glorious baseballer's throw. He could bowl either slow leg-breaks or medium-pace 'seam-up'. Above all, he had immense charisma; crowds flocked to see him, not only in Australia, but all over the world – notably in India.

Bill O'Reilly called him 'a second Bradman'; while Wally Hammond described him as the most brilliant post-war batsman. As a schoolboy there was a move to make him a sprinter; but his imagination was captured by cricket – and by Keith Miller in particular.

In 1956-57, at nineteen, he averaged 43.61 in his first season for New South Wales and toured New Zealand – scoring a century in the unofficial 'Test' and averaging 72.66 for the tour. Yet, amazingly, he was not chosen for the following tour of South Africa. When he returned home he delivered a reply to the selectors with a most spectacular 233 against Victoria, made in little over four hours: an innings of such virtuosity and power as roused the crowd to immense enthusiasm. It received, wrote the local reporter, an ovation reminiscent of the days of Don Bradman. It was then that Bill O'Reilly made his claim for the young man.

In the next Australian domestic season – 1958-59 – Peter May brought the England side there and such was the interest in O'Neill – five first-class centuries already at his back – that substantial crowds turned out to watch even the net practice before the MCC *v* Combined XI match at Perth. O'Neill duly made a highly responsible 104 (in 200 minutes); and followed it with 84 not out for New South Wales against the touring side, which virtually guaranteed his place in the side for the first Test. Then his 34 (highest score but one in the Australian first innings) and the highest score of the match – 71 not out in the second, effectively gave them an eight-wicket win. They duly won the rubber by 4-0; and O'Neill finished second to Colin McDonald in the batting averages of the two countries with an average of 56.40, though without a Test century.

That came on the following tour of Pakistan (134) and India (163 and 113). His highest Test score followed in Australia, 181 in the historic tied Test with West Indies. So, in 1961, he made his first tour of England; and it was a happy success. The crowds enjoyed him; he was now coming to the richest period of his cricket: he scored 1981 runs at 60.03; and made seven centuries, including his first in a Test against England.

No one had ever seriously faulted his technique; now, however, the flaw emerged, and it was purely psychological. He simply became a bad starter; probably it was due to a combination of public pressure and team responsibility on his mind. Certainly, he began to fidget, to shift his grip down the bat handle and to lose his nerve at the beginning of an innings. Shrewd English professional bowlers diagnosed the problem and applied pressure on him as soon as he came in. Significantly, on his second (1964) tour of England he scored 1,369 runs at 45.63; and did not convey his former certainty. At the start of the 1964-65 tour of India and Pakistan he went down with stomach trouble and did not play a Test for the rest of the series. After an indifferent 1965 tour of West Indies (he did not play in the fifth Test), he put his name to an article by a Sydney journalist which attacked Charlie Griffith – for throwing – and his old idol, Keith Miller. The Australian Cricket Board alleged he had broken regulations and, although he

Norman O'Neill sweeping a ball from David Allen during his 82 against England in the Edgbaston Test of 1961

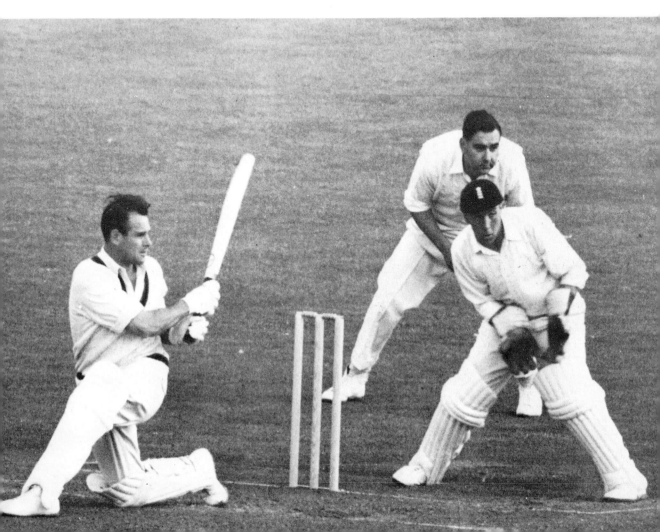

made plenty of runs in Australian cricket that season, that was the end of his Test career.

He was not chosen for the subsequent tour of South Africa. So the Test career of one of the most brilliant of modern players ended at twenty-eight, and at thirty he declared his knees could no longer sustain the strain of first-class cricket and retired from the game. It is too facile – and inaccurate – to say he was not an outstanding performer. In a highly competitive period, and despite temperamental problems, in 42 Tests Norman O'Neill averaged an impressive 45.55. It remains to ponder how much more he might have achieved if star treatment had not unsettled him. Might he have justified Bill O'Reilly's prophecy? Those who watched him at his best would hesitate to deny that.

FIRST-CLASS CAREER RECORDS

Career	M	I	NO	HS	Runs	Avge	100
1955-1967	188	306	34	284	13859	50.95	45

Ct/St	Runs	Wkts	Avge	BB	5wI	10wM
104	4060	99	41.01	4-40	—	—

TEST CAREER RECORDS

Tests	I	NO	HS	Runs	Avge	100	50
42	69	8	181	2779	45.55	6	15

Ct/St	Balls	Runs	Wkts	Avge	BB	5wI	10wM
21	1392	667	17	39.23	4-41	—	—

Zaheer Abbas

Clive Lloyd

Gordon Greenidge

Ian Botham

Graham Gooch

LEFT: *David Gower*   *Allan Border*

Martin Crowe

TUPPY OWEN-SMITH

'TUPPY' OWEN-SMITH was one of the most likeable, potentially masterly, temperamentally magnificent and athletic all-round sportsmen and cricketers. If his first-class cricket career was brief, it was significant enough to stamp him as outstanding.

His nickname stemmed from a comment that he was 'no higher than tuppence worth of coppers' and certainly he was physically short – and somewhat bow-legged to boot – but fast of thought and movement, with splendid coordination, fine ball-sense and a natural aptitude for games. In both South Africa and England he was a university light-weight champion and, at rugby football, in turn a fly-half, centre three-quarter and, eventually, a superb full-back who captained England.

He learned his cricket at Diocesan College, Rondebosch, where he was coached by a series of visiting English professionals, of whom Jack Newman probably had the most profound effect on his cricket. He played for Western Province against R.T. Stanyforth's MCC team to South Africa in 1927-28. Then, however, he went to England and to Oxford University, so he had never played any Currie Cup cricket when he was picked for 'Nummy' Deane's side to England of 1929.

He was barely twenty years old; and by first-class cricketing standards utterly raw. Yet his impact on the English game was immense. Indeed, his cricket reputation rests largely upon the five Tests of that tour – all he ever played.

His quality was never better captured than by the old master, Raymond Robertson-Glasgow: 'Just a few bat in a Test Match as they would in a practice-net, only more so. Among them pre-eminently of modern cricketers, is H.G. Owen-Smith. When he takes guard … convention sleeps, and cricket awakes.'

He revelled in cricket; in the field he chased the ball at quite remarkable speed, picked up and threw in with unusual celerity. He bowled his leg-breaks and googlies quite prodigally; they were not always accurate, but they were spun like tops and, for that reason, puzzling in flight. As a batsman, however, he captured a nation's imagination. His fine tactical sense made him hard to contain; he attacked off front foot or back; on both sides of the wicket, cutting, driving, pulling, hooking: he was unquenchable.

On that single tour – he was chosen for only fifteen of the side's first thirty-four days of first-class play – he made virtually no impression until, as the fifth bowler used, he took six for 38 against the Minor Counties.

That and his fine fielding took him into the first Test where he batted gamely for 25 (out of 250) in his only innings and was

Dr Harold Geoffrey Owen-Smith (1909 -) Western Province, Oxford University, Middlesex and South Africa Right-hand bat; leg-break bowler and brilliant field, especially at cover-point.

*Tuppy Owen-Smith,
whose Test career was
brief but glittering*

again magnificent in the field. So to the Lord's Test where, in the first innings, batting at number seven, he was joined by 'Sandy' Bell at 279 for nine; and, to the surprise of the English bowlers, the two put on 43 in 20 minutes for the last wicket which, in the end, probably averted an English win and drew the match.

At Headingley in the third Test, England led on the first innings by 92 and then reduced South Africa to 116 for seven in their second, a bare 24 ahead. Then Owen-Smith with Quinn put on 51; with Van der Merwe, five; that was 172 for nine; then came what remains the South African record for the last wicket and changed the entire complexion of an apparently lost match. Owen-Smith and – again – 'Sandy' Bell scored 103 in 65 minutes. 'Tuppy' made his 129 in two-and-three-quarter hours, with two sixes and 15 fours, in what *Wisden* said ' ... as a display of skilful and plucky batting could not have been bettered ... When Owen-Smith and Bell returned to the pavilion the cheering was so loud and prolonged as to suggest they might have won the match for their side.'

Owen-Smith went on to make 102 (v Durham); 126 (v Warwickshire) and to finish the tour with an average of 42 in Tests, 35.39 in all first-class matches, and was top of the bowling in all matches with 39 wickets at 23.20. Thereafter Oxford University (a blue in all three years), medical training and practice, claimed him; except in vacations. Between 1935 and 1937, he played 28 matches for Middlesex (993 runs at 24.83; 100 wickets at 21.50) and in isolated games for Western Province up to 1949-50; but, over a career of twenty-three years, he appeared in only 101 first-class matches, 21 of them on that single tour.

Wisden's opinion on that visit may sum up: 'Nothing stood out more than the dazzling exploits of H.G. Owen-Smith, one of the youngest members of the team and an object lesson to everyone against whom he played.' It might have added that he was an unforgettable joy to watch.

FIRST-CLASS CAREER RECORDS

Career	M	I	NO	HS	Runs	Avge	100
1927-1949	101	162	11	168*	4059	26.88	3

Ct/St	Runs	Wkts	Avge	BB	5wI	10wM
93	7410	319	23.22	7-153	20	3

TEST CAREER RECORDS

Tests	I	NO	HS	Runs	Avge	100	50
5	8	2	129	252	42.00	1	1

Ct/St	Balls	Runs	Wkts	Avge	BB	5wI	10wM
4	156	113	0	—	—	—	—

EDDIE PAYNTER

EDDIE PAYNTER WAS a true Lancashireman – from Oswaldwistle – short, lean, wiry, competitive, who regularly and historically rose to the challenge of the great occasion, but was desperately unlucky in his opportunities. He had the remarkable Test average of 59.23, and proved a match-winner against Australia; yet he played in only 20 Tests over eighteen years.

His first stumbling block was the massive Lancashire batting which won the Championship four times in five seasons between 1926 and 1930. They were virtually impregnable in their team places, wherefore Paynter had to languish in the second eleven until he was twenty-eight for a regular team place.

Even after that, little went right for him. His omission from the England sides in 1934 and the touring team to Australia in 1936-37 remains quite incomprehensible. Then, O'Reilly, with first Grimmett and then Fleetwood-Smith, was the effective Australian bowling influence. Eddie Paynter was, first of all, a left-hander, and therefore well equipped against the right-hander's leg-break, which came in to him. Secondly, he was a splendid reader and player of wrist spin – and also sound against pace. His first recognition by the selectors had been in 1931, when he was chosen for the third (and last) Test against New Zealand, in which only half a day's cricket was possible. Then he was picked for the solitary Test against India in 1932, when he made

Edward Paynter (1901-1979) Lancashire and England
Left-hand bat; right-arm medium change bowler; fine outfield.

Eddie Paynter, resolute in defence and powerful in attack, as he pulls another boundary on his way to a double century against Australia at Trent Bridge in 1938

14 and 54. His first real opportunity, and his initial success, was in Jardine's team to Australia in 1932-33; even then he was not chosen until the third Test, when he went in at number seven. This was the peak of the 'Bodyline' series, when, and despite the tensions, he scored 77 in the first innings and helped to avert a crisis, after England had subsided to 30 for four. In the next Test he was taken ill and sent to hospital with tonsilitis; but, when England were 216 for six in reply to Australia's 340, he left his bed to play a historic innings of resistance – 83 against O'Reilly and Ironmonger. Characteristically, he returned in the second innings to hit the six which won England the match, and decided the rubber in their favour. His reward was to be sent in at number eight in the next Test.

Not involved in the defeats of 1934 or 1936-37, in 1938 at Nottingham he made 216 not out, which included a share in a record fifth-wicket stand of 206 with Denis Compton. At Lord's he came in when England were 31 for three and scored 99 in another record partnership – of 222 for the fourth wicket with Wally Hammond. In 1938-39 in South Africa, his Test average was 81. Two Tests against West Indies in 1939 ended his Test career, and he retired at the end of that season.

Although he had lost two fingers in an accident in his youth, he was a superb outfield, as both catcher and thrower. At Lord's in 1938 when Leslie Ames broke a finger, Eddie Paynter kept wicket throughout the Australian second innings; although he had virtually no experience of keeping, he allowed only five byes and took a catch. He had played only one match since 1939 when, in 1947, he turned out in the Harrogate Festival and scored 154, 73 and 127.

He never failed England, whose selectors relied on him too little. Eddie Paynter had any amount of guts and although over a decade lesser batsmen were often picked in preference to him, he never failed to give his utmost.

Eddie Paynter: loyal professional and undervalued batsman

FIRST-CLASS CAREER RECORDS

Career	M	I	NO	HS	Runs	Avge	100
1926-1950	348	533	58	322	20075	42.26	45

Ct/St	Runs	Wkts	Avge	BB	5wI	10wM
160	1317	30	43.90	3-13	—	—

TEST CAREER RECORDS

Tests	I	NO	HS	Runs	Avge	100	50
20	31†	5	243	1540	59.23	4	7

Ct/St	Balls	Runs	Wkts	Avge	BB	5wI	10wM
7	—	—	—	—	—	—	—

GRAEME POLLOCK

GRAEME POLLOCK IS undoubtedly the finest post-war South African batsman and is challenged only by Garfield Sobers as the finest left-hander of the period. Tall, wide-shouldered and relaxed, his easy timing invests his strokes with considerable power. He has always blended style and an attacking bent with striking deliveries which would force the majority of batsmen on to the defensive.

He has cricket in his blood: his Scottish-born father kept wicket for Orange Free State and, like him, Graeme does everything except bat with the right-hand dominant; his elder brother Peter was a Test fast bowler, and he himself exhibited quite precocious skill as a boy. At nine, playing for Grey Junior School against Union High, he scored his first century and took all ten wickets for 25. He played for Greys on his thirteenth birthday, continued in the team for an unheard of four years, and for Eastern Province Schoolboys in the Nuffield Schools Week set

Robert Graeme Pollock (1944-) Eastern Province, Transvaal, South Africa and Rest of World XIs
Left-hand bat; slow right-arm leg-break bowler.

Graeme Pollock scatters the spectators again, for South Africa against Hampshire in 1965

an individual record of 152. A month short of his seventeenth birthday he was the youngest player to score a century in the Currie Cup; at nineteen he became the youngest South African to make a double century, and scored his first Test hundred. Still nineteen, he went to Australia under Trevor Goddard, made a century in the third Test and then, in the fourth – still short of his twentieth birthday – with Eddie Barlow, put on 341 for the third wicket. That remains South Africa's highest stand for any wicket in Tests; and it was made in only 283 minutes.

Back home he had initial difficulties with the two England off-spinners, Fred Titmus and David Allen, on responsive pitches; but in the last Test, to his immense satisfaction – it was on his home ground at Port Elizabeth – he made 137 and 77 not out.

So to England, where he batted splendidly; notably at Trent Bridge when, particularly against that master of swing Tom Cartwright who, in humid conditions ideal for his technique, had reduced South Africa to 80 for five, Graeme struck a quite majestic 125.

That was followed, in 1969-70, by the last Test series played by South Africa; when Pollock set a new South African Test record score with 274 at Durban; and, in the four-Test series which South Africa won by four to none, averaged 73.

That perforce was the end of his Test cricket. Since then he has scored heavily in the Currie Cup but resisted most invitations to play abroad until, in 1968, he accepted a generous contract to take part in the Sunday matches of the International Cavaliers which he much enjoyed and where he gave great pleasure.

He had already established himself as a world-class batsman at an unusually early age; and the memory remains of him leaning into the ball and with an almost lazy, long swing of the bat, striking it quite classically, and with splendid force through some skilfully identified gap in the off-side field.

FIRST-CLASS CAREER RECORDS

Career	M	I	NO	HS	Runs	Avge	100
1961-1984	247	414	51	274	19813	54.58	60

Ct/St	Runs	Wkts	Avge	BB	5wI	10wM
237	2062	43	47.95	3-46	—	—

TEST CAREER RECORDS

Tests	I	NO	HS	Runs	Avge	100	50
23	41†	4	274	2256	60.97	7	11

Ct/St	Balls	Runs	Wkts	Avge	BB	5wI	10wM
17	414	204	4	51.00	2-50	—	—

BILL PONSFORD

BILL PONSFORD WAS the first of the modern batting record-breakers; eight years older than Don Bradman, and retiring relatively early – after effectively only eleven years in the first-class game – he left behind a massive list of scores. Those who watched the two closely maintained that Ponsford was the only partner whom 'The Don' did not overshadow.

Ponsford was heavily built, with large buttocks which made him look ponderous and which deceived some into believing he was slow in movement. He was, however, extremely fast on his feet; a master of spin bowling and of placing strokes through gaps in the field, and massively sound against medium-fast bowling. Although he settled as an opening batsman, he was not at his best against fast bowling, tending to move too far into – indeed, across – it, so that he was sometimes bowled behind his legs. His stamina and concentration were immense; and, although he disliked publicity, mistrusted the press and especially photographers, his batting temperament was sound. He was an undemonstrative batsman; his main mannerism was that of tugging his cap towards his left ear as his innings wore on. Indeed, Ray Robinson always asserted that when Ponsford's cap was over his left ear he was on the way to his second hundred.

He first appeared for Victoria in 1920, but used to observe, ironicaly, that to break into that immensely strong State side he had to break a world record; that record was 429 (made in 477 minutes) against Tasmania in 1923; and only the second time anyone scored over 400 in a first-class match. In only his third first-class innings he made 334 in a day, against New South Wales (and he repeated the feat in 1927-28, with 437 against Queensland). For the moment, though, he had achieved a place in the Victorian team. In the following season he was chosen for the opening game of the (1924-25) series with England, and in his first Test innings made a century (110). He continued to roll out massive scores: 13 over 200. At one point he shared the record partnerships for the first, second, third and fourth wickets in Australia: his 456 for the first wicket with Edgar Mayne (1923-24) still stands. Throughout his career his one great weakness was not against pace as such, but against the pace of Harold Larwood. He did not flinch from him; in fact, especially in the Adelaide Test of the 'Bodyline' series, he deliberately took the fast bowling on his body. He shared in 22 century stands – five of them over 200 – with Bill Woodfull. Their partnership of 375 against New South Wales in 1926 was the foundation of Victoria's great total of 1,107. Victoria had made 573 for one by

William Harold Ponsford (1900-   ) Victoria and Australia Right-hand bat; bowling negligible; deep field; fine thrower.

the end of the first day and Ponsford was to make 352.

He had an indifferent tour of England in 1926 (playing in the last two Tests only), though in 1930 he averaged 55. In the 'Bodyline' series his figure dropped to 25.50. In 1934, however, he made 181 in the fourth Test at Leeds, and 266 – with a partnership of 451 with Bradman – in the fifth Test at The Oval. Larwood was not playing, but Bill Bowes, Nobby Clark and G.O. Allen were – yet Ponsford finished top of the Test averages – ahead even of Bradman – with 569 runs at 94.83. A quiet man, not given to extravagant gestures, no doubt he felt he had made his point with a century in his last Test as in his first: he went back to Australia and retired from the game.

FIRST-CLASS CAREER RECORDS

Career	M	I	NO	HS	Runs	Avge	100
1920-1934	162	235	23	437	13819	65.18	47

Ct/St	Runs	Wkts	Avge	BB	5wI	10wM
71	41	0	—	—	—	—

TEST CAREER RECORDS

Tests	I	NO	HS	Runs	Avge	100	50
29	48	4	266	2122	48.22	7	6

Ct/St	Balls	Runs	Wkts	Avge	BB	5wI	10wM
21	—	—	—	—	—	—	—

Imperturbable openers: Ponsford (Right) and Woodfull

K.S. RANJITSINHJI

'RANJI', AS EDWARDIAN England happily and admiringly called him, was a highly accomplished batsman; probably better than is generally allowed. Certainly he was highly dextrous and popularly renowned for the leg-glance which he executed nearer to the stumps – in fact, often off the middle – and later, than anyone else. He had, though, all the strokes, and if at first he favoured those behind the wicket on the leg-side, he became a splendid cutter and a powerful and punishing driver.

Kumar Shri Ranjitsinhji, later H.H. Shri Sir Ranjitsinhji Vibhaji, Jam Sahib of Nawanagar (1872-1933) Cambridge University, Sussex and England
Right-hand bat; slow right-arm bowler; slip field.

The impressive point about his cricket is its concentration. The records give his career as from 1893 to 1920, which is statistically accurate, but it did not effectively begin until he qualified for Sussex in 1895; and virtually ended in 1912, while there had already been two four-year breaks in that period. Yet, amazingly, in the course of only about 307 matches he scored nearly 25,000 runs and made 72 centuries. That is a most unusual degree of cricketing achievement.

By birth a Rajput, Ranji had played only a little cricket at home before he came to England on a visit in 1888 when he was fifteen. It seems that he then became obsessed with the game and decided to stay. He had no organized cricket until he went up to Trinity College in 1890. Those who knew him there recalled his engaging Bill Lockwood, Tom Richardson, 'Old Jack' Hearne and Tom Hayward – the first two then as fast as any in the world and whom he instructed to bowl at their fastest to him – for his extremely long practice sessions. Advised not to take such protracted nets, he replied: 'I must now master endurance'.

He won a Blue only in 1893, his fourth year; and although his intuitive batting had attracted unusually large crowds to watch his matches on Parker's Piece, he remained an unsophisticated batsman. Intensive practice, though, ensured that by the time he qualified for Sussex in 1895 his natural gifts had been channelled into controlled brilliance. In his first match for the county – against MCC at Lord's – he scored 77 not out and 150. That season he went on to make 1,775 runs at nearly 50. His next year, however, was quite historic; it was only his second season of major cricket. In his first Test (v Australia) at Manchester he not only became the first Indian to play Test cricket, but only the second batsman, after W.G. Grace, to score a hundred (62 and 154 not out) on his initial appearance. Indeed, in his second innings he made 100 before lunch on the third morning. Soon afterwards he scored three centuries in successive innings, and such centuries – 165 against Lancashire; 100 and 125 against Yorkshire; the last two made in a single day. By the end of the

summer he had, too, broken W.G. Grace's record of 1871 by scoring 2,780 runs in a season (average 57.91, with 10 centuries). In 1897-98 he went in A.E. Stoddart's side to Australia, where he scored 189 in his first match of the tour, and 175 in his first Test there.

He now possessed the power effectively to destroy even the best bowling. In 1899, when he became captain of Sussex, he scored 3,159 runs; in 1900, 3,065, including his remarkable 202 against Middlesex made in three hours on a difficult wicket, where the rest of the Sussex side could muster only 198. His highest score was 285 not out, against Somerset (1901), made after having been up all night – fishing. He resigned the captaincy of Sussex in 1903; but played there in the next season and was again top of the national batting averages.

He last played for England in 1902 when, like his friend C.B. Fry, he failed in the decisive Old Trafford Test. He left some considerable records: three times – twice in 1899 and again in 1900 – he scored 1,000 runs in a month; he twice made double centuries in successive innings, while his partnership of 344 with Billy Newham (v Essex, 1902) remains the English record for the seventh wicket.

The cricket of Ranji, though, was not to be measured in statistics; he was inventive, elegant, exciting to watch – as spectators of three countries testified. Perhaps the last word should rest with Gilbert Jessop, a man always cool enough about others' merits, and who described Ranji as: 'indisputably the greatest genius who ever stepped on to a cricket field, the most brilliant figure in what, I believe, was cricket's most brilliant period'. A year after his death, the Ranji Trophy – the major championship of Indian domestic cricket – was named after him.

OPPOSITE *'Ranji', aristocrat, diplomat and possessor of a virtually magical leg glance*

FIRST-CLASS CAREER RECORDS

Career	M	I	NO	HS	Runs	Avge	100
1893-1920	307	500	62	285*	24692	56.37	72

Ct/St	Runs	Wkts	Avge	BB	5wI	10wM
233	4601	133	34.59	6-53	4	—

TEST CAREER RECORDS

Tests	I	NO	HS	Runs	Avge	100	50
15	26	4	175	989	44.95	2	6

Ct/St	Balls	Runs	Wkts	Avge	BB	5wI	10wM
13	97	39	1	39.00	1-23	—	—

JOHN REID

John Richard Reid, OBE (1928-   ) Wellington, Otago and New Zealand Right-hand bat; right-arm fast-medium bowler; wicketkeeper; close field.

JOHN REID WAS a mighty man; not merely physically powerful – as he was – but a very strong man; a kind of Atlas-figure of New Zealand cricket as all-rounder and captain through the formative period from 1949 to their first Test wins in the mid-1960s.

It is surprising that he should have become so strong for, in his youth, over-indulgence in sport brought on two attacks of rheumatic fever, the second of which resulted in four months in hospital and his having to give up Rugby football. However, by twenty-three he was fit enough to score 283 for Wellington against Otago and never reported any subsequent ailments.

The senior John Reid – nicknamed 'Bogo' – was a basically correct right-hander constantly prepared, when his side was in trouble, to hit his way out of it. He was a splendid attacker; and when he made his highest score – 296 for Wellington against Northern Districts in 1962-63 (with a world record of 15 sixes) – he took his score on the second morning from nought to 174 at lunch, and on to 296 before tea.

As a bowler he trafficked in brisk outswing until experience in the Central Lancashire League persuaded him that it was uneconomic, when he changed to off-cutters which he often made rear most hostilely. He took to wicketkeeping at school, when a dislocated shoulder prevented him from bowling; and for the remainder of his career he was capable of keeping at Test level. His large hands, coupled with his determination to play the game hard, made him also a safe – sometimes brilliant – close fieldsman.

Chosen in Walter Hadlee's team to England in 1949, he shrewdly and rapidly assessed the demands and his own shortcomings. In the first place, as a basic change, he resolved not to play forward so often. He kept wicket capably when needed; and, on his day, was as fast as any bowler in the country.

Superb competitor as he was, even when the going was toughest, he had a splendid and generous smile, which completely lit up his face. The 1953-54 New Zealand tour to South Africa went far towards rounding off his cricketing education; that may seem a grudging statement since on it he became the first player to score 1,000 runs and take 50 wickets in a season there. He himself, however, believed that by watching Eric Rowan he learned much that he had not understood about back play against fast bowling (and he had Adcock at his bounciest for practice). New Zealand at this time played – for them – an unusually concentrated series of Tests. For the second of 1955-56 against West Indies, John Reid was appointed captain and, in the fourth, as captain and top scorer, he took New Zealand to the first Test win of their history. He led them, too, in their second and third Test wins.

At one time, John Reid held nearly all their national records; most Tests, most Test runs, wickets, catches, captaincies and appearances; he ended his career having played in more consecutive Tests – 58 – than anyone else. He established himself beyond doubt as a – even *the* – major figure in his country's cricket: game, strong and unflinching.

FIRST-CLASS CAREER RECORDS

Career	M	I	NO	HS	Runs	Avge	100
1947-1965	246	418	28	296	16128	41.35	39

Ct/St	Runs	Wkts	Avge	BB	5wI	10wM
240/7	10535	466	22.60	7-20	15	1

TEST CAREER RECORDS

Tests	I	NO	HS	Runs	Avge	100	50
58	108	5	142	3428	33.28	6	22

Ct/St	Balls	Runs	Wkts	Avge	BB	5wI	10wM
43/1	7725	2835	85	33.35	6-60	1	—

The sturdy John Reid, who led New Zealand to her first Test Match victory

BARRY RICHARDS

*Barry Anderson
Richards (1945-   )
Natal, Gloucestershire,
Hampshire, South
Australia, Transvaal,
and South Africa
Right-hand bat; slow
off-spin bowler; slip
field.*

BARRY RICHARDS WAS a batsman of staggering talent; and, surely, the most 'purely' mercenary of all the mercenary cricketers largely produced by the British 'immediate registration' legislation of 1968. Because South Africa ceased to play Test cricket after 1969-70, he had little opportunity to play at the highest level. It may well be, as Roy Marshall has maintained, that proof of world class is sustained only by consistent performance at Test level. Richards never had that opportunity, but in his mere four Test match appearances – against no less opposition than Australia, and at the age of twenty-four – he achieved an average of 72.57.

No one who ever watched him bat could conceivably doubt his ability. He picked up the line of the ball early, had a wide range of strokes and, when he was in the mood, could toy with the best bowling. The tragedies of his career are the fact that he played so little international cricket; that his own country saw so little of his great skill; and that – probably because he did not have the stimulus of Test play – he lost his zest for the game.

Barry Richards captained the South African schools team to England in 1963; and immediately afterwards he and Mike Procter, from the same side, spent a summer with Gloucestershire, during which he played a single match for the county – against the South African side which was touring England at the time. In 1968, he was engaged by Hampshire, and he played a major proportion of his first-class career with them. He turned out, too, for a full season with South Australia; in the course of which he scored 356 (including 325 on the first day of the match) against Western Australia. After the 1978 season, however, he returned to South Africa and became a Kerry Packer player.

He will be remembered by those who watched him as one of the most brilliant players of bowling of modern times. Nine times he scored a century before lunch, and he completed his first Test century in the first over after lunch on the first day. Especially in over-limit matches he would perpetrate strokes of an unparalleled extravagance. He would, for instance, step away to leg to an off-break pitched on, or outside, the leg stump and play it, against the spin, for four through the covers; or pick up a left-arm breakaway from outside the off-stump and, with something near to laughing contempt, simply whack it over mid-wicket for six.

When he cared to do so, he could bowl off-spin to an extremely high standard; and, at slip, he constantly and almost casually picked up extremely difficult catches. He was seen to be brilliant; yet it is doubtful if he ever exhibited his full ability.

FIRST-CLASS CAREER RECORDS

Career	M	I	NO	HS	Runs	Avge	100
1964-1982	339	576	58	356	28358	54.74	80

Ct/St	Runs	Wkts	Avge	BB	5wI	10wM
367	2886	77	37.48	7-63	1	—

TEST CAREER RECORDS

Tests	I	NO	HS	Runs	Avge	100	50
4	7	0	140	508	72.57	2	2

Ct/St	Balls	Runs	Wkts	Avge	BB	5wI	10wM
3	72	26	1	26.00	1-12	—	—

*A measured cover drive
from Barry Richards*

231

VIV RICHARDS

Isaac Vivian Alexander Richards (1952-   ) Leeward Islands, Somerset, Queensland and West Indies Right-hand bat; slow off-spin or medium-pace bowler; cover or close fieldsman.

VIV RICHARDS IS the most brilliant and prolific batsman in world cricket of the 1980s. He might be described as a towering figure, but he does not seek to tower so much as to compete and enjoy – almost revel in – batting. His career began in his native Antigua when he was suspended for dissenting from an umpire's decision. Nowadays he accepts their rulings graciously and philosophically.

Basically Viv Richards is an orthodox batsman. He has all the strokes and he plays them with such power that even his mis-hits constantly go to the boundary. He is fast into position to play his strokes and he dominates bowling. He hits through the entire arc in front of the wicket with masterly pacing; cuts, glances and hooks gloriously. In short, an excitingly murderous batsman against any opposition. Even Sir Donald Bradman never exerted quite such headlong mastery. In the losing series against Australia with Lillee and Thomson, Richards grew up with experience of the conditions and opposition to score 44, 2, 30, 101, 50 and 98.

He was only twenty-two when he joined Somerset and relatively immature, but learnt quickly from Brian Close and made 1,223 runs for the county in that season. He, and many others, were sad when for 1987 he was not offered a new contract by the county and his friendly rivalry with Ian Botham was broken up. So in 1987 he played for Rishton C.C. in Lancashire League cricket.

Taken by West Indies to India, Pakistan and Sri Lanka in 1974-75 to gain experience, he made 192 not out against India and established himself as a Test cricketer. In England in 1976 he missed the Lord's Test through illness but still scored 829 runs in the series. Australia was to be the trial of his quality when, in all matches, he averaged 71.09; but in the Tests, 91.

Virtually his only bad patch came in 1982 when, through weight of concentration on cricket, even he lost some of his zest; but with rest he overcame it, as he seems to have done with his eye trouble.

To recite his outstanding performances would make this merely a string of statistics, but Viv Richards is bigger even than his figures. He has become the first West Indian to score a hundred first-class centuries; has played his hundredth Test and held his hundredth Test catch.

As captain of West Indies he is happy, and so are the players under him. He has all the orthodox strokes – even those in defence which he prefers not to use – and he plays them all with

The peerless Vivian Richards: delight of spectators, despair of bowlers

killing power; he can also improvise brilliantly. His favourite stroke at Lord's – where he has recorded many successes for both West Indies and Somerset – is a most improbable heave to cart a ball from outside the off-stump over mid-wicket into the Mound Stand – and then he laughs.

With his aquiline nose, flashing smile, small beard, and elegant silk shirts, he is a striking figure both on and off the field. He catches well and his apparently amiable off-breaks or medium-pace seamers are often valuable: indeed, in 1982 he performed a hat trick against Essex in a Sunday League match.

He loves his cricket but he also gives much, and it was striking that his anxiety to succeed for Somerset often invested his batting with unusual care.

In the Fifth Test of 1985-86 against England (and Botham) Viv Richards scored the fastest recorded Test hundred – off 56 balls: since it happened in his native Antigua, the delight can be imagined – or can it?

Viv Richards is a joy to watch and there is no more relishable cricketer in the world.

FIRST-CLASS CAREER RECORDS

Career	M	I	NO	HS	Runs	Avge	100
1971-1988	420	656	43	322	30591	49.90	98

Ct/St	Runs	Wkts	Avge	BB	5wl	10wM
385/1	8218	193	42.58	5-88	1	–

TEST CAREER RECORDS

Tests	I	NO	HS	Runs	Avge	100	50
99	147	9	291	7268	52.66	22	33

Ct	Balls	Runs	Wkts	Avge	BB	5wl	10wM
99	3826	1383	28	49.39	2-17	–	–

ANDY SANDHAM

ANDREW SANDHAM – OTHERWISE 'Sandy' – was the dapper, quiet, modest, generous, opening batsman who spent sixty years as player, coach and scorer with Surrey. Yet in his early days he must have doubted if he would ever become a fully-fledged county player. A combination of the size of the Surrey staff – thirty (plus some amateurs) – and the incidence of the First World War meant that he was twenty-nine years old before he won a regular county place. Nevertheless, by the time he was forty-seven he had made over 41,000 runs with 107 centuries and, for good measure, another 207 scores of 50 or over.

Andrew Sandham (1890-1982) Surrey and England
Right-hand bat; sound outfield.

Present-day county players would find it hard to believe how hard the going could be for a young man in the early years of this century. At twenty, after scoring centuries in four consecutive matches – for Mitcham, Young Players of Surrey, Surrey Club and Ground, and the second XI – he was given a game against Cambridge University, scored 53, and returned to the second team. Then, one day, he was bowling in the nets when Tom Hayward fell out at the last moment and he was told at the last moment to play against Lancashire. After scoring 60 he was dropped again. In 1912 he played only a single innings – 23 not out – before he dropped back; and in 1913, even his first century – 196 against Sussex – could not keep him afloat at first-team level.

He had watched Tom Hayward intently and modelled his batting on him, and was delighted to take his place when Hayward retired after the Great War. Even then, however, he was dropped when the young Donald Knight came from Malvern. In early August, though, an innings of 175 not out – just after his twenty-ninth birthday – resolved the problem.

He settled down to open the Surrey innings with Jack Hobbs in a partnership which lasted fifteen years until the senior partner retired in 1934. They shared 63 opening stands of over 100 in 1926, including one of 428 against Oxford University. They became famous for their running between wickets; indeed, Sir Jack used to say that 'Sandy' was the best runner of all his partners. They so refined that skill that eventually they ran without calling, constantly creating runs where none seemed to exist.

Quick on his feet, fearless and accomplished against pace, Andrew Sandham was strong on the leg-side, a bold, controlled hooker, and a skilful deflector; he was a neat cutter, with a fine square drive. He hardly ever bowled, but was a highly efficient outfield; fast over the ground, dexterous in picking up and a quick, accurate thrower.

Andy Sandham walks out to bat at The Oval in 1922

When the English batting was on the run against Australia's fast bowlers in 1921, he was chosen for the fifth Test, and batted usefully if unspectacularly. In 1922-23 in South Africa he was the most successful batsman over the entire tour, but had little sucess in Tests; the same was the case in Australia in 1924-25. By now Herbert Sutcliffe was established as Jack Hobbs's opening partner in Tests, so Sandham had little chance at representative level until he was chosen for the West Indies in 1929-30. He scored 152 at Bridgetown, and 325 at Kingston, the latter still the highest by an English player in a Test in West Indies.

He had a dry wit, a clear mind and a modest approach; he never seemed to resent Jack Hobbs being the senior partner, and there was a warm feeling between the two. When Hobbs equalled W.G.'s record number of centuries at Taunton and had the chance to beat it in the second innings, Sandham, who might have had a hundred himself, deliberately gave him the bowling: it was a characteristically unselfish gesture. Andrew Sandham, was a generous man; if he achieved less than his ability merited, he never resented the fact, taking infinite pleasure in his cricket and his friendships.

FIRST-CLASS CAREER RECORDS

Career	M	I	NO	HS	Runs	Avge	100
1911-1937	642	1000	79	325	41284	44.82	107

Ct/St	Runs	Wkts	Avge	BB	5wI	10wM
158	560	18	31.11	3-27	—	—

TEST CAREER RECORDS

Tests	I	NO	HS	Runs	Avge	100	50
14	23	0	325	879	38.21	2	3

Ct/St	Balls	Runs	Wkts	Avge	BB	5wI	10wM
4	—	—	—	—	—	—	—

ARTHUR SHREWSBURY

'GIVE ME ARTHUR,' said W.G. Grace when asked who was the *next best* batsman (to himself, of course). He meant a man apparently his direct opposite. Arthur Shrewsbury was a slight, retiring, quiet man – and bald as an egg; but, like W.G., he had a virtually perfect batting technique. Based on an almost impregnable defence, it won him general recognition in the last twenty years of the nineteenth century as one of the finest professional batsmen in England.

His promise was implicit in his selection for the Colts of England against MCC when he was barely seventeen; for Nottinghamshire – then quite the strongest county – at nineteen; and for the Players against Gentlemen at twenty. Ill health held him back; he was always frail, until at twenty-five the long sea voyages and the sun of his first visit to Australia in 1881-82 steadied him physically and he settled to twenty years of utter consistency. He had an extremely high average for his period of 36.66 (59 centuries) in all first-class cricket; 35.47 in his 23 Tests; with three centuries.

In his early days he was a fine deep fieldsman; later a safe catch at point. He scarcely ever bowled, but after his death A.W. Shelton, reading through his diaries, found an entry: 'I bowled out William Gunn' – and it was trebly underlined; it was not, though, in a first-class match; he never took a wicket in his life at that level.

He was a purist batsman; patient, poised and regarded as the master on bad wickets. It is one of the traditions on Trent Bridge that, as he walked out of the pavilion to bat after lunch in the days before a tea interval was allowed, Shrewsbury used to say to the pavilion attendant: 'Bring me out a cup of tea at half-past four, Kirk', and the story has it that he was usually there waiting for it.

He jointly managed three touring teams to Australia; and after 1887-88 remained out there to manage a football side from England. He is credited with playing two of the great innings of Test cricket, both against Australia: 164 out of a total of 353 – on a pitch which one of his opponents considered 'impossible' – in 1886; and, in 1893, 106 out of 334 (in the course of which he became the first batsman to reach 1,000 runs in Tests) against Turner – 'The Terror' – on a hideous 'sticky'. Both innings were at Lord's.

In his last season (1902), at the age of forty-six, he scored two centuries in a match for the first time and was top of the first-class averages (1,250 runs at 50). But he believed that his cricket career was at an end and, convinced that he was suffering from an

Arthur Shrewsbury (1856-1903) Nottinghamshire and England Right-hand bat; fine deep fielder.

Arthur Shrewsbury, a model of personal and professional integrity and W.G's first choice batsman

incurable disease, he shot himself. Famous, popular and modest, Arthur Shrewsbury was much mourned and is still remembered with great respect in Nottingham.

FIRST-CLASS CAREER RECORDS

Career	M	I	NO	HS	Runs	Avge	100
1875-1902	497	811	90	267	26439	36.66	59

Ct/St	Runs	Wkts	Avge	BB	5wI	10wM
376	2	0	—	—	—	—

TEST CAREER RECORDS

Tests	I	NO	HS	Runs	Avge	100	50
23	40	4	164	1277	35.47	3	4

Ct/St	Balls	Runs	Wkts	Avge	BB	5wI	10wM
29	12	2	0	—	—	—	—

BOBBY SIMPSON

BOBBY SIMPSON WAS a physically compact, highly accomplished batsman with a striking penchant for compiling high scores. His 359 for New South Wales v Queensland at Brisbane in 1963-64 is the highest innings played in Australia since the 1939-45 War. His 311 for Australia v England at Old Trafford in 1964 is the second highest for them in Tests; and, at 762 minutes, the longest ever played for them. Incidentally, that was his first century, made in his thirtieth Test. He scored 12 double centuries in his career which is the most made in the post-war 1945 period by any player. With Bill Lawry he put on 382 for the first wicket against West Indies at Bridgetown in 1964-65, which remains an Australian Test record.

Neat on his feet and a correct stroke-maker, Simpson had a clear mental picture of batting. A brilliant square-cutter and driver, he rarely hooked but moved out of the line of the short-pitched ball, preferring not to hazard his wicket; on the other hand, he exploited the pull stroke with immense profit.

The son of Scottish parents (his father had been a soccer professional with Stenhousemuir in the Scottish League), he was an assured but courteous man who controlled his teams well. His talent was early apparent, and he first appeared for New South Wales at the age of sixteen in 1952-53. In 1956-57 he joined Western Australia and played there for four seasons. He retired from first-class cricket in 1967-68, but returned in 1977-78 to take over the captaincy of New South Wales and of Australia during the Packer period, and captained them in 39 Tests altogether.

He had had four seasons with New South Wales without winning a Test place before he moved to Western Australia and, in 1959, played a season in Lancashire League cricket with Accrington. The whole basis of his success in fact resided in three changes. Until he first went on to the ground as 12th man for New South Wales he had always been a deep fieldsman. Keith Miller, though, his State captain, waved him to slip, where he made two catches within half an hour and remained a slip fielder for the rest of his career, with sufficient ability to be described as the finest catcher in that position in his time. Many good batsmen – including Len Hutton – were amazed by the catches he made off them; he never seemed to hurry, yet his certainty was extraordinary.

Similarly, he had always been a middle-order batsman until Jimmy Burke retired, when Neil Harvey suggested that Simpson should attempt to fill Australia's lack of an opening bat. He

Robert Baddeley Simpson (1936-   )
New South Wales, Western Australia and Australia
Right-hand bat; right-arm wrist spinner; outstanding slip fieldsman.

Bobby Simpson, highly efficient batsman and shrewd captain

galloped away with 902 runs in six innings; a successful tour of New Zealand and a first – 1961 – tour of England, when he made 1,947 runs including six centuries. His other major change was technical: switching his batting method from square-on to sideways-on, which enhanced the quality of his driving. He spun the leg-break and googly well, and would probably have bowled more at test level if his career had not coincided with Benaud's.

When he first retired, after the 1967-68 series with India, he had made 4,131 runs in Test cricket at an average of 48.60. When the Packer moves began, and the Australian Cricket Board invited him back to captain their side against India in 1977, he was forty-one years old. He batted well through that rubber, but in the following series, against the West Indies, he was less successful, though he was top scorer in the first innings of the third Test which Australia won narrowly by three wickets. Moreover, his skill and leadership was beginning to have marked effect on an Australian side heavily plundered by the Packer demands. He asked, therefore, to be promised his place in the first Test against England in 1978-79. The Australian Board, in the manner which has antagonized their players over the years, refused. Simpson therefore moved to the far more financially rewarding occupation of commentator and newspaper reporter. Yallop, whom Simpson has helped throughout his career, took over; but despite a century in the first Test he had an unhappy series, losing not only the Australian but also the Victorian captaincy. Simpson, for his part, had taken his tally of Test catches to 110 with his revitalized career – five more than Ian Chappell; his Test batting record finally included 10 centuries and – importantly – twenty-seven other scores of more than 50.

He was a pleasant, personable cricketer, and a captain with genuine feeling for his players. Those who watched him will never forget the masterly ease of his slip-catching.

FIRST-CLASS CAREER RECORDS

Career	M	I	NO	HS	Runs	Avge	100
1952-1977	257	436	62	359	21029	56.22	60

Ct/St	Runs	Wkts	Avge	BB	5wI	10wM
383	13287	349	38.07	5-33	6	—

TEST CAREER RECORDS

Tests	I	NO	HS	Runs	Avge	100	50
62	111	7	311	4869	46.81	10	27

Ct/St	Balls	Runs	Wkts	Avge	BB	5wI	10wM
110	6881	3001	71	42.26	5-57	2	—

GARY SOBERS

Sir Garfield St Aubrun
Sobers (1936-   )
Barbados, South
Australia,
Nottinghamshire and
West Indies
Left-hand bat; left-arm
finger spinner, wrist-
spinner and fast-medium
bowler; brilliant close
fieldsman.

THERE HAS HARDLY been a more absorbing or exciting experience in modern cricket than watching the progress of Garfield Sobers to the status of, surely, the greatest all-round cricketer in the history of the game. To be sure, W.G. Grace set most of the exalted standards, but no one has done so with such immense elan nor excelled so diversely as Sobers. Everything about his cricket was memorable; for even if that strange, forward-leaning, sag-kneed walk which his young admirers delighted to imitate probably was the precursor of the knee-damage which eventually hobbled him, it did not inhibit him until he had scaled all the heights – and done so with a gloriously joyous athleticism.

Born with an extra – fifth – finger on each hand (amputated early) he excelled at ball games from childhood. He began his first-class cricket, chosen for Barbados as an orthodox left-arm finger spinner, at the age of sixteen. In the next year (1954) he played his first Test, still as an orthodox slow left-armer; but he was already starting to develop his batting. Surely enough, four years later in 1957-58, against Pakistan at Kingston, he made his first Test century – it was 365 not out, one more than the Test record Sir Len Hutton had set in 1938.

Now, indeed, the cricket world was his oyster and he relished it in princely fashion. He perceived the value of wrist spin – in his case the 'Chinaman' and its associated googly, especially on plumb wickets; mastered the technique and exploited it most effectively. Later, to balance his team's bowling economy, he bowled fast-medium left-arm with a born-perfect action which gave him swing, movement off the seam, and the nip of the natural pace bowler. In the field, he was spectacular in the outfield or the covers as a young man, became a fine slip and, ultimately, a quite phenomenal short-leg.

As a captain he was bold; some might say he felt he could change and win a match by himself, as indeed he frequently did. In 1967-68, after three long-winded draws against England in the West Indies he declared in the fourth Test, setting England 215 runs in 165 minutes: they achieved it. All those who subscribed to the argument that a captain should never make a declaration which allows the other side a chance to win blamed Sobers for 'throwing away the match – and the series'. Later those same critics chose to ignore the immense all-round effort of Sobers – 152 and 95 not out; three for 72 and three for 53 — which took West Indies to within a single wicket of squaring the series.

The most desirable playing property in the game, he was much sought after and, for both South Australia and Nottinghamshire, he proved an immense attraction, a most successful all-rounder and an inspiration as captain. For Nottinghamshire against Glamorgan in 1968, of course, he historically and at that time uniquely, struck Malcolm Nash's medium-pace left-arm for six sixes in a six-ball over (this great feat was equalled by Ravi Shastri in 1985).

The statistics of this book show the records Garfield Sobers set and broke; but those who watched him recognized, and still recall, that his cricket transcended records.

Gary Sobers, utterly brilliant all-rounder

Sobers hits, Long admires

FIRST-CLASS CAREER RECORDS

Career	M	I	NO	HS	Runs	Avge	100
1952-1974	383	609	93	365*	28315	54.87	86

Ct/St	Runs	Wkts	Avge	BB	5wI	10wM
407	28941	1043	27.74	9-49	36	1

TEST CAREER RECORDS

Tests	I	NO	HS	Runs	Avge	100	50
93	160†	21	365*	8032	57.78	26	30

Ct/St	Balls	Runs	Wkts	Avge	BB	5wI	10wM
109	21599‡	7999	235	34.03	6-73	6	—

A.E. STODDART

TALL, HANDSOME, ATHLETIC and a gifted all-round games player, Andrew Stoddart was a great batsman, now accorded less than due credit in England. Like several other English cricketers he achieved his major successes in Australia, where he played 11 of his 16 Tests, and captained England in a winning rubber (1894-95). In England he played less than regularly for Middlesex, but much club cricket with Hampstead, for whom, in 1886, he scored 485 – then the highest recorded innings – against The Stoics.

In his small corner of the last decade of the nineteenth century, he was a public idol; the choice of music hall songsters and the light verifiers as the image of cricket. Yet the manner of his going was poignant enough to stifle that kind of popularity.

Essentially, Andrew Stoddart was a Victorian, a typical Victorian amateur sportsman, though far above average in performance. It was fitting that his last innings for Middlesex should have been played in 1900 – and typical of the man that it was one of 221. His life had the ingredients of a Victorian novel.

Stoddart was a stockbroker who lived in Hampstead, and was of impressive appearance; an Australian lady columnist described him as having 'quite a Piccadilly manner'.

He met the highest cricketing demand of a higher average in Tests than in all cricket (35.57 to 32.12). Generally an opening batsman, he was quite fearless; naturally a forcing player, he also played some outstanding innings on bad pitches. A capable fast-medium bowler he was, according to Haygarth, 'unsurpassed as an outfield'; and a thoughtful and well-liked captain. As an outstanding rugby three-quarter for Blackheath, he was capped ten times for England. In addition he could have boasted – but he did not boast – good amateur standard at real and lawn tennis, horse riding, golf, hockey, boxing and billiards. To back those activities, F.B. Wilson declared him, after he had scored 906 runs in four innings spread over ten days, 'one of the most tireless men who ever lived'.

He did not come into county cricket until 1885, when he was twenty-two; and his 170 matches for Middlesex were spread over the next sixteen seasons. For Hampstead he achieved some surprising figures: between 1885 and 1907 he scored 13,912 runs at 70.61; in 1887 his average was 155.16; in 1893, 111; in 1899, 104.84.

In Australia, in Melbourne, he played a crucial innings of 173, and had a Test batting average of 39.00 in the winning series of 1894-95. He also had an outstanding 134 at Adelaide in

Andrew Ernest Stoddart (1863-1915) Middlesex and England Right-hand bat; right-arm fast-medium bowler; outfield.

A.E. Stoddart, dashing
Victorian and
dominating batsman,
whose life ended
tragically

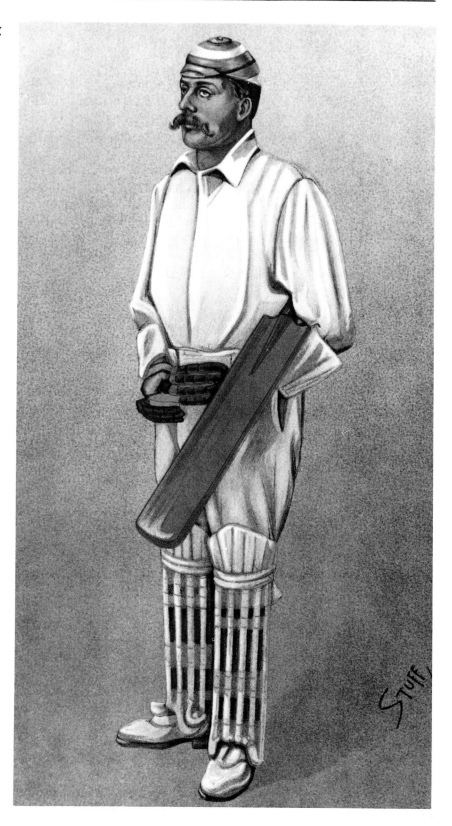

1891-92; but he had, too, some great days in England. In 1893, when he played a full season, he made 2,072 runs at 42.28. In that season, when Middlesex followed on 179 behind Surrey, he and T.C. O'Brien put on 228 for the first wicket to create a win by 79 runs; and, in the three consecutive innings which they opened against the Australians, he and W.G. Grace made 120, 114 and 151. Two years afterwards they went in first for the Gentlemen on a bad wicket at Lord's against Tom Richardson and Arthur Mold; they put on 151; otherwise only O'Brien (21) made double figures. It was said that Stoddart never played better than in 1890 for South against North, who had Attewell, Peel, Briggs and Barnes to bowl; and Stoddart made 115 out of 169 scored while he was at the wicket. In one phase he made 50 while W.G. scored 3.

Stoddart took another team to Australia in 1897-98; but before the Tests began, a cable came telling him that his widowed mother had died. The news distressed the unmarried Stoddart into shock and melancholia; he did not play in the first two Tests; batted himself at number eight in the third and fourth and withdrew from the fifth. He averaged 20 in Tests; 18 in all eleven-a-side games. Nevertheless he returned to head the Middlesex averages in 1898, but announced that he was 'tired of first-class cricket', and leaving it in favour of golf and the club game. In 1899 he appeared only once for Middlesex – in an emergency – scoring nought; then, in 1900, when he was thirty-seven, came that melodramatic 221 in Jack Hearne's benefit match as farewell.

His stockbroking business did not flourish; in 1906 he married a widow he had met in Australia and took the £300-a-year sinecure as secretary of Queen's Club. In 1907 he made his last appearance for Hampstead – with a century against Old Westminsters. He had put on weight; tennis elbow ruined his golf, and the ageing sportsman was simply an ageing sportsman; his marriage was a petulant affair. On 3 April 1915, Andrew Stoddart, the famous cricketer, shot himself through the head.

FIRST-CLASS CAREER RECORDS

Career	M	I	NO	HS	Runs	Avge	100
1885-1900	309	537	16	221	16738	32.12	26

Ct/St	Runs	Wkts	Avge	BB	5wI	10wM
257	6571	278	23.63	7-67	10	2

TEST CAREER RECORDS

Tests	I	NO	HS	Runs	Avge	100	50
16	30	2	173	996	35.57	2	3

Ct/St	Balls	Runs	Wkts	Avge	BB	5wI	10wM
6	162	94	2	47.00	1-10	—	—

JEFF STOLLMEYER

Jeffrey Baxter Stollmeyer (1921-   ) Trinidad and West Indies Right-hand bat; leg-break bowler; good all-round field.

THE YOUNGER BROTHER of Victor Stollmeyer – also Trinidad and West Indies – Jeff played for Trinidad at seventeen in 1938-39, and almost immediately afterwards toured England with Rolph Grant's side. He scored 59 in both the first and third of the three Tests. He matured considerably, of course, over the War period, and in 1946-47 made the highest score ever recorded in inter-colonial cricket – 324 for Trinidad against British Guiana – when he and his close friend Gerry Gomez put on a record of 434 for the third wicket.

Slim and elegant in appearance, Jeff Stollmeyer was a stylish batsman with a relaxed air, easy timing, strong on the leg-side and undisturbed by pace. After he had made 78 and 31 in the first Test of the home series with England in 1947-48, he missed the second and third of the four through injury. He settled down early in his career as an opening batsman, with Allan Rae of Jamaica as his partner for many years in the West Indies team. On the India tour of 1948 they shared a record 239 partnership for the first wicket at Madras, when Stollmeyer scored his first Test century (160).

On the tour of England in 1950 which proved so historic for West Indian cricket – first win and first rubber in England – the major, and certainly the most spectacular, batting honours were taken by the 'three Ws'. Thus many have overlooked the

consistently valuable opening partnerships which took the edge from the England attack. For the first wicket Stollmeyer and Rae made 52, 32, 37, 48, 77, 103 unbroken, and 72 over the four Tests. Against Sussex at Hove, too, the pair put on 355 together.

Elevated to the captaincy, Stollmeyer had good series against Australia/New Zealand, England and India in 14 Tests between 1951 and 1955; and over his Test career maintained an average of 42.33.

He has since become a senator in the Trinidad government, a Test selector, President of the West Indies Board of Cricket Control and wise and popular in the International Cricket Conference; and he has never lost his sense of humour.

FIRST-CLASS CAREER RECORDS

Career	M	I	NO	HS	Runs	Avge	100
1938-1956	117	194	16	324	7942	44.61	14

Ct/St	Runs	Wkts	Avge	BB	5wI	10wM
93	2482	55	45.12	3-32	—	—

TEST CAREER RECORDS

Tests	I	NO	HS	Runs	Avge	100	50
32	56	5	160	2159	42.33	4	12

Ct/St	Balls	Runs	Wkts	Avge	BB	5wI	10wM
20	990	507	13	39.00	3-32	—	—

Jeff Stollmeyer's leg glance beats a diving Hubert Doggart in the Old Trafford test of 1950

BERT SUTCLIFFE

*Bert Sutcliffe
(1923-   ) Auckland,
Otago, Northern
Districts and New
Zealand
Left-hand bat; left-arm
wrist-spinner; capable
all-round field.*

BERT SUTCLIFFE WAS a happy-looking, fair-haired, handsome and athletic cricketer. He was one of the finest left-handers in the world of his period and in the post-war years broke one record after another. Playing in 58 Tests between 1946 and 1965 he was, in historic terms, one of the leading figures in building up New Zealand cricket from 'poor relation' level to their first Test win (1956).

Like all the best batsmen, he was strong off front foot or back – and his forward strokes were quite scholarly in method – his driving was handsome, but his hooking and pulling were equally effective. Modest and humorous, he was a dedicated cricketer; he enjoyed going in first, and his inclination was to attack; but because he was a team man, and his side had its batting problems, he became a middle order batsman. He had to curb his early impetuosity, though it was never in his nature to adopt a purely defensive attitude. By profession he was for many years a physical training instructor – and later coach to Otago – and was always in fine condition; which may account for the fact that as many as eight of his 44 three-figure scores were of 200 or over.

He was amused to bowl slow left-arm wrist-spin which produced a lot of turn, but only rarely wickets; though his faster ball was well concealed. In the field his natural speed and unfailing keenness made him valuable anywhere.

Although he was something of a batting prodigy at school, he played little first-class cricket before the war, during which he served with the New Zealand army in Egypt, where he created a reputation as a cricketer which was to precede him to England in 1949. He played Services cricket there in company with some others who were later to make reputations, such as Ron Aspinall, Jim Laker and Peter Smith. Returning home, he turned out in a few unremarkable games for Auckland; but in 1946-47 he compelled attention by scoring 197 and 128 for Otago in their match against the MCC touring side. From that point he set off on his career of record-breaking.

Of his eleven Test-playing tours with New Zealand, only on that of England in 1965 was he not outstandingly successful; then, after being hit on the ear by a ball from Fred Trueman in the first Test, he did not play in another. He captained his country in four Tests, and was made an honorary member of MCC. Bert Sutcliffe is remembered as a brilliant and fearless stroke-maker and a modest, pleasing personality. Together with Neil Harvey and David Gower he is one of the most fluent left-handers since the war.

FIRST-CLASS CAREER RECORDS

Career	M	I	NO	HS	Runs	Avge	100
1941-1965	232	405	39	385	17283	47.22	44

Ct/St	Runs	Wkts	Avge	BB	5wI	10wM
158/1	3264	86	37.95	5-19	2	—

TEST CAREER RECORDS

Tests	I	NO	HS	Runs	Avge	100	50
42	76†	8	230*	2727	40.10	5	15

Ct/St	Balls	Runs	Wkts	Avge	BB	5wI	10wM
20	538‡	344	4	86.00	2-38	—	—

Bert Sutcliffe, New Zealand's backbone for nearly twenty years, batting against England on the 1949 tour

251

HERBERT SUTCLIFFE

Herbert Sutcliffe
(1894-1978) Yorkshire
and England
Right-hand bat; outfield.

HERBERT SUTCLIFFE WAS a batsman of immense concentration, unflinching courage, imperturbable temperament and consistent success. From his birthplace in Summerbridge, his family took him, while still quite young, to Pudsey, where 'Long John' Tunnicliffe and, later, Len Hutton also grew up, and where all three played for local clubs. He had the ritual Yorkshire trial at eighteen; but then, in the First World War, was commissioned into the Green Howards. On his return he was taken into the Yorkshire team for 1919, the first post-war season. He scored 1,839 runs, so impressive a start that, after a single season, he was chosen as one of *Wisden*'s 'Five Cricketers of the Year'. He now embarked on a distinguished career: indeed, he was the only player to top 1,000 runs in all of the twenty-one inter-war seasons. In twelve of those seasons he scored over two thousand; in another three, three thousand. Altogether he made 149 centuries, 17 of them of 200 or more; over his entire career, he averaged 51.95: and, as measure of his capacity for rising to the great occasion, in all Test cricket his average was 60.73; in Tests against Australia, 66.85. In the English season of 1931 his average, for 3,006 runs, was 96.96.

His first season saw the launching of his opening partnership with Percy Holmes; in the course of its fourteen years they put on

Herbert Sutcliffe and his family leaving Southampton for a winter cruise in 1933. His son, christened William Herbert Hobbs Sutcliffe, later captained Yorkshire

The determined Herbert Sutcliffe, scorer of over 50,000 first class runs

100 or more for the first wicket seventy-four times; and, of course, historically, against Essex at Leyton in 1932, they made 555, which remained the world record for the first wicket until 1976, when the Pakistanis Waheed Mirza and Mansoor Akhtar made 561 for Karachi Whites against Quetta.

253

Herbert Sutcliffe began his Test career by winning – against strong opposition – selection as opening partner of Jack Hobbs in the first Test of 1924 with South Africa. In England's only innings they made 136; in the second Test they put on 268 together: Hobbs 211, Sutcliffe 122; and the finest opening pair of cricket history had made their mark. Altogether they opened the innings for England on thirty-eight occasions, of which they marked fifteen with partnerships of over 100, and ten others with more than 50.

Herbert Sutcliffe was not, as he happily admitted, as stylish a player as Jack Hobbs; but he had a studied technique, knew his limitations, and played within them. His judgement was based on masterly reading of length and line. At Yorkshire's or England's need, his defence – with masterly use of the dead bat – could be all but impregnable. Strong off the front foot, especially in well-controlled driving, he was a tidy, though careful, cutter; and probably as powerful and safe a hooker – particularly fine of square – as anyone. Influenced by Jack Hobbs, and through much experience with Percy Holmes, Herbert Sutcliffe became a fine judge and taker of a run.

Quite apart from the statistical side of his career, essential here because it was both significant and impressive, Herbert Sutcliffe was an interesting character. Emerging from the wartime officers' mess, he set out, unlike his Yorkshire contemporaries, to convert his native accent to standard southern English. This gave rise to some suspicion in the dressing room until in 1927 he was offered the Yorkshire captaincy as a professional. Refusing it, he said that he would be happy to play under any other captain. Herbert Sutcliffe was, as his subsequent successful business career demonstrated, a man of cool, clear mind and purpose.

Always immaculately turned out, he was, too, infallibly courteous – to everyone, which is the true courtesy.

FIRST-CLASS CAREER RECORDS

Career	M	I	NO	HS	Runs	Avge	100
1919-1945	748	1088	123	313	50138	51.95	149

Ct/St	Runs	Wkts	Avge	BB	5wI	10wM
469	527	10	52.70	2-16	—	—

TEST CAREER RECORDS

Tests	I	NO	HS	Runs	Avge	100	50
54	84	9	194	4555	60.73	16	23

Ct/St	Balls	Runs	Wkts	Avge	BB	5wI	10wM
23	—	—	—	—	—	—	—

HERBIE TAYLOR

HERBIE TAYLOR MUST indeed be nearly the finest batsman ever produced by South Africa. Certainly no other approached him in his own period. That is not a fact likely to be conclusively proved by figures but, against what was by common contemporary consent the most dangerous bowling of all – that of S.F. Barnes on a matting wicket – his performance in South Africa's losing series of 1913-14 was utterly outstanding. In that Test series, when Barnes had the amazing figures of 49 wickets at 10.93, Taylor's aggregate was 408 runs at 50.80; the next aggregate on the South African side was 281; and the next average 39.83. England lost only one match on that tour, when – including Barnes – they were beaten by Natal, for whom Taylor scored 91 and 100 out of 153 and 216 for six. So well and so consistently did he bat against Barnes that the bowler himself became exasperated to the point of an outburst on the pitch: 'Taylor, Taylor, Taylor all the time.'

Taylor's career was seriously interrupted by the Great War, but on either side of it he played in 42 Tests – eighteen of them as captain. Incidentally, all his seven centuries for South Africa were made against England.

Herbert Wilfred Taylor MC (1889-1973) Natal, Transvaal and South Africa
Right-hand bat; only very occasional right-arm off-break bowler; fine all-round fieldsman.

Herbie Taylor, freescoring strokemaker and a rare match for the great Sidney Barnes

He was of sound temperament, and regularly successful against all types of bowling. Utterly correct – and with a handsomely vertical backlift – he had no particular strength or favourite stroke; he was – as several who played with or against both observed – like Jack Hobbs in the completeness of his technique. Invariably sound in his judgement of length, his footwork was neat and fast, though unhurried. Perfectly balanced, he was strong on both the leg and off-side of the wicket; and he had every stroke, using them all generously. Many emphasized the strength of his back play – and he would go back almost on to the stumps when necessary, especially against Barnes. On the other hand, when, coming together at 20 for three against England at The Oval in 1929, he and 'Nummy' Deane put on 214 (in 190 minutes). Taylor used his feet to go down the pitch to drive ball after ball from 'Tich' Freeman in an attack which effectively put Freeman – 0 for 169 – out of Test cricket.

A natural games player, Taylor was a fine rugby half-back for Natal and, after the end of the War of 1914, when he stayed for a short while in England, he played rugby for Blackheath. A quiet, modest, likeable and reliable man, so sound was his technique that he played capably until he was forty-seven. For many years after his retirement he used regularly to coach local schoolboys on Sundays.

FIRST-CLASS CAREER RECORDS

Career	M	I	NO	HS	Runs	Avge	100
1909-1935	206	340	27	250*	13105	41.86	30

Ct/St	Runs	Wkts	Avge	BB	5wI	10wM
75	560	22	25.45	4-36	—	—

TEST CAREER RECORDS

Tests	I	NO	HS	Runs	Avge	100	50
42	76	4	176	2936	40.77	7	17

Ct/St	Balls	Runs	Wkts	Avge	BB	5wI	10wM
19	342	156	5	31.20	3-15	—	—

VICTOR TRUMPER

IN HIS LIFETIME Victor Trumper was the most charismatic figure in Australian cricket. Despite the fact that no one can now be alive who watched him in an informed fashion, he has become an Australian legend. Much has been written about him, as a man and cricketer, perhaps more than a little of it extravagant; Johnnie Moyes expressed the feeling about him: 'He has a special place in the hearts of all who knew him and in the memory of those who watched him bat.'

He was a right-hand opening bat, on whom C.B. Fry made two illuminating comments: 'He had no style and yet he was all style'; and: 'He had three strokes for every ball.' Certainly he had all the strokes, and he used them prodigally, if not consistently. He played innings of epic quality, but genius is never uniform. He was a serviceable right-arm medium-pace bowler, and a splendid outfield with a throw in the best Australian tradition: but the touch of magic lay upon his batting.

Legends have sprung up around him, most of them true and some immensely revealing. It was always said that Trumper's cricket bag was the untidiest in any dressing room; full of dirty shirts, crumpled trousers and odd socks. It was told, too, that once on a British tour, a group of the Australians came out of a theatre late on a stormy night. Trumper saw a boy newspaper-seller huddled, wet and cold in a doorway; he went over and bought his entire stock. It is related, too, that once when Warren Bardsley had made about 120 and was batting as seriously as ever, Trumper ran him out. When Bardsley taxed him with doing it deliberately, Trumper admitted it, saying: 'You've got one hundred, why do you want to make another when other men are waiting to come in?'

His talent was observed early, but Charles Bannerman, who coached him, gave it up because he played recklessly at wide balls far off the wicket. He was picked for New South Wales at seventeen but twice failed, and was not chosen again for two years.

He was originally left out of the 1899 team to England but, in a warm-up match at Adelaide, the selector Joe Darling realised the mistake, and he was taken as an 'extra player' at a reduced bonus. He failed in early matches, including the first Test, but in the second, at the age of twenty-one, he made a chanceless 135 not out to launch the Australian win. Immediately afterwards he scored 300 not out against Sussex.

His office job affected his eyesight, and when MacLaren's 1901-02 side went to Australia he had a poor season. He was still

Victor Thomas Trumper, New South Wales and Australia (1877-1915) Right-hand bat; right-arm medium-pace bowler; fine outfield.

picked in Darling's side of 1902, said to be the finest ever sent to England; and, even in that company, Trumper stood out. In a miserable summer of rain-affected wickets he scored 11 centuries, plus 92 against Gloucestershire and 96 against the Players. In that epic series he scored a century before lunch on a sodden wicket at Old Trafford in the Test which Australia won by three runs to take the rubber. He came again in 1905 and 1909, but without immense success; still, though, he produced memorable innings.

He played in 48 Tests and scored 3,163 invariably gracious runs. In Sydney grade cricket huge crowds followed him to watch his amazingly fast and gloriously attractive scoring. As Harry Altham wrote, though: 'The measure of Trumper's genius is not to be found in any figures.' Trumper was so gentle and generous that Frank Iredale, who played much with him, recalled that: 'To be near him seemed to me to be an honour; it felt good to live in his presence.'

He was a teetotaller and non-smoker, a loving and loyal husband and father, and only thirty-seven when he died from Bright's disease. For those who never experienced his play or his personality, probably the soundest opinion is Sir Pelham Warner's: 'No one ever played so naturally. Batting seemed just part of himself, and he was as modest as he was magnificent.'

FIRST-CLASS CAREER RECORDS

Career	M	I	NO	HS	Runs	Avge	100
1894-1913	255	401	21	300*	16939	44.57	42

Ct/St	Runs	Wkts	Avge	BB	5wI	10wM
172	2031	64	31.73	5-19	2	—

TEST CAREER RECORDS

Tests	I	NO	HS	Runs	Avge	100	50
48	89	8	214*	3163	39.04	8	13

Ct/St	Balls	Runs	Wkts	Avge	BB	5wI	10wM
31	546	317	8	39.62	3-60	—	—

GLENN TURNER

*Glenn Maitland Turner
(1947-   ) Otago,
Northern Districts,
Worcestershire and New
Zealand
Right-hand bat; slow
right-arm off-break
bowler; capable all-
round field.*

GLENN TURNER WAS consciously a career cricketer; who most
appropriately entitled his autobiography *My Way*. Born in
Dunedin, he was coached by Bert Sutcliffe and 'Billy' Ibadulla of
Warwickshire, and played for Otago at seventeen. Soon
afterwards Ibadulla recommended him to Warwickshire who
undertook to engage him. So determined and urgent was Turner
that he gave up his job in an insurance office to work night-shifts
in a bakery to earn the extra money to pay his fare to England. On
his arrival Warwickshire broke the news to him that they already
had their full quota of overseas players, but undertook to arrange
trials for him with other counties. The first one was with
Worcestershire, who engaged him instantly; and after a year's
qualification period with the second team (where he averaged 50),
he passed into the county side (1968).

He had to endure some criticism and leg-pulling as he put his
head down and set out doggedly to make his place certain.
Midway through that season it was decided to convert him into an
opening batsman where his obduracy would be best employed; he
settled into a good partnership with Ron Headley; achieved 1,000
runs for the season, and won his county cap.

During the winter he returned home to begin his Test career for
New Zealand against West Indies – with nought – but
immediately established his team place. He then went back to
England where he played for Worcestershire for the first two
months of the season before joining the New Zealand touring
side, for whom he made a hundred against Middlesex at Lord's.
Then in the Test on the same ground he carried his bat for 43 not
out in a total of 131.

On the following New Zealand tour of Asia he made his first
Test century – against Pakistan – and returned an altogether wiser
and more experienced player, though still obsessed with defence.
Fairly early in the following season, though – to the delight but
not complete surprise of his county captain, Tom Graveney – he
suddenly opened out in a Sunday League match and revealed a
range of strokes which he incorporated into his normal routine.

In addition to his basic correct and sound defence, he had
always had the capacity to tuck the ball away, especially on the
leg-side. Now he expanded, especially into off and straight
driving and a particular stroke of his own, in which he drove
through midwicket with a perpendicular bat, the face angled.

He then settled down to break records. In 1977 (Worcestershire
v Glamorgan) he carried his bat for 141 not out of a total of 169, a
first-class record of 83.4% of the team's score. In 1973 (for the

New Zealand touring team) he scored 1,018 runs before the beginning of June in an English season, the first time that feat had been achieved since 1938; and, so difficult have present-day fixture lists made it, that it may well be as long again before it is repeated. He holds, too, the remarkable record of having scored a century against all seventeen first-class counties, including his own – that was done for the New Zealand touring side against Worcestershire. He made more centuries (103 between 1964 and 1983) and more runs (34,346) than any other New Zealand cricketer. For Worcestershire, he made the highest score (311*) and more centuries in a career and in a season than anyone else. In 1982 he became only the nineteenth man and the second non-Englishman to reach 100 centuries, most fittingly in a Worcestershire match at Worcester, where 33 of them had been scored (v Warwickshire who had passed him on and over) when he scored 100 before lunch, and 311 not out in the day.

His figures, especially in Tests, would probably have been even more impressive but for a season away from touring to prepare

The purposeful Glenn Turner, only New Zealander to score the coveted century of centuries

for his benefit; and the disagreement with the New Zealand authorities which led to him resigning the captaincy; and in the rest of cricket because he retired from the English county game after the 1982 season.

He made himself unavailable for New Zealand when he became a Test commentator but came back to tour Australia and play against Sri Lanka in 1982-83. Who knows if or when he will come back again – or take some fresh course? Glenn Turner has always been his own man; and a great batsman.

FIRST-CLASS CAREER RECORDS

Career	M	I	NO	HS	Runs	Avge	100
1964-1982	455	792	101	311*	34346	49.70	103

Ct/St	Runs	Wkts	Avge	BB	5wI	10wM
410	189	5	37.80	3-18	—	—

OPPOSITE *Vishwanath sweeps, Keith Fletcher watches, during Vishy's double-century against England at Madras in January 1982*

TEST CAREER RECORDS

Tests	I	NO	HS	Runs	Avge	100	50
41	73	6	259	2991	44.64	7	14

Ct/St	Balls	Runs	Wkts	Avge	BB	5wI	10wM
42	12	5	0	—	—	—	—

GUNDAPPA VISWANATH

'VISHY' WAS, AND is, a batsman of considerable character who probably has been overshadowed by the record books. He holds one most unusual record: he scored 100 on his first appearance in a first-class match – indeed, he made a double century (230 for Mysore v Andhara) and another century in his first Test match – after nought in the first innings he scored 137 in the second innings for India against Australia at Kanpur in 1969-70. That dual feat is equalled only by the Australian, Dirk Wellham.

Even shorter than his brother-in-law, Sunil Gavaskar, at 5 feet 4 inches, Viswanath has always been an extremely fast mover, a masterly and wristy player off front foot or back but apt to take

Gundappa Ranganath Viswanath (1949-   ) Mysore and India Right-hand bat; occasional leg-break bowler; specialist slip fieldsman.

risks outside the off-stump. A splendidly aggressive batsman, with extremely powerful wrists and fine timing which invest his strokes with considerable power, a bowler of leg-breaks – he insists 'strictly in the nets' – and a safe catcher. He played more consecutive Test matches than any other cricketer: between that at Kanpur for India against Australia in 1969 and at Karachi v Pakistan (December 1982) he played in 87 consecutive Test matches, two more than Garfield Sobers' earlier record.

After long as an automatic choice he began to lose both speed and concentration. Although he had a good home series against Australia in 1979-80 (518 runs at 74 and 161 not out at Bangalore), on the tour of 1980-81 to Australia and New Zealand, apart from a characteristically exciting 114 at Melbourne, he fell below his old standard. Back home against England he made 107 and then his highest Test score of 222 – (when he and Yashpal Sharma put on 316 for the third wicket) – to keep his place. Then, suddenly, his form at Test level disappeared. It was an almost dramatic end to such a career for, after passing Sobers by two matches, he never played for his country again.

Oddly enough, although they were companions and related by marriage, and 'Vishy' went in number four, he never shared a big partnership with Gavaskar. Geneticists, as well as cricketers, will be interested in any son born to such a marriage as his.

OPPOSITE *Vishy salutes the Madras crowd on reaching 200*

FIRST-CLASS CAREER RECORDS

Career	M	I	NO	HS	Runs	Avge	100
1967-1985	293	464	43	247	17230	40.92	43

Ct/St	Runs	Wkts	Avge	BB	5wI	10wM
219	723	15	48.20	2-21	—	—

TEST CAREER RECORDS

Tests	I	NO	HS	Runs	Avge	100	50
91	155	10	222	6080	41.93	14	35

Ct/St	Balls	Runs	Wkts	Avge	BB	5wI	10wM
63	70	46	1	46.00	1-11	—	—

'THE THREE W'S'

THE THREE BARBADIAN-BORN cricketers who were dubbed 'the three Ws' have so much in common that, despite their contrasting methods and characters, they should initially be treated together, if only to avoid repetition. They were born within a few miles of each other – two in Georgetown and one in St Michael – in Barbados, within the space of seventeen months. The three were chosen for Barbados within three years – indeed, Walcott and Worrell in the same match of 1941-42 – all began to play for West Indies within little more than a fortnight of February-March 1948; and all emerged as major Test batsmen.

CLYDE WALCOTT

*Clyde Leopold Walcott OBE (1926-   )
Barbados, British Guiana and West Indies
Right-hand bat, medium-pace right-arm bowler; close field or wicketkeeper.*

CLYDE WALCOTT WAS only sixteen when he first played for Barbados, but his early batting was not completely successful, and he took to wicketkeeping in order to hold his team place. Then, though, in 1946, when he was just twenty, he had an unbroken partnership of 574 for the fourth wicket with his schoolmate, Frank Worrell, for Barbados against Trinidad. That remains the record West Indian stand for any wicket; and his 314 not out remains the highest score of his career.

He was 6 feet 2 inches tall, and weighed at his fittest some 15 stone. His splendid physique and good timing enabled him to hit with immense force and if his driving and square cutting probably brought him the majority of his runs, he could also hit murderously straight off the back foot.

On the historic English tour of 1950, his 168 not out decided the issue at Lord's and brought West Indies their first Test win in England. He had a disappointing tour of Australia in 1951-52, but against them at home in 1954-55 he performed the unparalleled feat of twice scoring two centuries in a Test match in the same series, when in fact his scores in the five matches were 108, 39; 126, 110; 8, 73, 15, 83; 155, 110.

The statisticians have unearthed, too, the fact that he was out for nought only once during his Test career: he played 74 innings for West Indies between January 1948 and March 1960, with a solitary 'duck' at Brisbane on 9 November 1951, when he was lbw to Ray Lindwall. An easy-going man with a good sense of humour, he was extremely popular during his years in the Lancashire League; managed several West Indian touring teams during the 1970s, and was awarded the OBE for his services to cricket.

Clyde Walcott turns a ball from Tony Lock during the Oval Test of 1957

FIRST-CLASS CAREER RECORDS

Career	M	I	NO	HS	Runs	Avge	100
1941-1963	146	238	29	314*	11820	56.55	40

Ct/St	Runs	Wkts	Avge	BB	5wI	10wM
174/33	1269	35	36.25	5-41	1	—

TEST CAREER RECORDS

Tests	I	NO	HS	Runs	Avge	100	50
44	74	7	220	3798	56.68	15	14

Ct/St	Balls	Runs	Wkts	Avge	BB	5wI	10wM
53/11	1194	408	11	37.09	3-50	—	—

EVERTON WEEKES

Everton de Courcy Weekes MBE (1925-   ) Barbados and West Indies Right-hand bat; leg-break bowler; capable close field.

A QUIET, CHEERFUL, short, powerful cricketer, Everton Weekes made a most amazing impact on English cricket when he arrived in 1950. Some had doubted his capacity to reproduce his form of West Indies domestic cricket or the Lancashire League against England and the counties. That doubt must have increased when it emerged to be a miserably wet summer. He was being compared with Bradman for his punishing power. Indeed, by mid-July he had scored five double centuries, including the highest sequence of runs ever scored by any batsman before being dismissed in the first-class game. He followed 246 not out against Hampshire with 200 not out against Leicestershire, and then 129 in the third Test at Trent Bridge – altogether 575 runs before he was out.

His defence was sound and he impressed by his speed of eye and foot. He was constantly likened to Headley and there was some similarity in build. Weekes had, though, an altogether

267

England players applaud Everton Weekes (Left) *and Frank Worrell as they return to the Trent Bridge pavilion, 21 July 1950. Their stand realized 283*

different stroke-range: for instance, he preferred the pull to the hook and used to hit devastatingly through the leg-side, though rarely as fine as square. Perhaps his most spectacular stroke was the square cut: constantly during that 1950 tour he played it with such power as forced opposing captains to post two cover points on the boundary. For preference he fielded at cover point, but he proved a fine slip catcher to Ramadhin and Valentine on that tour. In 1953-54 he made 206 against England at Port of Spain when he and Worrell put on 338 for the third wicket, then a West Indian record for any wicket against England.

Against India in 1952-53 he had the amazing Test return of 716 runs at 102.28 and in New Zealand in 1955-56 he made 940 runs, including six centuries at an average of 104.44 in eight first-class matches. He played League cricket successfully in England, was awarded the MBE for services to cricket, and returned happily to his native Barbados.

FIRST-CLASS CAREER RECORDS

Career	M	I	NO	HS	Runs	Avge	100
1944-1963	152	241	24	304*	12010	55.34	36

Ct/St	Runs	Wkts	Avge	BB	5wI	10wM
125/1	731	17	43.00	4-38	—	—

TEST CAREER RECORDS

Tests	I	NO	HS	Runs	Avge	100	50
48	81	5	207	4455	58.61	15	19

Ct/St	Balls	Runs	Wkts	Avge	BB	5wI	10wM
49	122	77	1	77.00	1-8	—	—

FRANK WORRELL

SIR FRANK WORRELL was the first cricketer to be paid the tribute of a memorial service in Westminster Abbey; and there were moving scenes in his native island when his body was brought home there for burial. He was a man who transcended cricket in his impact on West Indian social life. George Headley was accorded the salute of captaincy of West Indies for a single Test in his 'home' island of Jamaica. Frank Worrell, however, destroyed the myth that no coloured man was fit to captain West Indies at the sport which is an integral part of their way of life.

He was a cricketer almost in isolation. There was no cricket in the family and he grew up with no encouragement to cricket, no coaching or instruction in it. He merely modelled himself on J.E.D. Sealy, his schoolmaster at Combermere, who had, of course, been the youngest West Indian Test player. Originally Worrell was a slow left-arm bowler who, at nineteen, played in the two matches of 1942 at Bridgetown between Barbados and Trinidad. In the first he scored 48; but it was regarded as more significant that, in the second, he took five wickets for 47. A year later, sent in as night-watchman against Trinidad, he scored 188 and 68. Then, in 1944, he made 308 not out in a world record partnership of 502 with John Goddard. In 1946, he and Walcott made 574 for the fourth – a West Indian record for any wicket – again off the suffering Trinidad bowlers. His reaction to congratulations was simply: 'The conditions were loaded in our favour: I wasn't all that delighted about it.'

In 1947 his mother moved to New York, and with his father usually away at sea, he tired of Barbados and went to live in Jamaica. Surprisingly as it may seem to people of other countries, many of his fellow Bajans never forgave him for this 'betrayal'.

He established his cricketing reputation against G.O. Allen's side in 1947-48: and in 1948 joined Radcliffe in the Central

Sir Frank Worrell (1924-67) Barbados and West Indies Right-hand bat, left-arm medium-pace bowler, capable close field.

*Frank Worrell,
outstanding as man and
cricketer alike*

Lancashire League. He brought over and married his fiancée, Velda, and settled in Radcliffe, and studied sociology and economics at Manchester University. In 1964 a street near the cricket ground was named Worrell Close (nothing to do with Brian Close!). In the great West Indian-English season of 1950, he was top of the Test batting with 539 runs at 89.83. It was then that he made his highest Test score – 261 at Trent Bridge – when Norman Yardley, the England captain, said that it was virtually impossible to set a field for him because his placing was so perfect.

Frank Worrell, amazingly for an uncoached player, was quite strikingly correct. A cool, unhurried stylist, he had all the purist strokes and he never played across the line, which meant that he never hooked, merely moved out of line with calm self-possession, even against the fastest bowlers of his time. He never forgot the lessons of West Indies' unsuccessful tours of Australia in

1951-52 and England in 1957. He perceived, and stated plainly, that those failures were due to the splits and dissensions in the side. There were none under him. When he was given the captaincy for the tour of Australia in 1960-61, some in West Indies had mental reservations about the appointment. In the event he did much to make it an immense success in every way. It began with the epic tie at Brisbane, then came a win for each side and, finally, Australia's two-wicket win in a tense finish at Melbourne to give them the rubber. It was a fine and urgently needed fillip to the game; marked by an amazing tickertape farewell to the West Indians and the establishment of the Frank Worrell Trophy for future Test rubbers between the two countries. Almost immediately after, in England – 1963 – when West Indies took the rubber by three to one – there was a similar immense public response to the team under Worrell. It was both a complete vindication of the coloured captain of West Indies and an indication of the health of the game there.

A master batsman, Frank Worrell balanced the economy of the side by bowling medium-pace left-arm most skilfully, and on even mildly helpful pitches, with considerable devil. He was an alert and safe field at cover or close to the bat. Above all, he was a superb captain who lifted the whole quality and standing of West Indian cricket. He had a splendid sense of humour and a fine dignity. He was knighted in 1964, became Warden of the University College of the West Indies in Jamaica, and a senator of their parliament. But for his death through leukaemia at the age of 42 he must have gone on to even greater eminence in West Indian history.

FIRST-CLASS CAREER RECORDS

Career	M	I	NO	HS	Runs	Avge	100
1941-1964	208	326	49	308*	15025	54.24	39

Ct/St	Runs	Wkts	Avge	BB	5wI	10wM
139	10114	349	28.97	7-70	13	—

TEST CAREER RECORDS

Tests	I	NO	HS	Runs	Avge	100	50
51	87	9	261	3860	49.48	9	22

Ct/St	Balls	Runs	Wkts	Avge	BB	5wI	10wM
43	7141‡	2672	69	38.72	7-70	2	—

DOUG WALTERS

Kevin Douglas Walters (1945-   ) New South Wales and Australia Right-hand bat; right-arm medium-pace bowler; all-round field.

THE QUIET, WRILY humorous Doug Walters scored more runs (5,357) in Tests for Australia than all but three other batsmen (Greg Chappell, Don Bradman and Neil Harvey). Moreover, he made them at an average of 48.26. Many of them, too, were scored brilliantly, like his century between lunch and tea at Port of Spain in 1963, or in difficult circumstances such as the unbeaten 104 (in a total of 221) against New Zealand when Richard Collinge exploited a horrible pitch at Auckland in 1973-74. He was also an extremely useful fast-medium bowler (49 Test wickets at 29.08); and a superb fielder either at cover or close to the bat.

Yet he is the only major Australian cricketer of modern times to visit England without being included in *Wisden*'s 'Five Cricketers of the Year'. This was explained by the fact that he never succeeded in England as he did in Australia, and also on wickets as different as those in West Indies, India and New Zealand. There he was an outstanding stroke-maker from front foot or back, cutting, hooking and driving with splendid temperament. Perhaps it was that the English bowlers – prompted by John Snow – detected and probed a weakness to a short ball on the off-stump which produced gully catches. Walters, with typical honesty, was not afraid to say that he found Australian pitches in general easier to bat on than English.

The son of an up-country New South Wales farmer, he showed a precocious talent; so he was bound to be labelled 'a second Bradman'. His first sight of Test cricket was a single day as a nineteen-year-old spectator at Sydney, whose imagination was fired by Graeme Pollock's century for South Africa. On his next day at a Test he himself scored 155 against M.J.K Smith's England at Brisbane, a few days before his twentieth birthday.

By then he had already shared with Lynn Marks the second highest partnership (378) in the history of the Sheffield Shield: gone on to make 253; and, for more than good measure, taken seven for 63.

He reached 1,000 runs in only 11 Tests, and his Test career – barely interrupted except by National Service and a spell with Packer – lasted until he was left out of the touring party to England in 1981. That decided his retirement: for behind the jokes, he was a perfectionist about cricket – especially Test cricket.

He was much missed; modest, a perfectly poker-faced poker player, a fine team man, unfailingly but not stridently cheerful, a godsend in the dressing room; and the crowds at the Sydney

Cricket Ground adored him from first to last; this, their poster proclaimed, was 'THE DOUG WALTERS STAND'.

FIRST-CLASS CAREER RECORDS

Career	M	I	NO	HS	Runs	Avge	100
1962-1980	258	426	57	253	16180	43.84	45

Ct/St	Runs	Wkts	Avge	BB	5wI	10wM
149	6782	190	35.69	7-63	6	—

TEST CAREER RECORDS

Tests	I	NO	HS	Runs	Avge	100	50
74	125	14	250	5357	48.26	15	33

Ct/St	Balls	Runs	Wkts	Avge	BB	5wI	10wM
43	3295	1425	49	29.08	5-66	1	—

A majestic cover drive by Doug Walters during the 1977 Trent Bridge Test

WALTERS

BILL WOODFULL

*William Maldon
Woodfull OBE
(1897-1965) Victoria and
Australia
Right-hand bat; bowling
negligible.*

BILL WOODFULL WAS arguably the most successful captain Australia ever had. Not only did he twice take sides to England which recovered the Ashes, but he was outstanding in terms of behaviour and manners. The son of a clergyman and himself awarded the OBE for his services as headmaster of Melbourne Grammar School, he behaved with immaculate good manners in face of provocation.

As a captain he was considerate of his players, understanding of their problems and always ready to accept responsibility. He was essentially a dour and defensive batsman whose nicknames – bestowed by his opponents – included 'The Unbowlable', 'The Rock' and 'The worm-killer', the last because of his barely existent backlift. His defence could be massive and unwavering. He was correct, but scored mostly from pushes in front of the wicket and deflections behind it. In 1926, when he scored 118 against Surrey, his last scoring stroke was his first four. When Wally Hammond bowled him in the fifth Test at Melbourne in 1928-29 it was the first time his stumps had been hit for a year.

Woodfull was immensely difficult to dismiss, and much of his best cricket was played in England: he toured there three times, and each time played in all Tests, scoring a thousand runs on the tour and averaging over 50. A physical handicap – muscular – meant that he played little cricket as a young man and did not develop as rapidly as many of the great Australian batsmen. He was twenty-three when he appeared for XV of Ballarat against the 1920-21 MCC team, twenty-four when he was first picked for Victoria, and twenty-eight when he played in his first Test match against England. That was the first – rain-ruined – fifty-minute first Test of 1926. In the third match of that series he made 141, and had a partnership of 235 with Charlie Macartney; on that tour he scored more runs than anyone else in the team.

It was at this point that Herbie Collins made him an opening batsman for Australia; he retained that position throughout his career, and he never missed a match in seven series. In 1928-29 when England put out Australia, with two men absent, for 66 at Brisbane, Woodfull batted throughout the innings for 30 not out. Australia were defeated in that series under the captaincy of Jack Ryder, and Woodfull was chosen to replace him on the 1930 tour of England, when he had the priceless asset of Bradman; he made the most of it in regaining the Ashes. In the so-called 'Bodyline' series of 1932-33 Woodfull probably emerged with more credit than any other of the major protagonists. Initially unsettled by both the tactic and the pace, he finished the series with innings of

Calmly efficient batsman, Bill Woodfull in action for the Australians against Worcestershire in 1934

26, 22, 73 not out, 67, 19, 14 and 67. Only once did he lift the shutters. After he had been hit over the heart by a short ball from Larwood, 'Plum' Warner came in to apologise. Thereupon Woodfull said: 'There are two teams out there, but only one of them is playing cricket.' To Woodfull's distress, someone leaked that story to the press. From then until the end of his life he refused to say anything that might in any way stir up the bitterness of that series. Altogether he captained Australia in 25 Tests, of which they won 14, lost 7 and drew 4.

Woodfull remained a highly respected figure, courteous, honest, clear-minded. He collapsed and died while playing golf near his home only a few days before his sixty-eighth birthday.

FIRST-CLASS CAREER RECORDS

Career	M	I	NO	HS	Runs	Avge	100
1921-1934	173	245	39	284	13392	65.00	49

Ct/St	Runs	Wkts	Avge	BB	5wI	10wM
78	24	1	24.00	1-12	—	—

TEST CAREER RECORDS

Tests	I	NO	HS	Runs	Avge	100	50
35	54	4	161	2300	46.00	7	13

Ct/St	Balls	Runs	Wkts	Avge	BB	5wI	10wM
7	—	—	—	—	—	—	—

FRANK WOOLLEY

Frank Edward Woolley (1887-1978) Kent and England
Left-hand bat; left-arm slow to slow-medium bowler; fine slip field.

FRANK – 'STORK' – WOOLLEY was tall – over 6 feet – but well-shouldered, a left-hander whose stroke play was quite beguilingly handsome to watch. Only Sir Jack Hobbs scored more than his 58,969 runs (average 40.75, with 145 centuries); but, especially in the earlier phase of his long career – 1906 to 1938 – he was a world-class all-rounder, who took 2,068 wickets (at 19.85) and made 1,018 catches, more than anyone else apart from wicket-keepers. He twenty-eight times scored 1,000 runs in a season (and took 100 wickets in eight of them); thirteen times he scored 2,000 runs and, in four of them, also took 100 wickets.

His considerable height gave his bowling valuable bounce; and coupled with his reach and his large hands, enabled him to make some apparently distant and difficult slip catches. Above all, he was perfectly equipped to play strokes; he had them all and played them, simply enough, 'as required '. He was professional enough to bat strongly off his legs against the amount of bowling – which increased during his period – directed, spun, or swung, in to his leg stump. His most handsome strokes, though, were his cut and drive; his timing was good, his leverage great, and his power furious. He was at his most handsome against pace; and he himself considered the two finest innings of his career were his 95 and 93 (in totals of 187 and 283) which saved England from being overwhelmed by the Australian fast bowling combination of Gregory and MacDonald at Lord's in 1921.

He was never a man to play for his average, nor even for hundreds; he was out thirty-five times in the nineties; but it is virtually certain it was not because he was nervous. Rather he seemed to glory in taking a chance at any time in his innings; he made 89 'ducks'; but he gave bowlers a mighty thrashing. When Ted MacDonald from Australia joined Lancashire, the two had some quite spectacular contests; indeed, Sir Neville Cardus wrote some of the most splendid prose of his life about their duels in Kent-Lancashire matches. Because Woolley would throw his bat so uninhibitedly, he would sometimes top-edge balls for four or six; but generally he played off the middle – and in most exciting fashion.

Frank Woolley was not one of the game's profound thinkers; and largely for that reason was never a good coach. He himself put his finger on the crucial point about his batting when, after his long career, he emphasised the fact that he had enjoyed it all so greatly. It is significant that, among the heavy-scoring batsmen, only Jessop exceeded Woolley's average scoring rate; and only Victor Trumper equalled it.

OPPOSITE *All ease and elegance: a Woolley cover drive*

History hung about his cricket from the start. Taken on the staff at Tonbridge, where he had been an enthusiastic attender since he was a small boy, he was played in the Kent first team in 1906, at twenty. In his third match – against Surrey at The Oval – Surrey batted first; Woolley took the wickets of Hayward, Hayes and Goatly; he then scored 72 (top score out of 200); in Surrey's second innings he took five wickets for 82; and, finally, scored 23 not out to win the match by one wicket. That season for the first time Kent won the Championship – narrowly from Yorkshire and Surrey. Woolley never needed to worry about his team place afterwards. Perhaps that helped him to enjoy batting so much.

FIRST-CLASS CAREER RECORDS

Career	M	I	NO	HS	Runs	Avge	100
1906-1938	979	1532	85	305*	58969	40.75	145

Ct/St	Runs	Wkts	Avge	BB	5wI	10wM
1018	41066	2068	19.85	8-22	132	28

TEST CAREER RECORDS

Tests	I	NO	HS	Runs	Avge	100	50
64	98†	7	154	3283	36.07	5	23

Ct/St	Balls	Runs	Wkts	Avge	BB	5wI	10wM
64	6495‡	2815	83	33.91	7-76	4	1

Woolley walks to the middle with Percy Holmes in July 1921

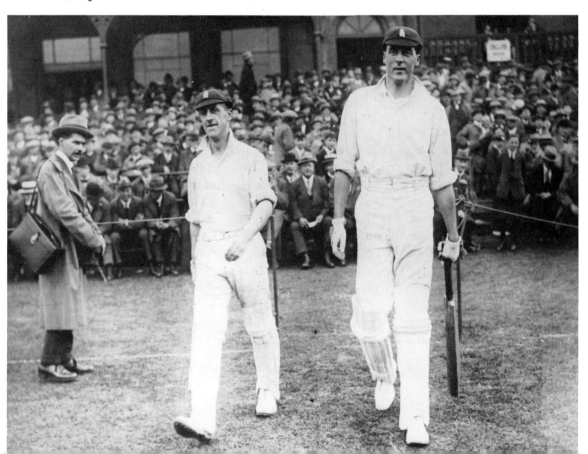

ZAHEER ABBAS

HIS ELEGANTLY RELAXED style and easy manner should never have been allowed to obscure Zaheer's cool, organized, single-minded attitude to batting. 'I have the same ideas about making runs as Boycott,' he once said.

Born in Sialkot (1947), he was keen on cricket from boyhood, and resisted the attempt by his family to persuade him to give it up. He first played with Karachi Whites in 1965-66, then, like many other promising young Pakistani cricketers, he was taken on to the staff of Pakistan International Airlines. He scored three centuries for them in 1969; and made 12 and 27 against New Zealand in his first Test (1969), but did not establish himself until his five hundreds in six matches – including 202 against Intikhab's Karachi 'A' Team in 1970-71 – which put him on the flight for the 1971 tour of England. He settled at once into English cricket and made a Bradman-like start with a brilliant 110 against Worcestershire; then, in the first Test – and only the second of his career – he scored 274 (putting on 291 in a Pakistan record second-wicket stand with Mushtaq). There simply was no mistaking his high ability, and there was instant competition among the counties to sign him. He decided on Gloucestershire, which may not have been an instantly apparent or fashionable choice, but it was a happy one. He played, at first, in gold-rimmed spectacles; later in contact lenses; but showed no handicap.

Simply enough, Zaheer was, and is, a world class player. Although he came to England prepared to modify his style, it proved completely unnecessary. From the start he had most of the strokes, and played them with an attractive lissom ease and surprising power. He has encountered few technical difficulties except, perhaps, on some of the livelier, greenish Australian wickets in the seventies – but he has not been alone in that – and against English bowling he has developed a masterly technique in the placing of strokes through the leg-side field. He is, too, a capable slip and occasional off-spinner. He set out in his modest, but utterly purposeful, way to break batting records: and he broke them. Perhaps the best example of his relentless appetite for runs is his record of scoring a double century and a century in the same match on no fewer than four occasions; two of them in the one regal season of 1976. He has also scored two separate centuries in a match eight times – another record. In 1982 he became only the twentieth man in the history of cricket to score a hundred centuries.

Zaheer always seemed to take pleasure in his game – he certainly gave it.

Zaheer Abbas (1947-) Karachi, Sind, PIA, Gloucestershire, Pakistan Right-hand bat; occasional off-spinner; capable slip fielder.

FIRST-CLASS CAREER RECORDS

Career	M	I	NO	HS	Runs	Avge	100
1965-1987	459	768	92	274	34843	51.54	108

Ct	Runs	Wkts	Avge	BB	5wl	10wM
278	1146	30	38.20	5-15	1	–

TEST CAREER RECORDS

Tests	I	NO	HS	Runs	Avge	100	50
78	124	11	274	5062	44.79	12	20

Ct	Balls	Runs	Wkts	Avge	BB	5wl	10wM
34	370	132	3	44.00	2-21	–	–

*Zaheer square drives
with absolute certainty*